The Child's Representation of the World

The Child's Representation of the World

Edited by

George Butterworth

University of Southampton
Southampton, England

PLENUM PRESS · NEW YORK AND LONDON

Library of Congress Cataloging in Publication Data

Main entry under title:

The Child's representation of the world.

Includes bibliographies and index.
1. Cognition in children—Congresses. 2. Drawing, Psychology of—Congresses.
3. Imagery (Psychology)—Congresses. 4. Space-perception—Congresses. I. Butterworth, George. II. British Psychological Society. Development Section.
BF723.C5C52   155.4'13   77-1046
ISBN 0-306-31025-2

Proceedings of the Annual Conference of the Developmental Section of the
British Society held at the University of Surrey, England, September 14–16, 1976

©1977 Plenum Press, New York
A Division of Plenum Publishing Corporation
227 West 17th Street, New York, N.Y. 10011

Printed in the United States of America

Contributors

E. Ampene
 Teacher
 University Primary School
 Lagos, Ghana

Elizabeth Bassett
 Graduate Student in Educational
  Psychology
 University of Stirling
 England

George Butterworth
 Lecturer in Developmental
  Psychology
 University of Southampton
 England

Karen Chessel
 Research Assistant
 Department of Experimental
  Psychology
 Oxford, England

Peter Coles
 Research Associate
 Department of Experimental
  Psychology
 Oxford, England

Mary Cox
 Lecturer in Psychology
 University of York
 England

Jan B. Deręgowski
 Lecturer in Psychology
 University of Aberdeen
 Scotland

Norman Freeman
 Lecturer in Psychology
 University of Bristol
 England

Paul Harris
 Lecturer in Psychology
 Free University
 Amsterdam, Holland

Liam Hudson
 Professor of Psychology
 Research Unit on Intellectual
  Development
 Edinburgh University
 Scotland

Lawrence Litt
 Tutor in Psychology
 The Open University
 North West Region
 Manchester, England

Gustav Jahoda
 Professor of Psychology
 University of Strathclyde
 Glasgow, Scotland

Lorna Selfe
  Area Educational Psychologist
  Hereford and Worcester County
    Council
  Bath Street
  Hereford, England

Marian Sigman
  Research Associate
  Department of Pediatrics
  University of California
  Los Angeles, U.S.A.

Susanna Millar
  Research Officer
  Department of Experimental
    Psychology
  Oxford, England

Elizabeth Newson
  Senior Lecturer in Child
    Development and Joint
    Director
  Child Development Research Unit
  University of Nottingham
  England

Cathy Urwin
  Research Associate
  Department of Experimental
    Psychology
  Oxford, England

John Willats
  Lecturer in Art and Design
  Faculty of Art and Design
  North East London Polytechnic
  London, England

N. Williams
  Lecturer
  Child Development Section
  Human Sciences Department
  University of Ghana
  Ghana

John Willsdon
  Lecturer in Art and Crafts
  Faculty of Education
  South Glamorgan Institute of
    Higher Education
  Wales

Richard Wollheim
  Professor of Philosophy
  University College
  London, England

Preface

Although central to theories of cognitive development, the concept of representation remains subtle and elusive. This collection of papers reflects a variety of individual emphases, none of which are mutually exclusive. The papers have been arranged in four groups, mainly along lines of related subject matter but also to illustrate different aspects of the development of representation.

In Piaget's theory, representation is defined as "the making present of an object which is not present to the senses" (Furth 1969). Representation has both a figurative and an operative aspect. The organisation of the content of the representation (the figurative aspect) depends on the operations of thought or on the schemes co-ordinating action. This use of the term is applicable both to internal representations, such as visual images and to external representation, such as children's drawings. However, it presupposes no necessary relation between a mental image and a graphic representation.

The first part of the book consists of papers on children's drawing. The operative aspect of representation emerges in the serial ordering problems encountered by young children who produce "tadpole" figures (Freeman Chapter 1). The figurative aspect of graphic representation is vividly illustrated by the drawings of the autistic child Nadia (Selfe Chapter 2). One further issue which emerges concerns the relation between linguistic and graphic representation. Difficulties experienced by the normal child in serially ordering the graphic components of the human figure may be another example of a parallelism between action and language (see Greenfield et al. 1972). Perhaps the development of graphic representation may be described best by a dual system in which a verbal-symbolic representational system and an imagery system interact (Litt Chapter 5).

Bruner (1966) defines representation as "a set of rules by which one conserves one's encounters with events". In addition to an imagery mode (ikonic representation) and a verbal mode

(symbolic representation) he describes an enactive mode.   The
enactive mode "serves to relate the requirements of action to the
visual field".

The papers collected in the second part of the book are mainly
concerned with the relation between action, perception and the
spatial field.   Evidence from studies of sighted and blind children
is reviewed.   One issue which emerges is the nature of so-called
"egocentric" errors in perspective-taking tasks.   Harris (Chapter 6)
argues that spatial development in children is best understood as the
progressive co-ordination of an egocentric and an allocentric spatial
code.   He maintains that "egocentric" errors may actually reflect an
undue reliance on allocentric spatial location information.   The
paper by Urwin (Chapter 10) examines the effect of blindness in
infancy on the establishment of frames of reference for language.

Two excellent papers had to be omitted from the published proceedings of the conference.   The first by Wendy Lawrenson (Department of Psychology, Plymouth Polytechnic), was on the coding of
stimulus-background relations in young children.   This will appear
in the British Journal of Psychology (in press).   The second paper,
by Dr Neil O'Connor (Medical Research Council Developmental Psychology
Research Unit, Gordon Street, London W.C.1), reviewed studies of
spatial and temporal coding in congenitally blind and congenitally
deaf school children.   This material will appear in a forthcoming
book.   Interested readers may wish to refer to O'Connor (1976).

The third part of the proceedings contains the invited address
by Liam Hudson.   Hudson's interpretation of the concept of representation is in the tradition of Bartlett (see Oldfield and Zangwill
1942).   Like Piaget, Bartlett distinguishes two aspects of representation.   In Bartlett's case they are termed the "dynamic" and
"material" aspects of representation.   The dynamic aspect is defined
as "an active organisation of past experience which must always be
supposed to be operating in any well adapted response".   Dynamic
organisation is the rule at all levels of psychological functioning
including the organisation of personality.   Hudson contrasts
"intuitive" and "rational" mental organisations which characterise
the "divergent" and "convergent" personality types.

The fourth part of the proceedings returns to the problems of
picture perception and production.   The philosophical criteria
defining a pictorial representation are discussed by Wollheim
(Chapter 12).   He argues that the fundamental criterion lies in
"seeing in" the third dimension, into the two-dimensional space
of the picture.   The paper by Willats (Chapter 13) on the development of the ability to represent perspective in drawings links
Wollheim's paper to the cross-cultural study of picture perception

reported by Jahoda (Chapter 14) and to the conference overview by
the discussant, Jan Deręgowski (Chapter 15).*

    A single and comprehensive definition of representation remains
as elusive as ever.   If this collection of papers at least affords
a glimpse of the variety of psychological processes which underlie
representational systems, it will have served its purpose well.

ACKNOWLEDGEMENTS

    The planning and organisation of this conference was carried
out by the committee of the Developmental Section of the British
Psychological Society.   Thanks are due to Dr John Coleman and Mr
Anthony Whitehouse who dealt with the administrative aspects of the
conference and to Dr Harry McGurk for his help in arranging the
programme.   I would particularly like to thank Mrs Sue Bonham for
her rapid and competent typing of the manuscript.

                                                G.B.

BIBLIOGRAPHY

BRUNER, J. S., OLVER, R. R. & GREENFIELD, P. M., Studies in
    cognitive growth, New York, Wiley, 1966

FURTH, H. G., Piaget and knowledge, Prentice Hall, 1969

GREENFIELD, P. M., SALTZMAN, E. & NELSON, K., The development of
    rule-bound strategies for manipulating seriated cups: a paral-
    lel between action and grammar, Cognitive Psychology, 1972,
    3, pp. 290-310

O'CONNOR, N., The psychopathology of cognitive deficit, British
    Journal of Psychiatry, 1976, 128, pp. 36-43

OLDFIELD, R. C. & ZANGWILL, O. L., Head's concept of the schema
    and its application in contemporary British psychology. In
    four parts: British Journal of Psychology, 1942, 32,
    pp. 267-286; 33, pp. 58-64, 113-129 and 143-149

PAIVIO, A., Imagery and verbal processes, New York, Holt, Rinehart
    and Winston, 1971

---

* At various points in the proceedings, discussions are included in
which most speakers are identified by name (or by name and university if they do not appear in the list of contributors).   Apologies
are offered to those individuals who may recognise themselves
described as "Member of the audience".   It was not always possible
to identify the speaker from the tape recording.

Contents

Part I

Children's Drawing

HOW YOUNG CHILDREN TRY TO PLAN DRAWINGS

Norman Freeman

INTRODUCTION

In their development, most children leave a trail of drawings
behind them. They are the most reliable and enduring of spontaneous
childish artifacts. Their study appealed to the "natural history"
instincts of the late Victorian era, and formed a valuable source
of propaganda for advanced pedagogues who wanted tangible evidence
that the "child mind" really did differ significantly from a small-
scale version of the adult mentality. With the manufacture of
cheap paper and pencils it became possible to amass vast amounts of
data; and the study of children's representational drawings was
one of the first areas of child psychology to become established
as a field of research. The 1890's saw the inauguration of massive
works which were outstanding in their scale of conception, amount of
raw material amassed and accuracy of observations. Certainly by
the end of the 1920's the number of potentially testable hypotheses
which had been produced formed a strikingly coherent corpus.

One would not guess that that had been the case from looking
at the content of modern textbooks and taught courses. Nowhere
are there sections on drawing which serve to generate ideas
inspiring research in associated fields. Contrast the role played
today by studies of children's games or language, and it becomes
very clear that drawing has become disestablished as a root of
child psychology, and now forms a side-branch, of not particularly
vigorous growth.

There is one way out of this position, and the last five years
has seen a sufficient number of researchers taking the way out to

warrant a statement on the state of the game. Basically, what
psychologists have begun to do is to conduct research which is
based on the same rules of evidence as other areas of experimental
psychology; and which is adapted to the raw material sufficiently
to be able to cast light on problems which are specific to the
development of graphic ability. Thus, there is now evidence on
the problem of linear order in drawing, the enhanced performance
obtained when precise assessing-cues are given, the existence of
strong response-biases, the effects of framework relations, the
role of scaled cues which reliably influence the relative strengths
of alternative graphic decisions, etc. Discussion of this type of
work forms the body of this paper. In view of the content of the
papers which follow this one at this conference, some of the issues
will be dealt with very briefly, whilst others, of no more intrinsic
importance, will be gone into in more depth to bring out methodological issues which will aid discussion of others' contributions.

These issues are basically familiar ones to students of human
performance characteristics. They can be picked up in many
different situations. If you give a young child a construction
game which is too complex for its stage of development, the child
may reject it or play simple games with it, often fantasy games,
which are not in the rule book, and which do not properly utilise
the potential relationships between the constituents. From this
point of view it is very instructive to watch a preschool child
playing with a Lego kit. Again, a three-year-old, given a doll's
house, often roughly segregates the furniture in a sort of parcelled-
out jumble or places them neatly against the walls in a non-veridical
way, i.e. using the walls as a baseline or frame of reference.
Having discovered a simple routine, the child may persist in it
repeatedly, on each occasion fully intending to repeat it. The
drawing situation is precisely comparable. The blank sheet and
salient edges of the page provide an immense number of potential
"degrees of freedom" which have to be reduced to workable order.
This is accomplished by drawing very simple routine configurations.
But here the child is faced with a real problem, almost unique in
its experience. There are literally no parts for the child to
assemble unless it produces them for itself. Lines do not even
fall into discrete bits in the way that plasticene may: lines are
essentially continuous until you learn, in effect, to make
controlled discontinuous movements. The creation of order is as
essential to graphic representation as syntax is to language and
rules to games.

It is the contention of this paper that experimental analysis
of the development of ordering and planning is essential to any
understanding of the development of representational drawing.
Analysis of the task-demands of pictorial representation must be
undertaken before we can devise appropriate units of analysis

whereby to scale drawings, or to speculate on the role of "mental
imagery" or "body image" in determining the variant forms produced
(Freeman, 1976).   Construction skills are never born fully-
fledged ab initio, nor do drawings spring automatically onto the
sheet, be the child's imagination never so powerful: pace Anna
Schubert (1930) with her confident assertion that "the Orotchen's
process of drawing must obviously be interpreted as the outlining
with a pencil of eidetic forms which are projected on to the paper".
Nothing is tipped out onto the paper: everything has laboriously
to be constructed (Freeman, 1975b).   Children's drawings are the
end result of an exacting, often exhausting, productive effort.
We shall present evidence that their abilities may be far in
advance of their unaided performance.   They do not access all that
they have available (for this distinction see Tulving and Pearlstone,
1966).

        These lines of research are really most readily related to the
field of perceptual-motor skills.   This is the favoured approach
for this paper.   But we take Burk's (1902) point that "the child's
pertinacity in carelessness as to accuracy, has only been equalled
by the pedagogue's pertinacity in his attempt to force the child to
be accurate...they should not be forced in drills of accuracy...the
child's hour for accuracy has not yet come" (p. 311).   The aim of
research upon their immense tendencies towards "inaccuracy" is not
designed primarily to help us design remedial programmes; nor
should it yet be.   The aim of the present paper is to point out
the types of planning problems which the child faces, and to explain,
by a consideration of these, why their drawing of the human figure
may look so very queer in its slow development towards the stereotyped "photographic" arrangement.   Note that the use of depth cues
will not be dealt with here, although there are similar issues
involved, and have been written up elsewhere (Freeman, Eiser and
Sayers, 1976).

                    FIRST EXPERIMENT ON THE TADPOLE FORM

        At first glance few versions of the human figure seem to be as
conspicuously inaccurate as those shown in Figure 1.   These
"tadpole people" are worthy of detailed attention, for they are
extraordinarily common, if not universal.   In what way are they
inaccurate?   Many authors assume that the trunk is omitted
(Lowenfeld and Brittain, 1964; DiLeo, 1970).   This provides as
good a starting point as any.   Assuming this therefore, either
the child did not mean to omit the trunk or he did.   If he/she
did not intend to, then the omission is what we may call a "performance error" or "production error".   The child knows that arms go
on a trunk but is somehow unable to accomplish that in his spontaneous drawings.   If we therefore provide a pre-drawn head and

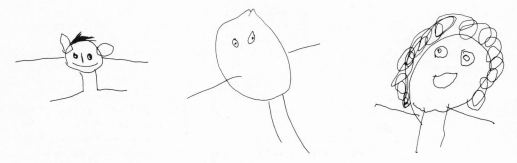

Figure 1.   Drawings of the human figure in "tadpole form" by
               pre-school children

trunk, then the child should be able to complete it by positioning
arms appropriately on the trunk.   On the other hand, if he did
intend to omit the trunk because he has some mental image which
specifies that arms go on the head, then he should position arms on
the head of the pre-drawn figure.   Therefore, playing a drawing-
completion game should discriminate between the two hypotheses.
Some people might object, and say that the relevance of such a test
is predicated on an oversimplified interpretation of the tadpole
form.   But even if it were the case that we should hold a sophisticated view, such as that of Arnheim (1954) who considers the tadpole
person to consist of a graphically undifferentiated head-trunk unit,
the test would still apply.   For here, if the tadpole form contains
an implicit trunk with arms attached, the provision of a pre-drawn
explicit trunk should attract arm-positioning.

When this experiment was first run, there at first sight seemed
to be no consistency in the pattern of results.   The same child
would sometimes position arms on the head, sometimes on the trunk.
The major determining factor turned out to be neither the absolute
size of the head nor of the trunk, but the relationship between them;
for the child would position the arms on whichever was the larger of
the two body parts.   Using this cue it became possible to get
individual children to alternate between head- and trunk-positioning
(Freeman, 1973).   The next step was to construct a properly scaled

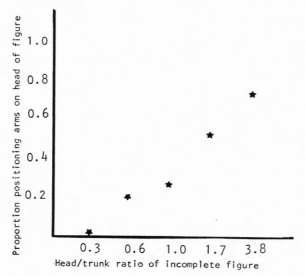

Figure 2. Scaled series of incomplete figures given one at a time, to children for them to complete. (Reproduced from Nature, 1975, 254, p. 416, by kind permission of the Editor and MacMillan Journals, London.)

Figure 3. The tendency to position arms on the head of an incomplete figure is a linear function of the head-trunk ratio. Data from tadpole-drawers ($\bar{x}$ = 3 rd. 7 mo.). (Redrawn from figures given in Nature, 1975, 254, p. 416, by kind permission of the Editor and MacMillan Journals, London.)

series of head-trunk ratios in which the ratios varied at approximately equal intervals on an underlying scale.   One such series
is shown in Figure 2.   Using series like these, giving the drawings
one at a time in random order, Freeman (1975a) found a reliable
linear relationship between the head-trunk ratio and the tendency
of tadpole-drawers to position arms on the head (see Figure 3).
This seems to show that the child is operating according to some
spatial cue which overrides the information in the drawing as to
which element is the trunk and therefore the appropriate place for
the arms.   It may be termed the "body proportion effect".   This
points to the necessity for an analysis of drawing in terms of:

  a) which cues the child is responsive to, and
  b) how he uses those cues.

     Of course, there are many questionable aspects of this
isolated initial study.   For example, some of the figures seem
very bizarre, although they were chosen to fall within the range
produced by normal preschool children.   Their bizarre appearance
may not be too grave a fault, for the linear relationship plotted
does neatly span the middle values, and is not an artefact of the
extreme values.   The next experiment was designed to accommodate
some of the more obvious design problems.   But before describing
it, we must consider a model of performance which would encompass
both the generation of the tadpole form and the results of this
type of drawing-completion study.   Freeman (1975a) attempted to
do that using the concepts of "accessing from semantic memory" and
"non-representational bio-mechanical bias".   But the model was far
too tied to the specific phenomena, so can only be regarded as a
place-holder.   In contrast, the procedure followed in the rest of
this paper is to attempt to analyse the task-demands outside the
drawing situation.   If a particular non-graphic problem imposes
similar constraints upon the subject, and if there be ample evidence
on how subjects respond to such constraints, then we should argue
that they will respond similarly in the drawing task.   In other
words, if we know some general characteristics of human performance,
then there is no reason why the drawing situation should confer
immunity from these.   For convenience we shall distinguish between
the production, positioning, orientation and size-scaling, of the
parts of the drawing, and begin with the first in this list.

                        PRODUCTION   OF   PARTS

               (a) Serial-Order Production Problems

     In order to draw the human figure the child has to be able to
analyse the relationships between the body parts.   The major axis
is vertical, and the poles are represented by head and legs.   Thus

the figure is drawn with the head at the top and the legs at the bottom in a constrained spatial serial order.   It therefore follows that its production should be subject to serial position effects. There is good reason for supposing that serial position phenomena are perfectly general: any series seems to elicit them.   Of course, they are probably produced by diverse mechanisms, but the end result is familiar to all experimental psychologists: if an ordered stimulus series is given to the subject, efficiency is higher with terminal items than with intermediate ones.   For convenience we shall term the most general form of the empirical phenomenon end-anchoring.   It seems to be an optimal strategy in the memorisation of temporal stimulus orders, in the response to spatial orders like those involved in the use of rating scales and perceptual judgement tasks, and in high level cognitive construction of order in dealing with three-term series.   Stimulus order produces differential serial position efficiency.

        We therefore expect early attempts at human figure drawing to show serial position effects.   Indeed, Freeman (1975a) reported that most tadpole drawers drew in the order head and legs, and only then the arms.   This is evidence for the child end-anchoring on the head and legs, and would account for the generation of the tadpole form.   In other words, the tadpole figure attests to the existence of a performance problem in accessing stored representations.   It is even possible to take the argument a step further. Considering the general phenomenon of end-anchoring, Trabasso, Riley and Wilson (1975) write: "The importance of this empirical finding is that the occurrence of a serial position effect may be taken as prima facie evidence of the construction or use of an underlying linear ordering of events" (p. 204).   According to such an argument, therefore, end-anchoring at the head and legs would be produced by an underlying ordered mental representation which includes the trunk as the intermediate item in the four-item series of head, trunk, arms and legs, otherwise, there would be nothing identifying the terminal items.   This is the strongest form of the serial-order argument, and the reader may prefer the weaker version in which it is left an open question as to the extent to which the tadpole drawer has a mental representation of a trunk. But certainly there are no grounds for supposing that the trunk is entirely unavailable from the internal store.   If one provides accessing cues, one can improve drawing performance, and this will be dealt with shortly.   For the moment the important point is that a basic drawing which depends upon the conjunction of the head and legs entails neither an aberrant body image nor peculiar perceptual experience, nor outlandish aesthetic aims.   If a perfectly general phenomenon like end-anchoring would generate the tadpole form, there may be no reason at all to think of it as attesting to a discrete stage in the development of mental ability.   End-anchoring would tend to occur whatever the child knew about the human figure.

There is further evidence which now falls into place.   Many
published surveys of spontaneous drawings show not only that the
head is more common than the trunk, but that the legs are more
common than the arms.   (Snyder and Gaston, 1970;   Shapiro and
Stine, 1965;   Ames and Ilg, 1963;   Hurlock and Thomson, 1934.)
Many authors comment on the variability in drawing of the trunk
and the arms.   In our own research we have found that the advance
towards employing double lines to represent the limb-contours occurs
with the legs before the arms, and that feet tend to be drawn sooner
than hands.   John Willsdon (Chapter 4), at Cardiff, has similar
data on a much larger sample of children than ours.   Graphic end-
anchoring seems to be a general phenomenon.

Finally, consider more closely the problem of temporal order
in drawing.   When we asked adults to draw a simple figure without
threading (i.e. without using a continuous line to represent the
outline) we found that they drew in order from top to bottom.   Thus
they made the temporal order of production map onto the spatial order
of the finished product.   This was also found when we asked them
verbally to describe a simple figure flashed briefly on a screen.
Such mapping is an essential discovery that children have to make.
End-anchoring helps in that the spatially polar head is drawn first
in the temporal series, but anchoring on the legs precisely prevents
the rest of the spatial-temporal mapping.   Somehow the trunk has to
be interpolated.   Indeed, Elisabeth Bassett (1976) (Chapter 3)
found that young children who managed to draw the trunk, still
produced the legs before the arms.   The conclusion is that the
appearance of the trunk in spontaneous drawings does not mean that
end-anchoring has entirely been overcome (as the evidence from
Willsdon's and our work, cited above, seems also to show).   Later
they move onto the more adult strategy of drawing in the order
head-trunk-arms-legs;   and Freeman (1975a) found that a large number
in his sample of preschool conventional drawers (mean age 4:0) had
discovered this.   Seriation is indeed a problem for young children.
Further discussion of temporal and spatial order in drawing may be
found in Liben (1975), and in Goodnow's articles.

(b) Accessibility and Availability

Thus far we have been dealing with indications that performance
has specific problems.   In experimental psychology, given such
indications, it is a standard tactic to assume that the subject has
more information available in store than he can easily deploy
unaided, and to provide some sort of help.   In the field of recall,
one commonly provides accessing-cues, and indeed it is commonly found
that cued recall is superior to unaided recall.   This reaches its
finest expression in the study of mnemonics.   If one suspects that
the drawing situation is similar, one should provide cues.   One way

of doing this is to dictate to the child the parts that are to be
drawn.   Interestingly, very young tadpole drawers are often very
resistant to dictation.   But if one waits a little for their
drawings to develop, they often respond extremely well to the
provision of verbal accessing cues (Gridley, 1938; Golomb, 1973,
1974).

     One can also include graphic cues in this context.   In our
research we have found that many inveterate tadpole drawers will
complete a pre-drawn head by attaching a trunk and limbs.   Now
this is not an unambiguous advance, since the children may really
only be drawing their basic tadpole configuration without the need
to put in facial features.   However, the fact that the majority of
tadpole drawers in our sample simply attached limbs to the pre-drawn
head, seems to indicate some advance on the part of those who turned
it into a conventional man.   Much more striking evidence comes from
studying the behaviour of children who can only produce scribbles
when drawing unaided.

Figure 4.   Scribbles by Sarah, aged 2 yrs. 0 mths.

    The first point about scribbles is that they are clearly non-
random.   Three scribbles by Sarah, aged 2:0, are shown in Figure 4.
They are clearly directionally biased.   Connolly and Elliott (1972)
asked young children to paint how they wished on a blank sheet, and
found a modal bias towards vertical rather than horizontal strokes.
Kellogg (1970) has even compiled a catalogue of twenty "basic
scribbles" which could, in principle, serve as a reservoir whence
later representational forms emerge.   Plausibly from this point of
view, the third scribble in Figure 4 was given the unsolicited title
"A Baby" by Sarah when she had finished it.   Early writers, such as
Luquet (1927) laid great stress on the role of post hoc recognition
in the development of form.   To a certain extent, these young
scribblers have graphic skills at their disposal which are relevant
to representation.   Instead of waiting until the children
spontaneously demonstrate their skills, one can provide cues which
bring them out, in the following way.

        Figure 5.   Scribbles by George, aged 2 yrs. 1 mth.,
                in response to two pre-drawn shapes

Consider Figure 5.   The only difference in technique is that
now the paper has something already drawn on it.   Here is a clear
interaction between the given abstract form and the scribbles
produced, obviously in response to it.   That is, there is clear
non-random positioning of the scribbles.   These are of course,
strictly speaking, still non-representational activities.   Even
apes will show that sort of behaviour, as Morris (1962) and Smith
(1973) have documented.   Fortunately we need no basic modification
of technique in order to bring out true representational skills, all
we have to do is make the pre-drawn shape represent something.
This is illustrated in Figure 6.   The child has scribbled over the
incomplete human figure.   But in each case the point where he
begins his scribbles is perfectly appropriate.   Here are position
skills, still buried in "noise", which one simply would not see if
one were confined to inspecting the finished product.

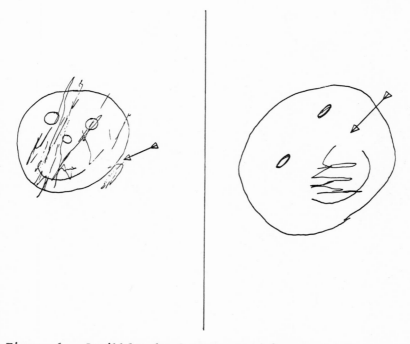

Figure 6.   Scribbles by George, aged 2 yrs. 1 mth.,
in response to pre-drawn incomplete human shapes.   In
each case, an arrow marks where the pen is positioned
to begin the scribbles. In the case of the first scribble,
he spontaneously said "ear", in the second, "nose", before
he began

In this child's case there was a sudden flowering of representation some weeks later.   One naturally wonders whether it was a
lack of motor control and co-ordination which was holding him back.
But notice how careful one has to be in accusing a scribbler of
lack of control.   For the drawings in Figure 7 are completion
responses made by a child whose spontaneous attempts to draw can
only be classified as scribbles.   Here suddenly appear limbs which
are correct in both shape and place.   Why could he not do that for
himself before our drawing started him off?   Indeed, why could he
still not do it when we had finished our experiments on him?   The
child is on the threshold of drawing but just cannot get himself
organised.

Figure 7.   Unprompted responses to pre-drawn head and trunk
         by scribbler aged 3 yrs. 10 mths.

The conclusion from this outline of serial order problems and drawing completion methods is that it is absolutely impermissible to posit that the contents of the child's internal store is directly and faithfully represented on paper in unaided drawing.   This is, of course, precisely the error made in the basis of the Goodenough-Harris test (Harris, 1963).   The same error is made by many of those who seem at first sight to be in a totally different tradition. Thus Machover (1949) also uses a model based on a one-to-one matching between observed performance and internal construct (Freeman, 1975b).

POSITIONING BODY PARTS

For the rest of the paper we shall assume that the subject can produce the essential body parts.   We now take up the question of how they position them on the page.   This involves the child in a search for position cues.   We shall confine ourselves to the question of the cues governing their decision as to where to position arms on the human figure.   This may be separated into two aspects. First we return to the question of which body part they will position arms on: introduced earlier as the body-proportion effect. Secondly we shall consider fine positioning upon the chosen body part.   If the previous analysis is correct, we expect that positioning will be more accurate with the end-anchored legs than with the intermediate arms.   To anticipate, this is precisely what we found.

It will be recalled that the body-proportion effect describes the tadpole drawers' lawful tendency to position arms on whichever is the larger of the pair, head and trunk.   The next step in research is intended to deal with an obvious doubt about the design, to control the child's responses more adequately and to test one explanation of the effect.   Let us consider these three points in order.   First, the design purports to put the head and the trunk into competition as position cues.   But we have no guarantee that it does so.   Thus, for example, when the head is very large, the children may conceivably classify it as a combined head-trunk and ignore the small appended trunk.   Therefore we need some prior indication that the body parts have been appropriately labelled; or, better, some prior indication that the head and trunk elicit different and appropriate graphic responses.   The solution adopted is to ask the children to draw either a nose or navel before adding arms and legs.   These are relatively easy responses, since all they demand is a gross "hit" upon the appropriate pre-drawn circle.   Secondly, we have already noted the importance of observing the temporal order of drawing.   In this experiment all children are asked to draw the arms before the legs, thus ensuring that temporal order is a controlled variable.   Finally, since the design controls and directs the children's movements, it becomes possible to test the following explanation of the body-proportion effect. The children are in the process of developing motor control, so that the effect could conceivably be explained in terms of lack of control. The children might intend to aim for the trunk, but be deflected by the more salient head, or even fear that they will not be as easily able to "score a hit" on the smaller trunk. The present design provides a common baseline for movement, in that each child will have centred the pen on a body part immediately before. Further, on this present account, those children who centre on the trunk in order to draw the navel will be immune to the body-proportion effect and those who draw the nose will show the effect most strongly, relative to a control group who simply begin by drawing the arms. The data showed that positioning was very accurate with the nose, navel and legs, and we now consider the arms.

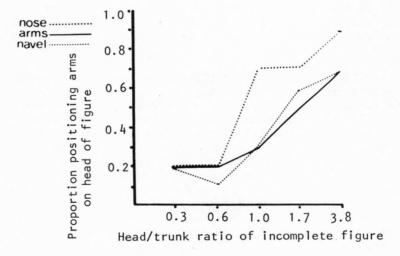

Figure 8. The tendency to position arms on the head of an incomplete figure is a linear function of the head-trunk ratio, whether the arms were preceded by centering on the head to draw a nose, on the trunk to draw a navel, or were the first elements drawn. (Reproduced from the Quarterly Journal of Experimental Psychology, by kind permission of the Editor and Heffer's Publishing House Ltd., on behalf of the Experimental Psychology Society

The results, from Freeman and Hargreaves (1977) are shown in
Figure 8. The three curves do not differ reliably, the same linear
trend adequately describes all three.   Thus the effect is a most
robust one, and inefficient movement-control cannot quite account
for it.   Of course, the results do not rule out the possibility
that some contribution to the effect may be made by undirected
movements, but they are more readily accounted for in terms of the
child's monitoring of position cues in a cue-competition situation.
The obvious question is why simple relative size should be the cue
to which the child responds, rather than the meaning of the body
part.   The only available evidence is as follows.

Figure 9. Early versions of figures with a trunk having the arms
   positioned on the trunk much lower than the shoulder region

First note that although one does find some tadpole figures
with the arms positioned on the legs, they are really very rare.
Tadpole drawers seem already to be in possession of a rule which
specifies that arms are positioned firmly on a body segment rather
than on another limb.   In this respect they resemble early versions
of the conventional form which also have the arms squarely on a body
segment (see Figure 9).   The transition to a fine positioning, at
the shoulder region comes much later.   It seems that the children
use relatively crude position cues, which ensures maximal <u>dispersion</u>
of the body parts.   That at least is a recipe for clear drawings.
Now, there was a little reliable data from these studies which
indicated that when an individual child positioned arms on the head,
he did so slightly lower than the midline, whereas he would put them
slightly above the midline when positioning them on the trunk.
This "centering" effect may mean that the way in which the head-
trunk ratio produces the body-proportion effect is in the way in
which he defines the visual centre of gravity of the pre-drawn
figure.   There is some suggestive evidence which may bear on this
point.

Measurements carried out on spontaneous drawings include a
great deal of error (a problem which dogged the massive work of
Schuyten, 1904), and the series of pre-drawn figures used here is
not optimal for measuring fine positioning.   Accordingly, we
replaced the trunk circle in the series with a single straight line
and repeated the experiment.   The results were clear.   For each
of the figures, tadpole drawers positioned the arms higher up the
trunk than did young conventional drawers.   Thus it seems possible
that the tadpole drawers were scanning the whole figure to find the
visual centre of gravity, whereas the conventional drawers were
analysing the figure and considering only the trunk.   This is the
first step towards fine positioning; and later the children will
specify the shoulder region as a cue <u>independent</u> of the rest of the
figure proportions.   That is to say, they will extract a cue which
is relatively context-independent.   But these preschool children
are not yet doing it (which, incidentally, argues against the
proposition that the trunk is drawn <u>in order to</u> represent shoulders).
These conclusions must remain tentative: we have not yet fully
analysed the data.

In the experiments on the body-proportion effect, we collected
data from two-hundred-and-ten preschool children.   Not all of these
were tadpole drawers, of course.   One interesting finding was that
scribblers also strongly showed the effect.   This means two things;
first that the pre-drawn figure elicited drawings of arms and legs,
of which one had no indication from their spontaneous productions,
and, secondly, that they were responsive to the same position cue
as the tadpole drawers despite never having successfully organised
limb positioning for themselves.   There is no sharp break between

the scribbling and the tadpole "stages" in this respect.   The
conventional drawers in the sample also showed the body-proportion
effect, to a small extent.   Thus the advance represented by being
able to draw the trunk spontaneously does not abolish that particular
position cue entirely.   We have already noted the similarity between
the tadpole figure and the early conventional man in gross arm
positioning on the body part.   Further, recall that both tadpole
drawers and early conventional drawers may show end-anchoring in
drawing the legs before the arms.   From all these points it is
clear that scribblers, tadpole drawers and young conventional
drawers do share important graphic behavioural similarities.   This
is what one would expect if all of them were trying to deal with
similar task-demands and overcome similar planning problems.   But
this must remain only a tentative conclusion, since the detailed
work necessary to explore the possible links between end-anchoring,
the body-proportion effect and the degree of fine positioning in
spontaneous drawings, has yet to be done.   If links do exist, one
would expect that those children who show end-anchoring in their
spontaneous drawings would be more prone to the effect than those
who show temporal-spatial mapping, and those who spontaneously draw
arms at the shoulder region to be completely immune.

When limbs are positioned on a drawing, the edge of the body
part to which they are attached acts as a baseline.   The concept
of a baseline, or reference line, is more conveniently dealt with
in considering problems of relative orientation.   Accordingly, we
now turn to general reference problems, and will later apply these
to the orientation of the arms and one role of the facial features.

ORIENTATION   AND   REFERENCE   LINES

In many serial order tasks, there are very strong context
effects constraining the child's actions.   It is very difficult
for young children to place objects in a straight line when this is
to run diagonally across a table, because they are tempted to use
the edge of the table as a reference cue (Piaget and Inhelder, 1956;
Laurendeau and Pinard, 1970, Experiment 2).   The table edge acts
as a distracting external frame of reference.   A similar difficulty
is found in drawing, judging and remembering the orientation of,
diagonal lines within a square frame of reference - the "oblique
effect" (Olson, 1970; Berman, 1976; Cunningham and Haskulich,
1974), or in placing cut-out shapes to match a model which is non-
orthogonal to the frame (Naeli and Harris, 1976).   There is thus
evidence that there may well be a general problem of how to isolate,
and act upon, cues which are internal to a display, and cues which
are external to it.   Perhaps the most rigorous set of studies in
this whole area are those done by Bryant (1974), on the basis of
which he says: "It can be suggested quite reasonably that between

the ages of four and eight years there is a transition from external
to internal categories in orientation perception". The same seems
to be true of his work on relative position responses (see also
Vurpillot and Berthoud, 1969). It should be emphasised that most
of the designs in this area are somewhat confounded; but the few
adequate experiments certainly sustain the proposition that young
children do utilise the external frame of reference in dealing with
orientation and position problems.

The role of external reference cues is most powerfully brought
out when they are placed in opposition to internal cues. But the
point must not be overlooked that if children rely on external cues,
this may actually aid them in the case of certain planning difficulties in drawing. Thus it is a great advance to learn to
construct baselines such as grass, sea and sky in a drawing. Such
lines directly map cues from the external frame onto the internal
structure of the picture. Barnhart (1942) has made some observations relevant to this problem; also see an interesting experiment
by Millar (1975). From the present point of view, it is a reasonable strategy for the children to adopt, and one which they may
hold to, quite firmly, to the despair of art teachers. Again, the
same mapping function is served in planning a drawing of a house
whereby the edges of the house can be drawn parallel to the edges
of the page. The roof remains difficult of course, because
obliques are involved, and many children draw curved roofs, then
graduate to asymmetrical ones. The edges of the house now act as
new reference lines, and the internal elements, such as windows are
often placed straight on them, as in Figure 10. Such stereotype
may be irritating to many adults, but it is an excellent solution
to a most difficult planning problem, that of internally structuring
a blank page with salient edges. The solution is to map external
cues onto internal ones, which then take over for the purpose of
relating "floating" features. Before we apply this argument to
human figure drawing, it is necessary to describe just one aspect
of placing lines on baselines, for it exemplifies the role of an
internal reference line as a cue for a potentially variable feature.

It will be noticed that the chimney in Figure 10 is out of
true with reference to the external framework and the walls of the
house. The most plausible explanation is that this results from
using the orientation of the proximal baseline, the roof, as a
reference cue, and, since the chimney cannot be put parallel to
it, normalising the acute angle to the perpendicular. We know
from Piaget's work that perpendiculars are reasonably easy. One
also finds the same phenomenon in drawings of trees on a hillside
or the water level in a tilted bottle. Ibbotson and Bryant (1976)
have succeeded in demonstrating this "perpendicular error" with
abstract stimuli. They asked children to draw a line, or to place
a rod, on a baseline to match a target line at an acute angle on a

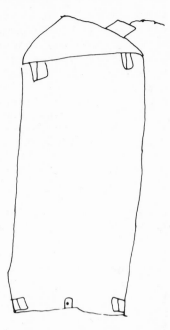

Figure 10. House by Sarah, aged 3 yrs. 10 mths.

Figure 11. Drawings by Sarah aged 3 yrs. 11 mths. showing
the arms in perpendicular orientation to the trunk baseline

model baseline.   The children typically normalised the relationship to the perpendicular when the baseline was tilted or horizontal.   This was not due to an inability to perceive or draw acute
angles, since they were relatively immune to the perpendicular
error when given a vertical baseline.   The normalisation may be
regarded as the result of response bias.   The children knew what
to do but had difficulties in doing it, except when the baseline
coincided with the most internal one possible, namely the child's
own vertical polar axis.   Recent work in psycholinguistics has
stressed the privileged status of the vertical axis in semantic
acquisition.   The perpendicular error reveals that the proximal
reference line may exert an important influence under certain
circumstances, and the vertical effect indicates that the error
has the status of a performance problem.   In this respect it
resembles the body-proportion effect, and Ibbotson and Bryant have
indicated this link between the two types of graphic behaviour.

     We may now apply these lessons to human figure drawing.
First, normalisation to the perpendicular is easily discernible in
the drawings in Figure 11, so we know that general orientation
problems apply here.   Let us consider the conditions under which
the axis of the whole figure is tilted.   In general, it should be
relatively easy to keep figures roughly vertical because there is
usually a salient reference cue in the edge of the page.   Of course,
the heterogeneity of the human figure drawing means that it will be
difficult to align perfectly, but error should be small.

     There is one internal cue which is often drawn in a perpen-
dicular relationship to the body axis, and that is the axis of the
eyes.   This is therefore placed to serve as an internal reference
cue for the body axis; and it is particularly well placed, given
end-anchoring on the head as a polar feature.   Many surveys have
commented on the reliability with which eyes are drawn.   Goodnow
and Friedman (1972) gave children a drawing completion task, in
which the eyes were sometimes given a vertical axis.   They observed
cue competition in the children's response to this, whereby horizontal and "compromise" tilted figures could be elicited.   This
certainly shows the emergence of an internal cue, but for present
purposes, the design is unsatisfactory, since the internal cue was
aligned with the horizontal external cue.   Elizabeth Bassett (1976)
corrected this by giving oblique eye-axes.   This produced clear
results.   Four-year-olds produced tilted figures, whilst six-year-
olds tried to utilise the external frame of reference.   The conclusion is that the match or mismatch between internal and external
cues can powerfully influence orientation in drawing; and it is
still an open research question as to the conditions under which one
or other cue will exert maximal effect on different aspects of a
drawing.   The development of routines for handling such operations
is a most important part of the child's mastery over planning

problems.   There is one further aspect of the frame of reference,
namely the way in which it serves to set a boundary to the drawing.
The problem of relative size in drawing forms the next section.

SIZE   SCALING

In order to draw properly it is necessary to plan properly so
as to avoid running into the edge of the paper, but this is a
particularly difficult trick to learn, especially for preschool
children.   However, if one begins the drawing in the middle of the
page, the external frame of reference is relatively remote, and
there is much space for the figure to become disorganised.   Unfortunately there is a scarcity of evidence upon the determinants of
children's choice of starting point in a drawing.   There is a
little evidence from Wallach's studies that individual consistency
may be quite high in respect of the typical size chosen for a
particular topic.   However, we do not know whether or not this is
correlated with consistency in choice of starting point position.
Certainly, on the basis of the present emphasis on planning problems,
we expect that systematic determinants should be relatively easy to
discover.   Gridley (1938) reported that children could, on request,
reduce the size of the human figure drawings by a small amount when
the size of the available paper increased in implicit competition
with the instructions;   and that when the two were in conjunction,
i.e. a larger figure requested and larger paper provided, the figure
was enlarged dramatically.   Her data are complex and her method
confounded.   Research in this area could be fruitful, and may
relate to the following problem of relative size amongst the body
parts.

Gridley (1938) noticed that her four-year-olds sometimes
responded to a request to draw another figure of a different size
by altering the proportions of the figure.   Thus, in reducing size,
a core construction, which she calls the "basal form" was reduced,
but other body parts may remain undiminished.   The children did
not necessarily scale down the figure harmoniously;   and rescaling
was more easily applied to some elements than to others.   It must
be noted that the data are extremely scanty;   and only sustain the
proposition that there is some indication of a viable area of study
here.   The reason why it may be of great importance is because of
children's immense tendency to draw the head larger than the trunk,
well into middle childhood.   But note that the head is drawn before
the trunk when there is far more space to utilise on the page;   and
it has to be large enough to include the facial features.   In addition, when drawing the trunk the child has to use the lower points
of the head as a position cue as well as ensuring that the trunk
joins the head.   By themselves, without detailed research it is
unwise to conclude that these factors would entail a _smaller_ trunk

than the head; but the existence of different planning problems
affecting the two body segments certainly leads us to find differential size entirely comprehensible.   It would be nice if we could
persuade young children to draw the trunk before the head on some
trials, but we have been quite unable to get them to do so.
Altering order throws their accustomed routines quite out of gear,
and they almost universally have refused to oblige us.   However,
there is one obvious technique which is applicable.   Children are
accustomed to putting parts together to make up a figure, and we
have found that they very readily agree to make a felt person out
of cut-out pieces in any order we select.   We have therefore been
giving them a choice between body parts of different sizes in order
to construct a person, and seeing whether differential temporal
order affected the relative size of the head compared with the
trunk, and arms compared with legs.   In one experiment we found
that it was the second element which tended to be larger than the
first, but this failed to appear with a slightly different technique,
and so far we have not yet succeeded in identifying the major determinants of relative size.   When we identify these, the body-
proportion effect, the influence of relative size on positioning,
may become clearer.

CONCLUSIONS

     The human figure presents design problems to the child when
drawing.   His performance characteristics help us make a task-
demand analysis of the problem.   This in itself is nothing new;
but what is new is the emphasis on a set of concepts all at the
same explanatory level, and taken from general experimental psychology, which should be utilised.   The child has to co-ordinate
the temporal and spatial ordering of parts, monitor position and
orientation cues, and scale relative size.

     Many earlier authors made excellent observations on such
issues.   In particular, it is well worth reading Rouma (1913),
Passy (1891) and Brown (1897) used dictation methods, Baldwin (1897)
both named and drew body parts for copying, and Ames (1943, 1945)
developed picture completion methods (continued by Ames and Ilg,
1963).   The development of integrated routines leading to stereo-
typy is implicit in Lukens (1896), and some illuminating comments
on this are contained in Eng (1931).   Perhaps the best source of
potentially testable hypotheses is the work of Luquet (1913, 1920,
1927).   In particular, Luquet discussed at length the possibility
that there was more than one type of tadpole figure, and sketched
out a sort of incomplete cue conflict model.   The proposal that
the tadpole category encompasses both figures with an undifferentiated head-trunk (Arnheim, 1954) and ones without a trunk needs
to be taken seriously.   The advantage of the present analysis,

favouring the latter possibility, is that the generation of the
tadpole figure can be treated by applying more general psychological
concepts than those commonly employed; and can lead to the application of simple scaling methods designed to control responses, which
can generate new phenomena.   The use of incomplete drawings, or
the provision of selected cues, helps us observe the kinds of
strategies which children employ in dealing with them.   Their
choice of strategy tells us a great deal about their drawing problems.   Convincing though post hoc analyses of finished products
may be, they cannot substitute for performance analysis of ongoing
processes.

     The present account has four useful aspects which may outweigh
its disadvantages.   The first is that it can be used to generate
many related new predictions, and identify new problem areas.   We
have particularly identified problems of integrating spatial and
temporal ordering and the utilisation of cues for position, orientation and relative size, and laid stress on new phenomena like the
perpendicular error and the body-proportion effect.   These may be
used to emphasise what scribblers, tadpole drawers and early conventional drawers have in common rather than what divides them.
What they have in common is that they are trying to plan their
drawings in the face of the same definable set of task demand
problems.   Thus both the tadpole figure and the early conventional
figure have the head and legs end-anchored in precisely the correct
position to define the top and bottom of the figure, the arms are
positioned very coarsely on the figure in a similar sort of way,
the temporal order of production is similar, and the body-
proportion effect can be discerned to a definable extent.   There
is bound to be much more in common, and it should be worth conducting
research to "close the gap" between scribblers and conventional
drawers.

     The second advantage of the present approach is related to the
first.   If there is a definable set of task demands to be responded
to, and if these are general in nature rather than being confined
to infantile aesthetics, then adults should show similar phenomena.
We have argued that the generation of the tadpole figure is precisely
because general serial order problems are a dominant task demand.
It is very likely that one would be able to deal with adults'
planning problems in the same terms if one asked them to draw
complex figures.   However it is neater if one can find the same
phenomena with the same stimulus materials in adults; and this
has been a major part of the work being conducted here in Bristol
by Brenda Barnard, using mentally subnormal adults.   They do indeed draw the tadpole form, show the body-proportion effect, the
temporal order effects etc.   This does suggest that we are here
dealing with general problems rather than peculiarly childish ones.
At the same time, it enables us to argue that certain accounts of

drawing which emphasise children's inadequate language, poor motor
control or peculiar visual experience, are not of central importance.
It is quite impressive to see an adult who can perform very complex
motor tasks, draw a tadpole figure with robust, determined strokes of
the pen.   Incidentally, since some adult tadpole drawers are above
average size, it does not seem plausible to level the same charge
against them that is commonly levelled against children, namely
that the tadpole figure represents a compulsory "worm's-eye view"
of a real person.   Again, the temptation to treat drawings as
though they were privileged photographs of a mental image should
be resisted.

The third advantage of the present approach is that we may now
return to the excellent literature of up to a half-century ago and
rework its material.   That is not to say that such literature is
commonly ignored, for many modern writers continually refer to it.
But they utilise it in an inappropriate way as a source of observations.   Primarily it should be used as a source for the generation
of testable hypotheses.   To cite their work at face value is to
take an impermissible short cut, to by-pass the need for the
application of laborious experimentation.   The present work stemmed
from an attempt to formalise Luquet's position (Freeman, 1972).

Finally, if there is any merit in this paper, it is as a
"ground clearing" exercise.   Concepts of mental imagery, aesthetic
aims, projective processes and interpretation have become entangled
in a thick undergrowth (if you will excuse the mental imagery used
here).   If we can define the level at which planning problems
operate, and categorise the variant forms of drawing which normally
result, we may then be able to clear the way for the infinitely
more important study of the operation of the passions (Freeman,
1976).   Until we do so, as Abercrombie and Tyson (1966) point out
we continually run the risk of interpreting variant forms as
obvious and deviant symptoms, on the basis of circumstantial
evidence, when such variants may easily appear in normal drawings.
The present account accords well with such a view (Abercrombie,
pers. comm.).   As a last thought, it is often suggested that
variation in orientation in drawings is correlated with brain
damage.   They may well be true, but it certainly is not proven
at all.

BIBLIOGRAPHY

ABERCROMBIE, M.L.J. & TYSON, M. C., Body image and draw-a-man test
    in cerebral palsy, Developmental Medical Child Neurology, 1966,
    8, pp. 9-15

AMES, L. B., The Gesell incomplete man test as a differential
    indicator of average and superior behaviour in preschool
    children, Journal of Genetic Psychology, 1943, 62, pp. 217-274

AMES, L. B., Free drawing and completion drawing: a comparative study of preschool children, Journal of Genetic Psychology, 1945, 66, pp. 161-165

AMES, L. B. & Ilg, F. L., The Gesell incomplete man test as a measure of developmental status, Genetic Psychology Monographs, 1963, 68, pp. 247-307

ARNHEIM, R., Art and Visual Perception, Berkeley, University of California Press, 1954

BALDWIN, J. M., Mental development in the child and the race (sic), New York, Macmillan, 1897

BARNHART, E. N., Developmental stages in compositional construction in children's drawings, Journal of Experimental Education, 1942, II, pp. 156-184

BASSETT, E. M., The young child's perception and representation of the human figure, Unpublished M.A. thesis, University of Lancaster, 1976. See also Chapter 3

BERMAN, P. W., Young children's use of the frame of reference in construction of the horizontal, vertical and the oblique, Child Development, 1976, (in press)

BERMAN, P. W., CUNNINGHAM, J. G. & HASKULICH, J., Construction of the horizontal, vertical and oblique by young children: failure to find the "oblique effect", Child Development, 1974, 45, pp. 474-478

BROWN, E. E., Notes on children's drawings, University of California Publications in Education, 1897, 8, pp. 1-75

BRYANT, P. E., Perception and understanding in young children, London, Methuen, 1974

BURK, F., The genetic versus the logical order in drawing, Pedagogical Seminary, 1902, 9, pp. 296-323

CONNOLLY, K. J. & ELLIOTT, J., The evolution and ontogeny of hand function, in BLURTON-JONES, N. (ed.) Ethological Studies of Child Behaviour, Cambridge University Press, 1972

DILEO, J. H., Young children and their drawings, New York, Brunner, 1970

ENG, H., The psychology of children's drawings, London, Routledge, 1931

FREEMAN, N. H., Process and product in children's drawing, Perception, 1972, 1, pp. 123-140

FREEMAN, N. H., A systematic study of a common production error in children's drawings, Paper presented to the Experimental Psychology Society, in Cambridge, 5-6 July, 1973

FREEMAN, N. H.,   Do children draw men with arms coming out of the
    head? Nature, 1975a, 254, pp. 416-417

FREEMAN, N. H.,   Drawing conclusions, New Behaviour, 1975b, 3,
    pp. 17-19

FREEMAN, N. H., EISER, C. & SAYERS, J.,   Children's strategies in
    drawing 3-D relations on a 2-D surface, Journal of Experimental
    Child Psychology, 1976 (in press)

FREEMAN, N. H.,   Children's drawings: cognitive aspects, Journal of
    Child Psychology and Psychiatry, 1976 (in press)

FREEMAN, N. H. & HARGREAVES, S.,   Directed movements and the body-
    proportion effect in preschool children's human figure drawing,
    Quarterly Journal of Experimental Psychology, 1977 (in press)

GOLOMB, C.,   Children's representation of the human figure: the
    effects of models, media and instructions, Genetic Psychology
    Monographs, 1973, 87, pp. 197-251

GOLOMB, C.,   Young children's sculpture and drawing, Cambridge,
    Harvard University Press, 1974

GOODNOW, J. J. & FRIEDMAN, S.,   Orientation in children's human
    figure drawings, Developmental Psychology, 1972, 7, pp. 10-16

GRIDLEY, P. F.,   Graphic representation of a man by four-year-old
    children in nine prescribed drawing situations, Genetic
    Psychology Monographs, 1938, 20, pp. 183-350

HARRIS, D. B.,   Children's drawings as measures of intellectual
    maturity, New York, Harcourt, Brace and World, 1963

HURLOCK, E. B. & THOMSON, J. L.,   Children's drawings: an
    experimental study of perception, Child Development, 1934, 5,
    pp. 127-138

IBBOTSON, A. & BRYANT, P. E.,   The perpendicular error and the
    vertical effect, Perception, 1976, 5, pp. 319-326

KELLOGG, R.,   Analysing children's art, Palo Alto, National Press,
    1970

LAURENDEAU, M. & PINARD, A.,   The development of the concept of
    space in the child, New York, International Universities Press,
    1970

LIBEN, L.,   Evidence for developmental differences in spontaneous
    seriation and its implications for past research on long term
    memory improvement, Developmental Psychology, 1975, 11,
    pp. 121-125

LOWENFELD, V. & BRITTAIN, W. L.,   Creative and mental growth, New
    York, Macmillan, 1964

LUKENS, H. T.,   A study of children's drawings in the early years,
    Pedagogical Seminary, 1896, 4, pp. 79-110

LUQUET, G. H.,   Les dessins d'un enfant, Paris, Alcan, 1913

LUQUET, G. H.,   Les bonshommes tétards dans le dessin enfantin,
    Journal de Psychologie Normale, 1920, 17, pp. 684-710

LUQUET, G. H.,   Le dessin enfantin, Paris, Alcan, 1927

MACHOVER, K.,   Personality projection in the drawings of the human
    figure, Springfield, Thomas, 1949

MILLAR, S.,   Visual experience or translation rules?   Drawing the
    human figure by blind and sighted children, Perception, 1975,
    4, pp. 363-371

MORRIS, D.,   The biology of art, London, Methuen, 1962

NAELI, H. & HARRIS, P. L.,   Orientation of the diamond and the
    square, Perception, 1976, 5, pp. 73-78

OLSON, D. R.,   Cognitive development: the child's acquisition of
    diagonality, New York, Academic Press, 1970

PASSY, J.,   Note sur les dessins d'enfants, Revue Philosophique,
    1891, 32, pp. 614-621

PIAGET, J. & INHELDER, B.,   The child's conception of space, London,
    Routledge, 1956

ROUMA, G.,   Le langage graphique de l'enfant, Paris, Mischel et
    thron, 1913

SCHUYTEN, M. C.,   De orrspronkelijke 'ventjes' der Antwerpsche
    schoolkindern, Paedologisch Jaarboek, 1904, 5, pp. 1-87

SCHUBERT, A.,   Drawings of Orotchen children and young people,
    Pedagogical Seminary, 1930, 37, pp. 232-243

SHAPIRO, T. & STINE, J.,   The figure drawings of three-year-old
    children, The Psychoanalytic Study of the Child, 1965, 20,
    pp. 298-309

SMITH, D.,   Systematic study of chimpanzee drawing, Journal of
    Comparative and Physiological Psychology, 1973, 82, pp. 406-414

SNYDER, R. T. & GASTON, D. S.,   Journal of Clinical Psychology, 1970
    26, pp. 377-383

TRABASSO, T., RILEY, R. & WILSON, E.,   The representation of linear
    order and spatial strategies in reasoning: a developmental
    study, in FALMAGNE, R. (ed.) Reasoning: Representation and
    Process, New York, Wiley, 1975

TULVING, E. & PEARLSTONE, Z.,   Availability versus accessibility of
    information in memory for words, Journal of Verbal Learning and
    Verbal Behaviour, 1966, 5, pp. 381-391

VURPILLOT, E. & BERTHOUD, M.,   Évolution génétique de la localisation
    dans un cadre de référence rectangulaire, Année Psychologique,
    1969, 69, pp. 393-406

A SINGLE CASE STUDY OF AN AUTISTIC CHILD

WITH EXCEPTIONAL DRAWING ABILITY*

Lorna Selfe

With an Introduction and Postscript by Elizabeth Newson.

'To marvel is the beginning of knowledge and when we
cease to marvel we may be in danger of ceasing to know'.

Gombrich

Gombrich's words are exquisitely pertinent to introduce Nadia,
a child who turns upside down all our notions of the development of
graphic representation. How incredible we found her, when we first
saw her at the Child Development Research Unit, Nottingham
University, may be understood when I explain that, some years
earlier, we had been the fortunate inheritors of twenty-four-thou-
sand children's 'pictures of mummy', the results of a Sunday newspaper competition, and had spent some time analysing the stage-
development of the ability to depict the human form. As a result,
we had mounted an exhibition** for the British Association for the
Advancement of Science; and we thought we knew what was possible
for a six-year-old and what was not.

Nadia was brought to my clinic at the age of 6:4, referred by
her mother, who was worried that she was not progressing in her
local school for severely subnormal children. In this clinic we

---

* This brief report is published as a much more detailed study (in
press): Selfe, L., Nadia: a case of extraordinary drawing ability
in an autistic child, Academic Press, 1977.

** 'The Innocent Eye', available as an illustrated audiotape:
Medical Recording Services Foundation.

use an integrated team approach; one person, working with the child
in the playroom, attempts to 'discover' the child to the rest of the
team, consisting of several observers, the parents and myself, all
sitting in the darkened observation-room.   Lorna Selfe worked with
Nadia on this occasion; Nadia's mother talked about the child.
During the session, she produced a sheaf of half a dozen drawings,
saying that perhaps I might be interested.   Nadia, meanwhile, was
scrubbing away with the fat wax crayon which had seemed suitable to
her general level, on the other side of the one-way screen.   How
were we to know that her medium was ball-point and that her performance depended obsessionally upon this?

My first reaction to the drawings was to marvel; my second, I
am ashamed to say, to doubt.   In the conference that followed the
clinic, we all examined the drawings, and the consensus was strong:
'She's having you on, Elizabeth, it's not possible for a six-year-
old to draw like that'.   Reluctantly, I began to agree; it was
more traumatic to me to think that in my clinic setting a parent
had lied to me than to have my 'understanding' of children's
drawing upset, yet clearly the drawings were not possible.   Lorna
said, without much hope, that if they did turn out to be authentic,
she would do a protracted study of this child.   A few days later,
Nadia showed her...

Nadia was born in Nottingham to Ukrainian emigré parents on
the 24th October 1967.   She is the second-born child in a family
of three children.   The development of the other two children is
proceeding normally.   They are bilingual.

Nadia failed to develop language properly and the few words
she had at nine months disappeared.   Her linguistic background is
unusual in so far as the family at home speak Ukrainian.   When
Nadia's language failed to develop the family adopted the policy of
speaking to her in English on the assumption that if she could only
master one language it had better be English.

I worked with Nadia from March to September, 1974, when she was
six-and-a-half years of age, and I should like to confine myself to
a description of her during this period.   I observed her in regular
two-hour sessions twice a week at school or in her home.   She had
an extremely limited vocabulary of some ten single-word utterances
heard over this five-month period.

The over-riding impression of Nadia was of lethargy and impas-
sivity.   She was very clumsy, poorly co-ordinated and excessively
slow in her movements.   She did not respond to command or instruction readily.   It was extremely difficult to know whether she
merely did not comprehend or whether she refused to co-operate.

At three-and-a-half years of age, Nadia suddenly displayed an extraordinary drawing ability which was marked from the outset by a high level of skill, manual dexterity and quality so sadly absent in all other areas of her functioning.   This ability continued to develop over the next three years.   I was fortunate to work with her during a very productive period.

I witnessed her drawing on many occasions during my work with her, although, owing to the problem of communication, she would seldom draw to order.   However, I was able to make a video film of her in action.   It is important to emphasise that these drawings were not copied from pictures.   In fact, she can draw from life.

I found that the inspiration for the drawings sometimes came from a child's picture book in which the quality of the original was often crude or highly stylised.   She studied the picture with great attention several weeks before she executed a similar drawing. However, her drawing showed many changes and embellishments from the original.   She could present the subject at a new angle, so that any form of simple imaging or eidetic memory as an explanation for this ability has to be abandoned.

Karl Buhler as early as 1930 said that by the time the child can draw more than a scribble - by age three or four - an already well-formed body of conceptual knowledge formulated in language dominates his memory and controls his graphic work.

Harris (1963) claimed that children do not draw what they see but what they know.   They draw in symbols and these symbols represent their concepts of the object.   To quote Harris:

"No data has ever appeared to controvert the general
import of Goodenough's observations and conclusions...
Drawings of objects are based on concepts;   concepts
are based on experience with objects.   Experience
increases the aspects of objects to be reacted to,
understood and incorporated in drawing".

In other words the normal child when drawing is dominated by his concepts - not by his percepts.   He draws what he knows rather than what he sees: although, as Gombrich (1960) has pointed out, one of the central dilemmas for any theory of representation is that seeing informs knowing and vice versa.   The two are logically related and are not independent.

The pictures largely speak for themselves;   however, some points of comparison can be briefly raised here.   In the drawings of the average child of this age, we can see many examples of the dominance of the concept over the percept.   For example, in Figure 1. the man is drawn with two legs where only one should be visible.

Figure 1. Man on a Horse – drawn by an average six–and–a–half–year–old child (Wechsler Intelligence Scale for Children IQ 105)

Figure 2. Man on a Horse - drawn by Nadia
at age six years three months

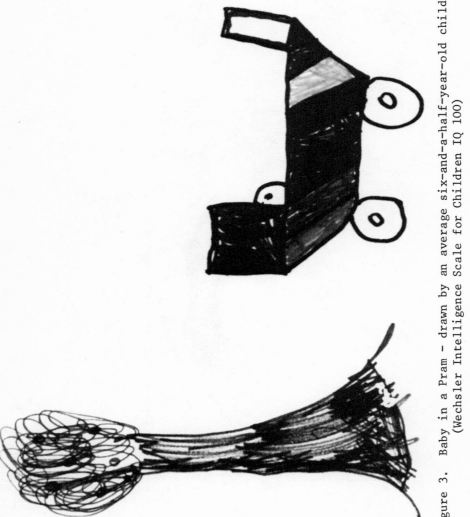

Figure 3.   Baby in a Pram – drawn by an average six-and-a-half-year-old child
(Wechsler Intelligence Scale for Children IQ 100)

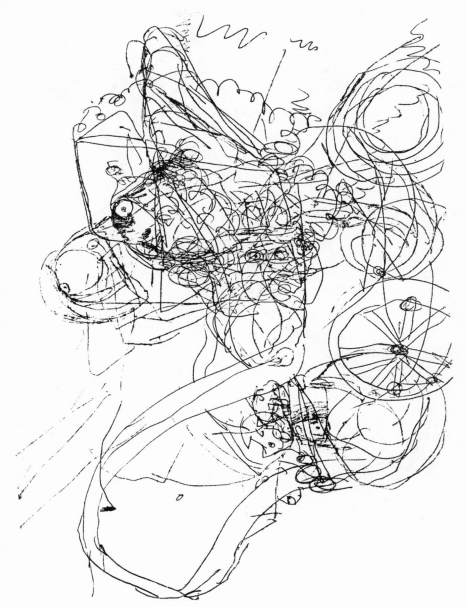

Figure 4. Baby in a Pram drawn by Nadia between four-and-a-half and five-and-a-half years

Figure 5. Horse and rider, with sketch for a cockerel, Nadia, 7:0

Normative studies, reviewed by Harris (1963), have pointed out the poorly developed use of relative size or proportion in young children's drawings.   McCarty (1924) says that proportion is not used effectively until after age eight.   Similarly, children rarely attempt perspective or foreshortening until after the age of eleven. Attempts at shading and shadow before eleven years are unusual and children of this age always use colour for preference.

Children, and even adults, regularly distort the image to fit it into the paper and tend to be governed by 'wholeness or complete- ness' at the expense of the true form.   Only three of Nadia's early drawings can be included here although it is important to state that she has a quite wide variety of subjects.   Generally she prefers to draw animals.   Average children typically choose humans or houses as their subject.

Finally, in children of this age, motor control is still poor. Connolly and Elliott (1972) have shown an age-related increase in grasp and precision movement.

COGNITIVE ASSESSMENT

Nadia was tested on a battery of standard assessment procedures. The results indicated a basal performance.   We have no real indica- tion of ceilings, nor could it definitely be concluded that she could not pass an item on the tests.   The composite results of testing indicated profound deficits on the language side both in comprehension and expression.

She also appeared to lack the prerequisites of language develop- ment.   She could not imitate and did not engage in symbolic or imitative play.   She could repeat monosyllables but not two syll- ables.   She did not use echolalia.

Gross motor development was very poor.   She could not hop or walk upstairs one step at a time.   Fine motor control was also surprisingly poor in view of her drawing ability.   For example, she could not do up buttons or use a knife and fork together.   She was tested for a receptive/expressive aphasia but she appeared to be uninterested or incapable of learning word and object associations through a visual means.

On some of the visual and perceptual tasks on standard tests she passed items at her age level.

Some of the relevant physiological facts pertaining to Nadia are of interest.   There was no evidence of birth trauma.   She was born in hospital after a normal pregnancy.   However, brain damage is suspected for the following reasons:

1) The EEG Report showed some abnormal activity located at the Sylvian Fissure (this being close to language areas) and some abnormal response to photic stimulation, suggesting the possibility of an epileptogenic focus.

2) Nadia is left handed. However, she has one sibling who is also left handed.

3) She has a flattened occiput.

4) There is evidence of abnormal substances excreted in Nadia's urine, suggesting a metabolic or endocrine disorder which could either be inherited or more probably the result of brain damage.

5) Skeletal and bone age are outside the normal limits.

THE   RARITY   OF   THE   CASE

My study of Nadia naturally led me to look for any similar cases of extraordinary drawing ability.

Even in normal children a representational ability well beyond their years is extremely rare. Goodenough (1923) was led to an intense search for talented child artists. She discovered that while child musicians and lightening calculators are not at all uncommon, the child with an outstanding representational ability is a very rare event. (In fact none are reported in her work!)

A search of the literature on children with special talents and mentally handicapped children with special abilities or 'idiot savants' revealed only three cases of outstanding ability reported since 1900. However, there were no real comparisons with Nadia's case, since all three subjects were adults. And although mentally handicapped, at least two of them had fairly well developed language.

Stotijn-Egge, 1952, studied drawing in mentally retarded children up to age fourteen. She found that most mentally retarded children draw at their mental age level. Some of her subjects failed to produce drawings and she reported that these subjects did not possess language. All children who could achieve recognizable drawings of objects had developed language. Her study concluded that language is a prerequisite for drawing a recognizable object. Nadia of course is an exception to this.

CONCLUSIONS

Finally, I should like to raise some speculative issues which have interested me in considering this case.

In the first place I believe that a case like Nadia is very important for two reasons. Single case studies are important because they can help to establish the parameters of a skill. I have been interested to note that recently there have been calls for a return to ideographic studies of this type (Buffery, 1974; Shotter, 1975). Also, any universal theory on the development of children's art must allow for the possibility of drawing ability at this level in a child like this. Nadia is the exception that tests the rule.

However, the second of my speculations is that Nadia's ability is essentially different from the drawing of normal children. It is not that she has an accelerated development in this sphere. Her development is anomolous; and her drawing ability is as much a sign of her abnormality as is her lack of language.

My extremely tentative hypothesis is that her drawing ability, and more especially her lack of language, are indications of an impoverished conceptual system which has allowed her to develop a perceptual representational ability to a very high level. The problem for this hypothesis is, however, that other children with similar deficits do not develop the same ability.

The third area of conjecture relates to her obvious exceptional ability to retain a visual image. However, this imaging or eidetic ability alone cannot account for her drawing skill. Eidetikers are not noted for their drawing ability. The process of getting the image down on paper is far more complex: for example, the level of motor control required.

We have only 'soft' evidence to indicate that Nadia is brain damaged; but a picture can emerge of left hemisphere damage to the language areas of the brain and the compensatory development of a highly organised ability possibly located in the right hemisphere. This hemisphere is thought to be dominant for visuospatial skills. These speculations are purely conjectural and the problems of testing her seem insurmountable since she is mute and unco-operative. My study of Nadia had to be diluted over the very wide field of psychology. She provided me with a very rich source of interest but she largely remains an enigma.

If, as Lorna Selfe has suggested, Nadia's ability in drawing is inextricably bound up with her failure to formulate concepts verbally, what will be the result of linguistic improvements in such a child?

Nadia entered a school for autistic children at the age of 7:7, and this postscript is written after three-and-a-half terms' work with her.   She has become more sociable, although her attachments to others, especially to children, are very obsessional;   she appears to gain a great deal of security from the continual presence of children she favours and is highly aware of their every action, and distressed by their absence.

Her verbal comprehension has improved steadily;   she is able to play certain table games in a group, and obey single-action instructions and a few double-action requests.   She has a full understanding of concepts such as big/little, up/down, open/closed.

However, Nadia's expressive language improves only very slowly. She uses little speech spontaneously, and these tend to be single word utterances, though no longer monosyllabic.   Most of her spontaneous speech is concerned with children with whom she is obsessed: 'where Martin?' - 'give Martin'.   If she becomes distressed, there is considerable delayed echolalia.   Her teacher reports that 'her awareness of the structure of the school day and its events is greater than her ability to express this verbally, and it is only when there is a change of routine (e.g. a late taxi arrival, or a child absent) that she will spontaneously use speech to note the event'.

Within 1:1 teaching sessions, Nadia's speech is better.   She is building up short sentences to describe actions and events, given a visual stimulus.   She has successfully acquired usage of the pronoun 'me', and this has been taught via her self-portrait.

Sadly, Nadia seldom draws spontaneously now, although from time to time one of her horses appears on a steamed-up window!   If asked, however, she will draw, particularly portraits of the thirty-odd adults and children in the school.   These portraits may or may not be posed (though she gives little attention to the sitter), and they are recognisable likenesses (in her most productive period between six and seven she drew only one portrait from life, and that unrecognisable).   In style her drawings are now more economical with much less detail (see Figure 6);   often they have a Thurberesque quality.   The fact that Nadia, at eight-and-a-half, can produce recognizable drawings of the people around her makes her talent a remarkable one for her age: but one would no longer say that it is <u>unbelievable</u>.

Is this a tragedy?   For us, who love to be astonished, maybe. For Nadia, perhaps it is enough to <u>have been</u> a marvellous child. If the partial loss of her gift is <u>the price</u> of language, even just enough language to bring her into some kind of community of discourse with her small protected world, we must, I think, be prepared to pay that price on Nadia's behalf.

Figure 6.   Drawing by Nadia after some language development

ACKNOWLEDGEMENTS

        The authors are grateful to Mr Sam Grainger for the photo-
graphs.

BIBLIOGRAPHY

BUFFERY, A.W.H.,   Asymmetrical lateralisation of cerebral functions,
        in DIMOND, S. J. & BEAUMONT, J. (Eds.) Hemisphere function in
        the human brain, London, Elek. Science, 1974

BUHLER, K.,   The mental development of the child, London, Routledge
        & Kegan Paul, 1930

CONNOLLY, K. & ELLIOTT, J.,   The evolution and ontogeny of hand
        function, in BLURTON JONES, N. (Ed.) Ethological studies of
        child behaviour, Cambridge University Press, 1972

GOMBRICH, E. H.,   Art & Illusion, New York, Pantheon Books, 1960

GOODENOUGH, E. H.,   Measurement of intelligence by drawings,
        New York, Harcourt, Brace & World, 1926

HARRIS, D. B.,   Children's drawings as measures of intellectual
        maturity, New York, Harcourt, Brace & World, 1963

McCARTY, S.,   Children's drawings, Baltimore, Williams & Wilkins,
        1924

SHOTTER, J.,   Images of man, London, Methuen, 1975

STOTIJN-EGGE, S.,   Investigation of the drawing ability of low
        grade oligophrenics, Luctor et Emergo, Leiden, 1952

DISCUSSION OF THE PAPERS BY

NORMAN FREEMAN AND LORNA SELFE

   Member of audience.   Dr Freeman, you rejected the mental
imagery and syncretic thinking theories of children's drawing.
Can you say a little more about the mental imagery view?

   Freeman.   There are different kinds of mental imagery theory
but their kernel is that you can read off the child's mental imagery
from the drawn product.   For example, if you get a tadpole man
drawn, such a theory would entail that the child had a mental image
that corresponds to the drawing.   My own view is that all drawings
involve the labour of production.   There is no privileged way of
reading off from the drawing what the mental image is.

   Member of audience.   This doesn't necessarily reject the
mental imagery view, it merely shows the limitations of drawing as
an index of mental imagery.

   Freeman.   I disagree.   Certainly we have mental imagery but
unless we have independent criteria for its use, unless we can
devise a task in which we can make it help or hinder us as Brooks
(1967, 1968) did, we cannot say how it relates to drawing.   There
are no independent criteria in mental imagery accounts of drawing.
Goodenough and Harris (1950) for example, confuse accessibility and
availability in their account.   The point is that what a child can
access at a given time does not entail that that is all he has
available.

   One child I encountered said: "I can draw a head and I can
draw a body but I can never get them to join up".   This is a good
indication of the labour involved in producing a drawing.

45

Scribblers aged two will satisfactorily complete a drawing of a
head and body.   The elements are available even though the children
have no way of accessing them.   There is no way of getting to the
mental image from the surface structure of the final product.   It
is as absurd as getting to the deep structure of language from the
surface structure of an utterance.

Harris.   In reply to Norman, the experiment by Elizabeth
Bassett (Chapter 3) gave the children cardboard cutouts instead of
drawing.   If children are suffering from production problems, they
should show the same difficulty in constructing a man as in drawing
one.   In fact, the children don't have any problems.   The figures
always have a body, a head and so on.   So, while there are production problems in drawing, it is reasonable to think in terms of a
syncretic mental image which the provision of cardboard cutouts
bisects for the child.   In other words, the child has a very
global mental image and if you provide a cutout figure, you bypass
that syncreticism.

With respect to Lorna Selfe's work, I have been tempted to
think about the relationship between serial order problems in
drawing and serial order problems in language.   One of the striking
things about Nadia is that her drawings suggest that these problems
are not necessarily so related as we thought.   At least that's the
first step.   Here we have a very competent drawer with little
language ability.   On the other hand, it is possible that she is
actually tackling the drawing in rather a different way.   In any
case, I would be tempted to say that something like the imagery
theory is more plausible but what one has to do is to specify it,
not in terms of an eidetic image but in terms of the type of image
which is potentially rotatable and manipulable.

The kind of findings I have in mind are those of Maier (1931),
where pliers are used to solve a problem.   Naming the pliers leads
to difficulty in realising that they could be used as a weight.
Conversely, if there is no naming involved, then people are more
susceptible to the basic perceptual features.   It is almost as
though Nadia doesn't think of a person as a list of features but
for want of a better word, as a concrete image.   Now she is
developing language, I am sad to see that maybe this will disappear.

Member of audience.   Was Nadia capable of non-verbal symbolic
play?

Selfe.   No.   She didn't use objects symbolically in play.
The spatial-perceptual things which she did well were non-symbolic.

Newson.   Nadia didn't draw in the kind of serial order one
might expect.   She was rather like a sophisticated adult artist

in that one couldn't see how the picture was going to come out.
She would draw a little bit here, a little bit there, in fact bits
seemed to come in from all over the place. She would then economically put in the strokes that were needed to pull it all together.
At first it seemed good evidence for an eidetic image but then she
produced so many orientations that this was no longer a good explanation. However, she would certainly have a very strong image to
do it in this unexpected way.

Harris.   It is fascinating to compare Nadia with Norman's
example where the head and body are separated.   In Nadia's case,
it is almost as though all the planning was done beforehand and
the drawing is just a simple execution.   All the features are
pre-arranged as part of a composite.

Newson.   A simple execution is perhaps the wrong way of
putting it.   For example, in drawing an eye she would produce a
perfect circle with a dot right in the middle.   This is not quite
so simple.

Freeman.   Nadia is doing what artists attempt to do; map the
topology of a surface.   With her I think you get a long way in
talking about mental imagery.   If she had communicative power, she
would almost certainly communicate some image but...

Newson.   But if she had communicative power she almost
certainly wouldn't have the drawing ability.

Freeman.   That's the point, you see.   When children draw,
the kind of problems they have aren't artistic problems any more
than language reflects poetic problems.   In the main, their problems are planning problems.   You can get very good drawings if you
dictate the order of parts to a scribbler.   The scribbler will
draw at the six-year-old level because the planning problems are
minimised.   The queer thing is that Nadia is not working on this
type of system.   When her language picks up, there is no way that
her drawings can pick up.   There is a radical transformation.
She is now struggling with the same old boring problems that other
children struggle with.

This is not due to language as such.   When you learn a
language you have to co-ordinate various relationships.   Language
and drawing make use of the same kind of co-ordination skills.
When the child is ready to struggle with one set, she struggles
with the other and this is the result.

Newson.   Yes, but I disagree that children don't reproduce
stylistic effects because when I was teaching five-year-olds, years
ago, I got very frustrated by the fact that they could be drawing

marvellous birds until some parent would tell the child to draw a
bird using a tick.   They would all start drawing birds in that
way.   One of my children was tremendously pleased with her solution
to the problem of how to make a face look catty, a round face with
a large X across it and pointed ears.   Perspective tricks become
stereotyped in the same way.   Children get very enamoured with
particular stylistic techniques.

BIBLIOGRAPHY

BROOKS, L. R.,   The suppression of visualization by reading,
        Quarterly Journal of Experimental Psychology, 1967, 19,
        pp. 289-299

BROOKS, L. R.,   Spatial and verbal components of the act of recall,
        Technical Report 17, McMaster University, Department of
        Psychology, 1968

GOODENOUGH, F. & HARRIS, D. B.,   Studies in the psychology of
        children's drawings II 1928-1949, Psychological Bulletin,
        1950, 47, pp. 369-433

MAIER, N.R.F.,   Reasoning in Humans II.   The solution of a problem
        and its appearance in consciousness, Journal of Comparative
        Psychology, 1931, 12, pp. 181-194

PRODUCTION STRATEGIES IN THE CHILD'S DRAWING OF THE HUMAN FIGURE: TOWARDS AN ARGUMENT FOR A MODEL OF SYNCRETIC PERCEPTION

Elizabeth M. Bassett

ABSTRACT

The young child's drawing of the human figure is often incomplete. Typically, the trunk and/or the arms are omitted. Does this mean that the child's mental image is incomplete or alternatively that the problem lies in the serial and spatial ordering of components on the paper?

Two experiments examine the nature of the child's mental image and the production strategies he uses to translate this image into a representation.

Results suggest that the error may be attributed to a third hypothesis. That is, the image is complete but individual components are not clearly differentiated within that image.

EXPERIMENT 1

The maxim, "children draw what they know, not what they see", has long been in use, but it seems unlikely that the tadpole drawer, for example, does not 'know' of the existence of the trunk. Yet he omits the component from his drawing.

Such an error may be attributed to three alternative hypotheses:

a) The internal representation is structured from specific features only and is therefore, incomplete. That is, a model of analytic perception is operating, e.g. Gibson, 1969.

49

b) The internal representation is complete but undifferentiated. That is, a model of syncretic perception is operating, e.g. Maccoby, 1968.

c) The internal representation is conceptually differentiated and the problem lies in the translation of this complete representation to a graphic form, i.e. in placing components successively in their correct spatial layout, e.g. Freeman, 1975.

In order to investigate which of these hypotheses best fitted the tadpole drawing, i.e. head and leg drawings of the human figure, Experiment 1 was designed to establish the existence of production strategies and at the same time to try and discover the accuracy of the child's internal representation. Whether this would be incomplete, complete but undifferentiated or complete and differentiated, it was hoped that if a production strategy emerged this might reveal a methodological explanation of how the internal representation is translated.

Children were presented with two tasks; a drawing and a construction task (construction of a man from six cut-out parts).

For each task the sequential and spatial ordering of each component was noted in relation to:

a) The completed figure, i.e. the number of components used, e.g. the head, trunk, legs and arms.

b) The serial order in which these components appeared, and

c) the spatial orientation of the figure.

From a comparison of the drawing and construction tasks within the context of these criteria, two predictions could be made.

First, drawing would be as accurate as construction:

a) If the child's internal representation contains only distinguishing features of the human figure, i.e. if it is incomplete.

b) If the problem is one of production. Although the construction task involves more simple motor actions the serial and spatial ordering of components in a construction task must be identical to that in a drawing task.

Second, drawing would be less accurate than construction:

a) If the child's internal representation is complete but undifferentiated since isolating the components for the child will eliminate the problem.

METHOD

Subjects: Twenty-eight children (mean age = 4 yrs. 9 mths.; S.D. = 3.2 mths.) were tested in local primary schools in the Lancaster area.

Procedure and Apparatus: Each child was tested individually and was asked to perform two tasks:

a) To draw a picture of a man on a plain sheet of A4 paper.

b) To construct a picture of a man with six pieces of plain white card: a circle (diameter = 5 cms.), a large rectangle (5 X 7 cms.) and four smaller rectangles (2 = 8 X 2 cms., 2 = 6.5 X 1.5 cms.).

Half the children received task (a) first, half task (b).   The subject sat at a small table with the paper in front of him.

Task (a): Each subject was presented with an H.B. drawing pencil and was instructed, "Would you draw me a picture of a man on this piece of paper".

Task (b): The six pieces of card were randomly placed beside the paper.   E. then instructed the subject, "I'd like you to use these shapes to make a picture of a man.   You can use as many of the pieces as you want".

Scoring: The serial order in which each component appeared was recorded, e.g. Head (H), Trunk (T), Legs (L) and Arms (A). When the construction task had been completed, E. suggested she drew around the shapes to see what the man looked like as this was the only way to record the orientation of figural parts to each other.

RESULTS

The number of components used: Twenty-four of the children drew partial figures, i.e. one or more of the salient components were absent.   In the construction task, however, no partial figures appeared – all constructions were representational in that all six pieces were put together correctly in relationship to one another to form a human figure outline.   The Sign test was used to establish the superiority of the construction task in the number of components used, $(p < .001)$.

Table 1.   To show the number of components
omitted in the drawing and construction tasks.

	Head	Trunk	Legs	Arms
Drawing	0	12	1	15
Construction	0	0	0	0

Table 1 sets out the components that were omitted in each task.
From this it appears that arms were most frequently left out.   This
would fit the general finding that tadpole men (usually head and
legs) and incomplete figures (head, trunk and legs) have no arms.

Serial order in which components appeared: Figure 1 shows the
serial order in which components were either drawn or placed.   It
can be seen from this that the head is significantly the first
feature to appear in both tasks (fifty-three out of fifty-six).
Of head starters, more than two-thirds (forty) put the trunk next
and more than half of head starters (thirty-two) put the legs after
the trunk.

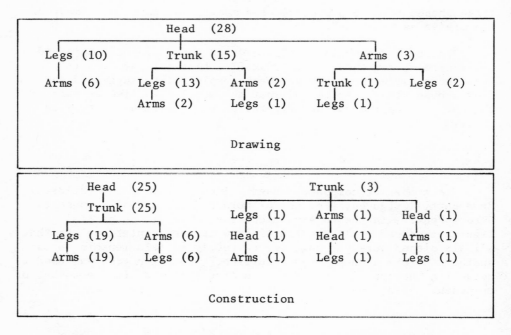

Figure 1.   To show Serial Order in which Components were
either drawn or constructed

Spatial orientation of the figure: Figure 2 demonstrates the typical orientation of the construction outline.   Children usually discriminated between arm and leg sizes choosing the slightly larger rectangles (8 X 2 cms.) for the legs, indicating proportionality.   Arms generally protruded from near centre of the trunk at 90°.

Drawings were spontaneously placed along the vertical axis, indicating that the internal representation of components does follow an upright orientation, viz. the head is always known to be at the top, and the legs at the bottom.   Spatial and serial top-to-bottom orders were thus synonomous.

Figure 2.   Typical orientation of construction:
Robert aged 4 yrs. 9 mths.

Thus, three major findings have emerged:

a) Children can construct a human figure more accurately than they can draw it.   This would imply that the internal representation is complete.   This rules out a model of analytic perception.

b) The results have shown that children typically do adopt a consistent serial order for production, i.e. the head first, followed by the trunk, legs and arms respectively.   Even when components are omitted in drawing this order remains

unchanged, e.g. tadpole men = head and legs.   Moreover,
spatial and serial top-to-bottom orders were synonomous.
This seems to rule out an hypothesis of a production error
on two counts.   First, there is no developmental change
in the drawing rules utilized by tadpole and representational
drawers in terms of serial and spatial ordering.   Second,
children do have a strategy for the spatial layout of
components.

c) Since the construction task was significantly more accurate
than the drawing task, the problem seems to be one of
differentiating components within the internal representation.

Before the results are discussed in the light of a syncretic
perception model, Experiment 2 attempts to discover more about the
child's production strategy.

EXPERIMENT 2

The results from Experiment 1 have shown that the young child
has a consistent mode of orienting and ordering his production in
both construction and drawing tasks, i.e. he will produce a human
figure from top to bottom.   To discover more about the child's
strategy, subjects were asked to draw a human figure upside down.
Three strategies might be observed:

a) The child may be using conventional rules of orienting the
figure on the paper, i.e. a page strategy.   He will work
from the top to bottom of the page placing the legs first.

b) The child may be adopting a figure to page strategy, i.e.
he would maintain serial order of production but work from
the bottom to the top of the page, placing the head first.

c) The child may be adopting a figure strategy, i.e. the head
appears at the top of the internal representation and will
be placed in its logical position at the top of the page.
Hence the figure will be upright.

In order to investigate these hypotheses, the above experiment
was replicated with a slight alteration in the instructions given.
The figure was to be upside down.

METHOD

Subjects: Twenty children (mean age = 4 yrs. 9 mths.;   S.D.
= 3.0 mths.) were tested in local primary schools in the Lancaster
area.

Procedure and Apparatus: Children were tested individually.
Before instructions were given, each child was presented with a

cardboard tree (8.2 cms. high) and was asked to make the tree upside down.   If this presented no obvious difficulty children were
instructed:

a) "Would you draw me a man that is upside down on this piece
   of paper."

b) "Would you put these pieces together to make an upside down
   man.   You can use as many of the pieces as you want."

The instructions were carefully given to avoid placement cues.
For example, an instruction to the effect 'draw a man standing on
his head' was not used in that children might immediately place the
head first and at the bottom of the page.

As before, half the children received task (a) first, half
task (b).

RESULTS

Children found the upside down tasks generally more difficult
than the upright tasks in Experiment 1.   This was demonstrated by
the length of time taken to perform.

Figure 3 shows the serial order in which components appeared.
Only one child deviated from the head start.   A Sign test indicated
the superiority of the construction task in the number of components
used, (p $<$.001).

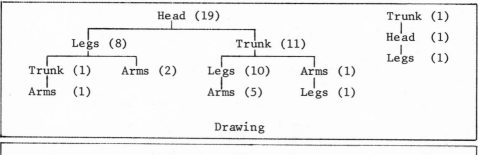

Drawing

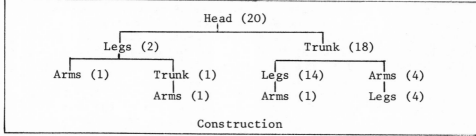

Construction

Figure 3.   To show Serial Order in which Components were
either drawn or constructed, in an inverted situation

Table 2 indicates the components omitted in both the drawing and construction tasks.   Again the arms, followed by the trunk are most likely to be omitted.   All figures were correctly oriented with the head towards the bottom of the page and the legs towards the top.

Table 2. To show the number of components omitted in the inverted drawing and construction tasks.				
	Head	Trunk	Legs	Arms
Drawing	0	7	0	11
Construction	0	1	0	0

It can be seen from the results that the second of the outlined hypotheses was supported.   That is, the child is adopting a figure to page strategy whereby the serial and spatial order of production remains consistent within the figure (i.e. head first, followed by trunk, legs and arms respectively), but the spatial arrangement on the page is reversed.   Thus, the serial order strategy of production for both upright and inverted figures remains consistent.

GENERAL   DISCUSSION

In order to make a representational drawing of the human figure, the child must:

   a) construct an image;   such an image must be perceived
      simultaneously;

   b) he must then break the image into separate components in
      order that he may

   c) serially order the execution of those parts onto the paper.

Explanations for the tadpole man have centred for the most part on (a), that the child's internal representation is incomplete, and (c), that the problem lies in "programming spatial layout rather than with any peculiar conceptual scheme".   Experiments 1 and 2 suggest that both hypotheses are incorrect.   Thus, the explanation must lie at (b), that is, in the differentiation within the image or with a model of syncretic perception.

Accuracy achieved in the construction task indicated that isolating the components for the child eliminated the need for (b) and consequently allowed the child to produce representational figures.

Syncretic perception, however, offers two distinct models:

a) The tadpole man may consist of a global portrait, i.e. the 'head' represents both head and trunk.

b) Owing to the lack of differentiation within the image the child's full attention is given to isolating each individual component within the image. This may cause the child to capture some components before losing the overall shape. Thus, the head and legs are separate and distinct features and the trunk has been completely omitted.

The first of these models has been supported by Arnheim (1957) and Paget (1932). However, an observation made by Gridley (1938) presents a sound criticism. Having requested a child to add the body to his tadpole drawing, he drew this component inside the head, below the mouth. Gridley then asked him to point to the part he had just drawn, on his own body. The child pointed to his chin. This suggests that the 'head' is drawn to contain facial features only and as such can only be intended to represent the head. If the differentiation of components is not complete, then although the child may, for example, draw components separately when given a specific label, when re-scanning his internal representation, since the head is a specific feature, he will re-interpret what he has drawn in relation to that feature.

This suggests that the second of the syncretic perception models is operating. The child can handle each individual component in isolation but when he comes to draw, all components must be isolated. The child's full attention is therefore given to isolating each component for himself and thus, he loses sight of the overall shape. The components he captures are the head and legs.

How these components are 'captured' and more readily differentiated from the internal representation may be explained by looking back at the child's production strategy or serial order of production. The spatial pattern of head, trunk, legs and arms could be termed top, middle, bottom and sides.

All children seem to pass through a 'bottleneck' in drawing, that is, they will draw tadpole men (top and bottom). The next stage appears to be the incomplete figure (i.e. top, middle and bottom) and finally the representational figure (top, middle, bottom and sides).

There is evidence to suggest that the young child scans objects along a vertical axis from top to bottom (Ghent, 1961). Thus, when scanning an internal representation of the human figure, the spatial locations of importance would appear to be the top (the

head) and the bottom (the legs).   Such features have been termed
'polar features' by Howard and Templeton (1966) and the axis
joining them the 'polar axis'.   The tadpole drawing, then,
consists of these polar features only.   The next step in this
scanning, still along the vertical or polar axis, would include
the concept of middle (the trunk) and hence the head, trunk and
leg drawings.   Concepts of left and right are reached at a later
stage and necessarily involve lateral scanning.   Thus arms are
the last components to be added.

Ghent (1961) has shown that this might also apply to abstract
figures.

Such an explanation may be termed an hypothesis of 'visual
scanning/component localisation' within the image which would
account for the number and character of components that appear in
incomplete drawings.   It would also provide a model by which the
child's initial 'whole' perception is differentiated into discrete
components.

BIBLIOGRAPHY

ARNHEIM, R.,   Art and Visual Perception, Berkeley, University of
California Press, 1954

FREEMAN, N. H.,   Do Children Draw Men with Arms coming out of the
Head? Nature, 1975, 254 (5499), pp. 416-417

GHENT, L.,   Recognition by Children of Realistic Figures Presented
in Various Orientations, Canadian Journal of Psychology, 1960,
14, pp. 249-256

GHENT, L.,   Form and its Orientation: A Child's-eye View, American
Journal of Psychology, 1961, 74, pp. 177-190

GIBSON, E. J.,   Principles of Perceptual Learning and Development,
New York, Appleton-Century-Crofts, 1969

GRIDLEY, P. F.,   Graphic Representation of a Man by four-year-old
Children in Nine Prescribed Drawing Situations, Genetic
Psychology Monographs, 1938, 20, pp. 183-350

HOWARD, I. P. & TEMPLETON, W. B.,   Human Spatial orientation, London
Wiley, 1966

MACCOBY, E. E.,   What copying requires, Ontario Journal of
Educational Research, 1968, 10 (3), pp. 163-170

PAGET, G. W.,   Some Drawings of Men and Women made by Children of
Certain non-European Races, Journal of the Royal Anthropolo-
gical Institute, 1932, 62, pp. 127-144

PIAGET, J. & INHELDER, B.,   The Child's Conception of Space, London
     Routledge and Kegan Paul, 1956

PREMACK, D.,   Putting a Face Together, Science, 1975, 188, pp. 228-
     236

RAND, C. W.,   Copying in Drawing: The Importance of Adequate Visual
     Analysis versus the Ability to Utilize Drawing Rules, Child
     Development, 1973, 44, pp. 47-53

VURPILLOT, E.,   The Visual World of the Child, G.B., George Allen
     and Unwin, 1976

A DISCUSSION OF SOME SEX DIFFERENCES IN A STUDY OF HUMAN FIGURE DRAWINGS BY CHILDREN AGED FOUR-AND-A-HALF TO SEVEN-AND-A-HALF YEARS

John A. Willsdon

The study of children's drawings, particularly of the human figure, was initiated by the Italian artist Ricci in 1887 when he wrote his famous article on 'The Art of Little Children'. Like many later studies, it was descriptive in style, though rich in perceptive comments. It drew attention, amongst other things, to the popularity of the human figure as a subject for drawing amongst children.

During the forty or fifty years which followed, many more investigations were carried out in both Europe and America. They included the work of James Sully (1895), Lena Partridge (1902) and Cyril Burt (1921) in Britain, Luquet (1913, 1920, 1927) in France, Kerschensteiner (1905) in Germany, and Helga Eng (1931) in Norway. Luquet and Eng were interested in the achievements of individual children, whilst the others looked at larger numbers. Kellogg (1969) in the U.S.A. writes of having studied nearly one-hundred-thousand drawings, and Kerschensteiner claimed to have examined the work of some three-hundred-thousand children.

One view that has emerged over the years is that children pass through a sequence of recognisable developmental stages (Kerschensteiner 1905, Rouma 1913, Burt 1921, Goodenough 1926, Lowenfeld 1947, Kellogg 1969). The Goodenough 'Draw-a-man' test of 1926 was based on the idea that the more complete the figure that the child draws, and the more realistic its appearance, then the greater the intellectual maturity possessed by the child. Kellogg's study, one of the more recent, is critical of Goodenough's simple link between drawing and intellectual maturity. In her view, children's drawings do not accurately reflect either conceptions or perceptions of objects or human figures.

Despite the popularity of the human figure as a subject for children to draw, not a great deal has been added to the studies made in the first few decades of the century and there remain many aspects of children's drawings of people about which we are uncertain or know very little.   This situation is due, in part at least, to the rapidly changing environment in which the child finds himself. For example, in the last fifteen years, a number of changes have taken place in Britain which could conceivably influence children's drawings of the human figure.   There are three that might be given particular mention:

   a) Most children now have access to television in both home
      and school.   The imagery presented by this means is powerful
      and vivid, and it has an immediacy which is designed to hold
      the attention.   The human figure appears frequently, both
      in action and in close focus.

   b) There has been a vast increase in the use of visual materials
      in schools.   Illustrated books, teaching apparatus, wall
      pictures, pictures for language development and so on have
      been far more readily available to young children, and the
      pictorial symbol, often of a human, is an integral feature
      of both the material itself and the teaching techniques.
      A great deal of attention is also paid in schools to the
      attractive display of children's drawings, paintings and
      other art products.   The children are thus having increased
      opportunities to see how others solve some of the problems
      which they themselves encounter in making a drawing.

   c) Because of playschool and nursery education, children are
      having earlier access to a much richer and wider range of
      pictorial material.   They also have greater opportunities
      to enhance their own body image through interaction with
      others.

Partly because of these changing circumstances I have been investigating what infants choose to include in their drawings of people so that I might make comparisons with earlier studies and attempt an evaluation of the extent to which developmental stages may have remained constant.

I obtained a human figure drawing from six-hundred-and-thirty-four boys and six-hundred-and-eight girls aged four-and-a-half to seven-and-a-half years in infant schools and infant departments of Infant and Junior schools.   The instruction given to the pupils was: "Draw someone.   It can be yourself, or Mummy, or Daddy, or someone you know.   Make the best drawing you can."   The teachers who supervised the actual drawing activity were asked not to give any help which might lead a child to include features which would otherwise have been omitted.   The drawings were done within a rectangle 23 cm by 15 cm vertically orientated on standard sheets of white paper using either a pencil or black crayon.   Each one was examined and scored for seventy possible features and the results were processed for computer analysis.   The volume of information which has emerged from all this is much too extensive to attempt to summarise here, but one aspect which has shown interesting results concerns the different achievements of the boys and the girls, and it is this area that I should like to consider in a little detail.

When Kerschensteiner published his study in Munich over seventy years ago he remarked on the much greater drawing ability of the younger boys compared with the girls.   He thought that the explanation for this lay in the fact that the boys were allowed more time for drawing in the curriculum, and so had greater experience. Cyril Burt (1921) found that the London boys in certain respects were 'eminently superior to the girls'.   Goodenough in 1926 and Harris in 1963, however, found that there were slight but consistent sex differences which favoured the girls.

If one takes the number of different features that the child puts into a drawing of a person as being one yardstick of achieve-ment, then the girls in my sample tend to be ahead of the boys in several respects.   This may be illustrated by reference to the drawing of the trunk in a figure.   Although both boys and girls between four-and-a-half and seven-and-a-half years favour a human with a distinct trunk, as in Figure 1, it is the boys who cling to the less mature style of the tadpole man in Figure 2 and indeed they do so for some six months longer than the girls.

The mouth of course is drawn in several different styles by children and some of the more common configurations are shown in Figure 3.   The most popular type with both sexes is undoubtedly the one where the line curves upwards in a 'saucer' shape.   How-ever, from the age of six onwards, the girls were more likely than the boys to draw cosmetic lips such as in Figure 4.   Kellogg, in her book "Analysing Children's Art" published only seven years ago, found that cosmetic lips were uncommon before the age of eight. Perhaps the Cardiff girls identify more readily with the older members of their own sex and at an earlier age.   Or is it that they are more susceptible to cosmetic advertisements than boys?

It may also be that identification explains the introduction by the girls of a waist into their drawings some six months before the boys.

Few of the children drew eye lashes and eye brows before the age of six.   When they did appear in the drawings, the eye brows were in greater evidence with both boys and girls.   Yet with both features the boys lagged behind the girls again.

Figure 1. Figure with separate and distinct trunk

Figure 2. Tadpole man

Figure 3. a) lips - curving upwards, b) lips - straight line
           c) lips - enclosing line, d) lips - curving downwards

Figure 4. Cosmetic lips

One feature however which seemed to appeal more to the boys
than to the girls is the ears.   It is perhaps easier to account
for this since a girl's hair style usually covers the ears.

But it is more difficult to explain the popularity of teeth in
the faces drawn by boys, especially between the ages of six-and-a-
half and seven-and-a-half years when they were most in evidence.
Could this be because the boys are more assertive, and because some
of their games and activities may have an aggressive bias?   Or is
it because the cosmetic and life-like lips, which appeal to the
girls, are too difficult for them to draw and a mouth with teeth
showing is considered by boys to be a more advanced stage of realism
than an upward-curving line as in Figure 3?   Perhaps cosmetic lips
are too closely associated with a feminine image and a display of
teeth is more suggestive of masculinity.

When arms and legs are depicted by children they may be drawn
with either single or double lines as in Figure 5, or occasionally
use may be made of single lines for the arms and double lines for
the legs, or the other way round.   Once the children began to show
their figure as having a distinct trunk, double lines for legs were
introduced by the girls at least as early as four-and-a-half years,
which was six months ahead of the boys.   And in the use of double
lines for arms the girls were as much as twelve months in advance
of the boys.

Figure 5.   Limbs - a) single line, b) double line,
                c) mixed single and double

The use of double lines for both arms and legs is clearly a
more advanced stage than one where the double lines are used for
one set of limbs only.   It was found that the girls, as young as
four-and-a-half years, were producing significantly more drawings
with double lines for all the limbs than were the boys who did not
catch up with them until six months later.

One of the most likely ways in which one might expect sex
differences to appear is in the sex of the figure which the child
draws when given a free choice.   But any attempt to determine the
sex of such figures is fraught with difficulties unless one has the
benefit of some verbal indication from the child.   This is due, in
part, to the schematic and symbolic nature of the drawing, and also
to the fact that contemporary hair and clothing styles make it
almost impossible in some cases to arrive at a firm conclusion.
Rhoda Kellogg has commented on the same difficulty in her work.
As the completed drawings were not discussed with the children, the
results relate to the appearance of the figure in the drawing, and
not necessarily to the child's intention.   Some details, of course,
are straightforward - a hair clasp or ribbon, a frock, a man's pipe,
or a collar and tie are fairly easily assigned to one sex or the
other, and allow one to score the drawing accordingly.

Throughout the three year groups studied, the girls showed a
significant preference for drawing the female sex.   The boys showed
a preference for male figures, but not until between five-and-a-half
and seven-and-a-half years.   Before an age of five-and-a-half years
it was not easy to decide which sex they had in mind.   There seems
to be a conflict of evidence about which sex children really prefer
to draw.   Jolles, according to Harris (1963), concluded that children aged five to eight years drew their own sex first in 80% of the
drawings, but Machover (1953) has found that in certain instances
girls drew the opposite sex first.

The present findings need to be treated with some caution.
The boys produced a great many more figures which were apparently
neutral or unisex and so they had to be classified in an
'indeterminate sex' category.   Some may have been intended to
signify one sex or the other - one could not be sure.

Be that as it may, it is evident that some children, and
especially the boys, have not succeeded in removing a source of
ambiguity here.   Either the differences between the sexes were not
regarded as important enough for them to feel that they had to
distinguish them in their figures, or they assumed that because
they knew what the figure represented, then others would do so also.

Or, perhaps, confronted with fashions in hair and clothing
which blurred some of the principal variants, the children, and

particularly the boys, found themselves lacking the perceptual and
technical skills necessary to make the distinction in a drawing.
One further possible explanation is that the boys are more readily
satisfied with a relatively simple schema or symbol for a human –
the function of the drawing may be met by a more abbreviated statement without the need for embellishment.   If this is so it may
indicate that the girls are more attracted by aesthetic considerations and see the drawing as having an end in itself, whereas the
boys may regard the drawing primarily as a symbolic gesture serving
other purposes.

Clothing is an obvious aid to determining sex.   Leaving aside
the question of whether the clothing is for a male or female, there
was evidence that the girls introduced clothing of some kind at
least as early as the youngest children in the study, that is at
four-and-a-half years;   and between four-and-a-half and six years
the girls produced significantly more drawings with clothing than
did the boys.

The drawings of children in infant schools sometimes contain
features which have apparently nothing to do with the topic which
has been set.   Some of these appear as non-pictorial scribbles,
i.e. the wandering lines, closed shapes, spots, angles and so on
which are more commonly found in the drawings of younger children
of up to about four years.   In this study they persisted in the
boy's drawings of the human figure to a significant extent compared
with the girls' drawings and especially between four-and-a-half and
five years of age.   This seems to suggest that the boys hold on
much longer than the girls to those more primitive elements of
scribble, even when they are producing a recognisable drawing of
the human figure.   It may be that the boys have a more playful
attitude towards their drawings, holding in balance both the
practical demands of the work set and their interpretative
fantasies.   More probably, the coexistence of pictorial and non-
pictorial forms indicates that these particular boys are in a tran-
sitional stage where the drawing objective is not strong enough to
suppress or reject a tendency to automatism.

In summary, then, the initial evidence presented on sex
differences appears to indicate at least four main points:

a) There are marked differences between boys and girls in
   terms of the ages at which they first produce particular
   features of the human figure in their drawings.   The boys
   took up to six months longer to produce a figure with a
   distinct trunk;   and up to eighteen months longer than the
   girls to introduce cosmetic lips, as well as six months
   longer to draw the waist.   In the drawing of double lines
   for legs the girls were in advance of the boys by some six
   months, and by as much as twelve months for double line arms.

> When it came to drawing both arms and legs in double lines
> in the one figure, the girls were at least six months
> ahead of the boys.   The girls produced far more clothed
> figures between four-and-a-half and six years than did the
> boys.

b) Girls, as a group, began to draw a figure of a clearly
   identifiable sex at an earlier age than boys.   For example,
   between the ages of four-and-a-half and five years 13% of
   the girls compared with only 2% of the boys were drawing a
   figure of a specific sex.   By the age of five-and-a-half
   – up to a year later – this sex difference had disappeared.

c) Lines and marks more suggestive of earlier types of scribble
   persist to a significant extent in the boys' figure drawings
   up to the age of five years.

d) Girls tend to show less interest in drawing ears and teeth
   than do the boys in this three year age range.

Interesting though these sex differences are, it would be
unwise to conclude too readily that because the girls' drawings
may show a greater number of features, or show them at an earlier
age than boys, then it follows that girls have a greater degree of
intellectual maturity.   As suggested, it may be that drawing serves
different purposes for boys and girls.   Other possible explanations
also present themselves.   For example, the girls may possess greater
skills in perceptual analysis, or have a greater concern with detail
and accuracy.   Burt (1949) expressed the view that girls were better
than boys at copying objects in front of them, and he said that they
excelled in delineating minute particulars.   That may still be true
of Cardiff girls.

Perhaps girls have a stronger body image than boys, or identify
more closely with it or with older members of their own sex.   The
results may also be interpreted as suggesting that girls have a
greater aptitude for resolving the difficult graphical technologies
involved in representing a three-dimensional object in two
dimensions.

ACKNOWLEDGEMENT

I am indebted to Professor Ronald Davie of University College
Cardiff, for his guidance regarding the preparation of this paper.

BIBLIOGRAPHY

BAKER, H. & KELLOGG, R., A developmental study of children's
    scribblings, Pediatrics, 1967, Vol 40, No 3, Part 1,
    pp. 381-389

BRITTAIN, W. L., Some exploratory studies of the art of preschool
    children, Studies in Art Education, 1969, Vol 10, No 3,
    pp. 14-24

BURT, C., Mental and scholastic tests, London, Staples Press,
    1921, 1949

ENG, H., The psychology of children's drawings, London, Routledge
    and Kegan Paul, 1931

GOODENOUGH, F. L., Measurement of intelligence by drawings, New
    York, Harcourt, Brace & World, 1926

HARRIS, D. B., Children's drawings as measures of intellectual
    maturity, New York, Harcourt, Brace & World, 1963

KELLOGG, R., Analysing children's art, Palo Alto, California,
    National Press Books, 1969

KERSCHENSTEINER, G., Die Entwickelung der zeichnerischen Begabung,
    Munich, Carl Gerber, 1905

KNOPF, I. J. & RICHARDS, T. W., The child's differentiation of
    sex as reflected in drawings of the human figure, Journal of
    Genetic Psychology, 1952, 81, pp. 99-112

LOWENFELD, V., Creative and mental growth, New York, Macmillan
    Company, 1947

LUQUET, G. -H., Les dessins d'un enfant, Paris, F. Alcan, 1913

LUQUET, G. -H., Les bonshommes têtards dans le dessin enfantin,
    Journal de Psychologie Normale et Pathologique, 1920, 17

LUQUET, G. -H., Le dessin enfantin, Paris, F. Alcan, 1927

MACHOVER, K., Human figure drawings of children, Journal of
    Projective Techniques, 1953, pp. 85-91

PARTRIDGE, L., Children's drawings of men and women, Studies in
    Education, 1902, July, Philadelphia, Earl Barnes, pp. 163-179

ROUMA, G., Le langage graphique de l'enfant, Paris, Misch. et Thron,
    1913

READ, H., Education through art, London, Faber, 1970

SCHILDER, P., The image and appearance of the human body, London,
    Kegan Paul, Trench, Trubner & Co., 1935

SULLY, J., Studies of childhood, London, Longmans Green, 1895

DISCUSSION OF THE PAPER BY WILLSDON

MEMBER OF THE AUDIENCE: What was your criterion for first appearance of any particular feature in the children's drawings?

WILLSDON: We only obtained one drawing from each child so the data refer to the trend of statistically significant occurrences. In some individual cases, a feature might appear earlier but this would not necessarily be statistically significant.

FREEMAN: We find that children use double lines for legs before double lines for arms and draw feet before hands. From our point of view this is comprehensible because if they are end-anchoring on the leg elements, you would expect the rest of the legs to be elaborated before the arms, just as the face is elaborated before any other body features. Do you find that the legs are elaborated before the arms in both boys and girls?

WILLSDON: Yes, that is assuming that in the tadpole they represent the legs.

FREEMAN: Of course, but in the conventional figure where they do represent the legs, we found that they double the lines before they elaborate the arms. If they are end-anchoring, it seems possible that girls are encountering the problem of elaborating the figure before boys are, judging by your results.

WOLLHEIM: It was not quite clear whether you were saying that the children were representing themselves according to their own sex or whether they just preferred portraying someone of a particular sex.

WILLSDON: We only looked to see if the picture was unambiguously male or female. I have no means of telling whether the children were portraying themselves or someone of their own sex.

NAMING OF PARTS: HOW CHILDREN DESCRIBE AND

HOW CHILDREN DRAW COMMON OBJECTS

Lawrence Litt

A recent paper (Litt 1976) described the implications of a dual coding model of thinking for establishing the imagery values of words for children. One of the deductions from the model that was briefly mentioned was that children's verbal descriptions of common objects should be compared with the way they draw them. The purpose of this paper is to amplify this idea; to describe techniques that can be employed and to discuss available evidence.

Before delineating the dual coding theory it is pertinent to the thesis to be put forward here to make some summary statement about the development of language and drawing.

Much information has accumulated about the way in which children come to represent common objects by drawing. In what is probably the best available summary of empirical research, Harris (1963) identifies three broad stages in the development of drawing. The toddlers first attempts at drawing are characterized more by enjoyment of the activity itself than by deliberate attempts at representation. Thereafter the child's drawing moves into a long stage extending from about four years to adolescence where the intent is clearly imitative and reproductive; where identifiable representations show progressively more and more discriminated detail. He identifies a third stage, not attained by most, where mastery of technical skills and appreciation of aesthetic principles allow the production of drawings which are both a source of meaningful communication with others and personal satisfaction to the artist.

Painstaking recording of the details in children's drawings, in the manner of Goodenough's pioneer enquiries, continues to

provide basic normative data.   Willsdon (Chapter 4) in the
proceedings of this conference illustrates significant differences
to be found in the drawings of boys and girls of infant school age.
Royer (1976) has re-standardised the draw-a-person test with a
European sample of children.   She has allowed for the use of
colour in children's pictures and has linked these productions with
personality differences as well as sex differences and general
intelligence.

     Even more information has accumulated about the development of
children's speech;   the development of vocabulary and their use of
language.   During the first year the infant babbles and plays at
making sounds.   Recognizable words are being spoken by the end of
the first year.   By eighteen months to two years new words are
accumulated at an increasing rate.   Nouns and verbs are most evident in the infant speech.   Other parts of speech, especially some
prepositions and personal pronouns, appear much later.   The toddler
quickly gains command over intricate syntactical structures apparently
without teaching.   Unless he is particularly disadvantaged he begins
school with an effective command of speech.

     Children's verbal responses to pictures are also well documented
in some respects.   Picture vocabularies have been used on a normative basis as intelligence test items since the days of Binet to
determine whether the portrayal of a familiar object in a picture
provokes recognition and calls up the appropriate name.   According
to the Stanford-Binet norms most 2+-year-old children can correctly
point out the hair, mouth, feet, ear, nose, hands and eyes on a
large cardboard doll.   This is notably earlier than most of the
same children could be expected to include all of these features in
a drawing of their own.   The correct naming of eighteen outline
drawings of common objects increases from three, on average, at the
two-year-old level to fourteen at four years of age.   The typical
verbal responses of the average two-year-old child to the more complex pictures entitled Grandmother's Story, Birthday Party and
Washing Day is to enumerate a few objects within the picture.
Only at the six-year-old level do the scoring norms on the Stanford-
Binet require the child to have described or interpreted the pictures.   The processes whereby children achieve picture recognition
and comprehension and the properties of pictures which aid or hinder
these processes seems to have been given little attention.   Likewise the rationale for the English Picture Vocabulary Tests is a
purely normative and discriminatory one.   The tests are claimed to
provide measures of listening vocabulary and general intelligence.
However, the procedures involved are theoretically curious.   The
preschool version for three to five-year-olds is largely acceptable
since with the exception of 'argument' and 'temperature' most of the
test pictures are chosen to represent concrete nouns and participles.
But for the seven to twelve-year-old version the child is required

to pick out pictures which are supposed to represent such abstract
notions as 'astonishment', 'assistance', 'wrath', 'communication'
and 'constrain'.   The curiosity of this procedure is enhanced if
one conjectures what would happen if one were to turn the procedure
around and ask children to produce drawings in response to such
words as 'constrain'.

Presumably, asking children to draw is one way of inferring the
functional existence of a mental representation.   Very little information has been recorded about this converse relationship:
whether the appropriate name calls up a mental representation of a
common object.   The more familiar and concrete the object then the
more likely is it to be capable of being represented in a drawing.
As a further extension of this line of thought the question then
arises as to whether children's descriptions of common objects
match the way they draw them.

This is a suitable point at which to return to the dual coding
theory of thinking as it provides a framework for dealing with this
question.   Striking parallels exist between the development of
speech and the development of drawing.   The similarities here have
often been commented upon.   Harris (1963) writes in his summing up
of the research literature on children drawing: "Increasingly,
however, the child's drawing becomes a form of language - a way of
expressing concepts and ideas.   It is thus a form of calligraphy,
a kind of stylized writing".

Willats (Chapter 13) in the proceedings of this conference writes: "Learning to use a particular type of drawing system does not depend directly on perception or on learning culturally
determined stereotypes but in its demands on creative ability
closely resembles the acquisition of verbal language".   At the
same time there are also important differences between the development of speech and drawing.   It is, however, insufficient simply
to note the similarities and differences.   Such features can be
encompassed within the thesis that thinking can be described by
two separate but inter-related symbolic systems: a verbal symbolic
system and an imagery or non-verbal system.

The evidence supporting this distinction has come mostly from
experimental psychology (Paivio, 1971).   Imagery variables have been
shown to have consistently facilitating effects on associative
learning in adults.   The definition of imagery is not restricted
to what is introspectively observable and reportable.   Imagery
may be inferred and operationally defined on the basis of a variety
of measures.   Drawing, it is assumed here, is one such measure.
To an extent that remains to be determined the development of children's drawing is an indication of the development of imagery or
representational thought processes.   Paivio has assigned specific
properties to the two symbolic codes and has specified measures
appropriate to five different levels of meaning.   Table 1 provides
an abridged statement of the theory.

Table 1. Abridged description of the dual codes and levels of stimulus meaning (from PAIVIO, A., Imagery and Verbal Processes (1971, pp. 52–59)

Levels of meaning	Verbal Code	Imagery Code
Iconic	The level of the rapidly fading perceptual image. Relatively untransformed information following stimulus exposure.	Functionally related to visual perception. Specialised for spatial representation. Primarily a parallel processing system.
Representational	Hypothetical symbolic representations stored in long term memory as concrete images in the case of stimulus objects and as implicit auditory-motor representations in the case of verbal stimuli. It corresponds intuitively to familiarity in the elementary sense of "knowing" the stimulus. Appropriate measures: speed of recognition, duration thresholds, familiarity ratings, frequency counts.	Relatively untransformed
Referential	This level assumes associative connections between imaginal and verbal representations such that an object or picture can be named, and the name can evoke an image. Appropriate measures: latency of labelling objects, latency of the arousal of images to words or sentences; ratings of the ease with which words evoke images or the words concreteness.	
Associative	Sequences or patterns of associations involving words, images or both. It encompasses the traditional meaning of association in terms of verbal association but also involves the assumption of similar associative structures between images. Appropriate measures: timings of associative latency.	

It is not assumed to be related to concreteness. Its mediating capacity is related to measures of verbal association and meaningfulness. Specialised for sequential processing by virtue of the temporal nature of the auditory-motor speech system.

Piaget (1971) in his particular terminology describes imagery as an active, internalized reconstruction of perception. These definitions provide a radically different epistemological status for imagery. The Associationist view of imagery as a facsimile or faded copy of perception was implicit in all the research on imagery during the early part of the century. (A further important difference is the methodological one. The early imagery research was conducted entirely in terms of individual differences. Paivio and Piaget deal with processes rather than individual differences.)

Freeman (Chapter 1) in the proceedings of this conference emphasises the constraints that the drawing task itself imposes on the child's drawing. He suggests, cogently and with justification, that children have many items available in memory but because of the difficulties the child has in retrieving them they are not included in their drawings. The child also has difficulty in executing the serial order of parts he has to include in his drawing. He is also influenced by external frames of references such as the edge of the paper and the lines he draws himself. For these reasons Freeman rejects drawing as a source of direct access to the child's mental imagery. This criticism has most validity if one is referring to imagery in the Associationist sense of the word. It does not necessarily affect the position adopted here.

The question of the accessibility of information for example is subsumed by the dual-coding model. Visual information accesses the imagery system directly at the iconic and representational levels of meaning; the verbal system is not involved. Freeman observes that some children when asked to draw could only scribble yet they could complete, with ease, pre-drawn figures implying that they did have the graphic elements available given appropriately eliciting cues but they could not organise their own drawings. Equally and more comprehensively one can say that this is an instance of the imagery symbolic system operating at the representational level of meaning. Asking children to draw accesses the verbal symbolic system directly; in this case, at the referential level of meaning and involves a transition to the verbal system. The model thus predicts that the latencies involved when children are asked to draw particular items will be longer than when they draw the same items cued by incomplete figures.

Having outlined the dual-coding theory and some of its implications we may now return to the question which is the focus of this paper: do children's descriptions of common objects match the way they draw them? The task involves the verbal system directly and the imagery system indirectly. Will then children's verbal accounts of familiar objects show any more detail than their drawings?

The technique adopted consists of asking children what they would like to draw. Then having ascertained this they are asked to describe it; to say all they can about it. The instructions are open-ended and non-directive. Their attention is not drawn to particular aspects of the thing in question such as size, shape, colour, location or use. When encouragement brings no further additions to their descriptions they are then asked to draw it. This completed, facets and details of the drawing are pointed to and a note made of what the child says it is.

So far the technique has been used on an exploratory basis with a small ad hoc sample of children of average intelligence or below aged between six and eleven years. For the younger subjects a house was the favourite choice. Older subjects chose to draw a helicopter, a car or a tank, for example. The responses are best summarised as naming of parts. Janet, a six-year-old girl of limited intelligence (IQ 83) says of a house, "It's got windows, doors...smoke and a door". Darren, a ten-year-old boy of average intelligence says of a tank, "It's got four wheels. A square-like body thing. A little box at the top. And there's a man in the box thing and at the front of the box there's three big shooter things. And they have big tread tyre things on the wheels. It's going up like a big hill". It can be seen from the illustrations (Figures 1 and 2) that the descriptions closely resemble the drawings themselves. This is typical of the responses collected so far.

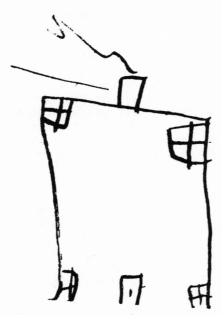

Figure 1.   Janet's Drawing

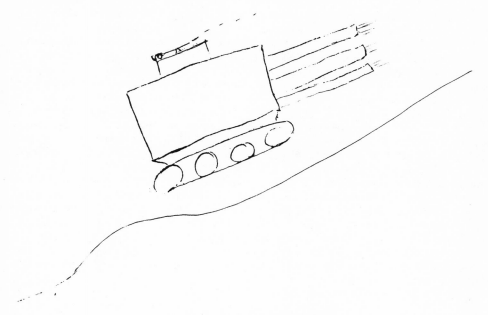

Figure 2. Darren's Drawing

They consist mostly of enumerating concrete items which together
compose the object in question.   In this the descriptions are as
schematic as the drawings.   Janet, for example, mentions most of
the features in her simple drawing of a house with the notable
exception of the chimney for which she did not know the name, nor
apparently had she heard it before.   With the older subjects the
drawings contain even more features not referred to in the descriptions though when they are pointed out in the drawings they can
usually be labelled or appropriately described.

There is a dearth of reported evidence on how children describe
objects which they can draw.   However Harris (1963) reports observations by Meili-Dworetzki (1957) which supports the evidence
reported here.   As part of a long term study involving observing
and collecting the drawings from over one-hundred children aged two
to seven years she asked a number of them to tell her how to draw a
man, what to draw first, and so on.   Most children described or
listed only those parts which they themselves included in their
drawings.   Their oral descriptions and their drawings were almost
identical, with the exception of the very youngest subjects who
could not draw at all.   The older children in her sample, five,
six and seven-year-olds, drew more parts than they mentioned orally.
The limitations of idea that appear in drawings also appear in

children's discussions of the drawings.   Meili-Dworetzki also
reports that the child at the scribbling stage can often tell more
about the human body orally than children who have already begun to
depict the human figure.   Selfe (Chapter 2) in the proceedings of
this conference reports a remarkable case of extraordinary drawing
ability in an autistic child.   Outstanding drawing ability is
apparently very rare.   When the child was first brought to her
attention at the age of six she had developed little language
ability.   When her speech began to develop her drawings began to
revert to more rudimentary forms.   Claire Golomb (1974) has ample
evidence on how well young children can draw when cues are provided
by verbal dictation methods.   It has also long been noted that
young children name their first drawings according to fancied
resemblances after completion.   Later, while engaged in drawing,
they will name the work in terms of some feature produced by chance.
It is only later still that children announce in advance what their
drawings will be.   Such observations support the hypothesis of
functionally distinguishable but interacting symbolic systems.   It
seems clear that the hypothesis has both theoretical and practical
applications.

BIBLIOGRAPHY

FREEMAN, N.,   How young children try to plan drawings, Chapter 1
     in this volume

GOLOMB, C.,   Young children's sculpture and drawing, Cambridge,
     Harvard University Press, 1974

HARRIS, D. B.,   Children's drawings as measures of intellectual
     maturity, Harcourt, Brace and World, 1963

LITT, L. H.,   Imagery values of words for children, 21st Inter-
     national Congress of Psychology, Paris, 1976

MEILI-DWORETZKI, G.,   Das Bild des Menchen in der Vorstellung und
     Darstellung des Kleinkindes, Bern, Verlag Hans Huber, 1957

PAIVIO, A.,   Imagery and verbal processes, Holt, Rinehart and
     Winston, New York, 1971

PIAGET, J., INHELDER, B. et al.,   Mental imagery in the child,
     Routledge and Kegan Paul, 1971

ROYER, J.,   La personalité de l'enfant à travers le dessin du
     bonhomme, Editions Editest, 1976

WILLATS, J.,   How children learn to draw realistic pictures,
     Chapter 13 in this volume

WILLSDON,   The development of human figure drawing in children
     aged four to seven years, Chapter 4 in this volume

Part II

The Child's Perception and
Representation of Space

THE CHILD'S REPRESENTATION OF SPACE

Paul Harris

Other speakers have discussed the child's difficulties in translating a mental representation into an external representation. I shall ask instead: what can we learn about the child's mental representation of space from the way he acts in space or from the way in which he constructs an external representation? In particular, the child's representation of the position of an object will be examined.

When he specifies the position of an object, the child must solve at least two problems. First, if he is going to act upon an object he must specify where it is in relation to his own current position. For example, if he is to reach accurately for an object, he must specify whether the object is straight ahead, or to his left or right, how far away and so forth. Even if the child simply wants to fixate something in the corner of his eye, he must be able to specify its position in relation to his own current fixation point - its direction and degree of radial eccentricity.

Eye movements and their co-ordination with head movements highlight one important requirement for the child's specification of position. Children are mobile organisms. Even from birth their head and eyes move spontaneously. This must mean that if the child is to specify the position of an object accurately, he must keep changing that specification simply because he constantly alters his own position vis à vis any given object.

Thus my first claim is that to act upon an object, the child must code its position relative to his own current position, and that such a specification must be constantly altered so that it remains up to date.

A second problem that the child must solve is a memory problem.
To find his way to the kitchen, to school or even to find a hidden
object, the child must remember where things are.   The child could
solve this problem by noting where things are in relation to self -
for example: straight ahead and at a certain distance - and then
altering this specification whenever he moved to a new position.
I think it is obvious that this system cannot be used for more than
a few objects.   Were all object positions specified in this way,
the upheaval in our mental geography every time we moved would be
enormous.   A solution to this difficulty is to specify the position
of an object not in relation to the current position of one's own
body but in relation to what I shall call adjacent landmark or
framework features (Bryant, 1974: Butterworth, 1976).

This is a more stable system because if the child remembers,
for example, that his toys are in a given cupboard, he does not
need to change this specification every time he moves.   His toys
remain "in the cupboard" irrespective of his own position.   Similarly the cupboard remains "in the attic".   Such a nested system
can be extended indefinitely.

I shall argue that one can make sense of the child's spatial
development by viewing it as a gradual co-ordination of these two
types of position specification - the self-related specification on
the one hand, the landmark specification on the other.   Certain
errors exhibited by the child in the course of development can be
attributed to the child's reliance on invariant landmark relations
instead of a combined use of both types of spatial code.

Such an analysis can be used to explain the child's difficulties in three areas: search errors during infancy, errors in perspective-taking tasks, and thirdly, the child's misunderstanding of
complicated spatial terms such as "in front of" and "to the left of".

SEARCH   DURING   INFANCY

Can the infant specify the position of an object accurately in
relation to self?   If we ask this question of the newborn baby, the
easiest action system to study is the eye movement system.   Recent
studies from different laboratories (Harris & Macfarlane, 1974:
Macfarlane, Harris & Barnes, 1976: Aslin & Salapatek, 1975) confirm
that the neonatal eye movement system codes target direction.   The
neonate makes an eye movement upwards, downwards, to the right or
left depending on the location of the peripheral target.

The very young infant also acts appropriately if we examine
other motor systems: he co-ordinates both head and eye movements
in localising peripheral targets (Tronick & Clanton, 1971) and

having fixated such peripheral targets can reach accurately toward
them (Bower, Broughton & Moore, 1970: White, Castle & Held, 1964).
He can also act appropriately toward objects which alter their
position relative to the self - for example, by avoiding potentially
colliding objects (Ball & Tronick, 1971) or by remaining fixated
upon laterally displaced objects (Tauber & Koffler, 1966).

These studies show that the infant exhibits spatially-adjusted
activity with the various motor systems of eye, head, hand and body.
To what extent a unitary spatial code serves these disparate motor
activities is not yet clear.   It is possible to conclude, however,
that the infant can specify position relative to self from an early
age in one or more ways.   In this respect the human neonate is
similar to many other species (Ganz, 1975).

When the infant and an object are displaced relative to one
another, accurate spatial action is still possible because the new
position of the object can be specified by the perceptual system.
For example, if the infant turns away from an object straight ahead
of him its new peripheral position ought to be specified given the
evidence cited above concerning saccadic eye movements toward peripheral targets.   Similarly if the object moves from the straight
ahead position the optomotor-reflex (Tauber & Koffler, 1966) or
pursuit tracking is initiated (Harris, Cassel & Bamborough, 1974)
indicating that the change of position is registered.   These pieces
of evidence support the claim made at the outset: for spatial action
to be accurate, it must be guided by a flexible spatial code - one in
which prior specifications of position are rapidly and continuously
replaced or up-dated to conform to the current situation.   It is
assumed here that afferent input provides the usual source of information for achieving such flexibility.   This input is presumably
visual in normal circumstances, since the visual modality provides
continuous feedback concerning change of position, but recent evidence (Bower, 1976) indicates that auditory surrogates are possible.

What happens when such perceptual feedback is eliminated - or
to put the question in more familiar terms - how does the infant
deal with hidden objects?   For hidden objects there is no perceptual feedback to specify any change in their position relative to
self.   To solve this problem I propose that the infant begins to
use a landmark code, instead of remembering that the object was
"straight ahead" when it was covered by a cloth, he now takes note
of the cloth itself and remembers instead that the object is "under
the cloth".   As argued earlier this is a more stable code, because
if he turns away from the cloth, the object position is still
accurately specified - it is still "under the cloth".   Conversely,
if he remembered that the object was "straight ahead" and then
turned to the right, the object would no longer be "straight ahead".
The only problem with the landmark code is that it appears to tempt
the child into perseverative errors.

In a recent review of the development of search during infancy, Harris (1975) noted the ubiquity of perseverative errors at different stages of search.   Having successfully found the object in one place, the infant returns there by orienting head and eyes (Bower, Broughton & Moore, 1974) or by reaching to the same place (Harris, 1973;   1974) even when he sees the object move or disappear elsewhere.   Piaget (1954) interprets these responses as egocentric errors - the infant assumes that the object can be made to appear at a given place simply by repeating a response that worked before; the infant acts as if the object's position will accommodate to his responses rather than accommodating his responses to the actual position of the object.

The hypothesis proposed here is that the infant treats the landmark code as an overly stable system, and fails to update it even when the object has moved to a new position.   Thus he returns to cloth A even if he sees the object disappear at cloth B, or he turns to the end of a tunnel from which an object has previously emerged, even though the object is visible at the entrance to the tunnel.

A recent experiment by Lucas (1975) provides a neat piece of evidence in support of this argument.   The to-be-hidden object was first placed near cover A.   In one condition the object was placed directly in front of cover A, and in a second it was placed to the side of cover A.   Accordingly we can expect infants to encode the object/cover proximity relation more readily in the first condition than in the second condition.   A second cloth B was then moved over the object, and this cloth and the object were moved across the table.   Cloth A remained in its original position.   Lucas (1975) found that infants were much more likely to search for the object at cloth A and to neglect the actual cover, cloth B, if the object had initially been directly in front of A.   This evidence suggests, then, that previously encoded landmark relations are treated as invariant even when they have actually been altered. This result is not easily explicable in Piagetian terms.   The infant has never acted at cloth A, so his search at A cannot be interpreted as the repetition of a previously successful search response.

This account can be extended to explain a variety of other findings concerning the infant's search for hidden objects (Harris, 1976).   For the moment the general conclusion can be stated: the infant gradually makes use of landmarks to specify the position of an object.   Reliance on this landmark code tempts the infant to neglect the more accurate but less stable self-related position code which guides his initial activities towards visible objects. Accurate search ultimately requires a co-ordination of these two codes.

PERSPECTIVE-TAKING

The classic finding in perspective-taking tasks was made by Piaget and Inhelder (1956).   Young children often pick out their own current perspective as being identical to what they would see if they were to move to a new position.   Piaget and Inhelder (1967) interpreted this finding in terms of the child's egocentricity – his tendency to assimilate all other perspectives to his current perspective.

There are numerous replications of these findings with different materials, but two pieces of evidence cast doubt on the validity of the egocentricity interpretation.   The first piece of evidence comes from the child's drawings; the younger child is much more influenced by alternative perspectives to his current perspective than is the older child.   For example, Freeman and Janikoun (1972) found that younger children invariably drew a cup with a handle even though the handle was turned away from them, but older children were much more likely to omit the handle.

One could attempt to reconcile this finding with the egocentricity hypothesis by claiming that the cup plus handle represented a canonical orientation – that is to say the most frequently encountered orientation.   The younger child draws this canonical perspective because he fails to acknowledge its equivalence to other perspectives.   Thus the child is egocentric in the Piagetian sense because he treats one perspective as representative of all other possible perspectives.   The three mountains display used by Piaget and Inhelder (1956) has no canonical orientation since it is unfamiliar; accordingly the child treats his current perspective as canonical, in the absence of other clues.

A recent experiment by Mclaughland (1976) suggests that this attempt to reconcile children's drawings with the egocentricity hypothesis will not work.   He repeated the experiment of Freeman and Janikoun (1972) but added a simple pattern to the cup (two coloured circles).   If children are drawing a generalised cup with a canonical orientation then the handle but not the circles should be included.   If, however, the child is drawing an orientation which is neither visible nor canonical but merely potentially visible from a different perspective, then the circles should be included.   Mclaughland obtained the latter result.   The tendency to include an invisible pattern was almost as strong as the tendency to include an invisible handle.   Both tendencies declined with age. Hence the child's drawings do indicate an awareness of invisible perspectives.

Thus development in the ability to convey a given perspective, more specifically the perspective available from a particular

location (Willats, 1976) appears to be a development of the ability
to draw such perspectives, not to imagine them as such.

The second piece of evidence against the Piagetian hypothesis
comes from an elegant study by Huttenlocher and Presson (1972).
They found that children make very few egocentric errors, if they
are asked to imagine the outcome of rotation of the display, as
opposed to imagining their own movement around it. This is a
surprising result from a Piagetian standpoint because whether the
display is rotated, or the observer moves around it, identical
transformations of the observer's perspective of the display result.
Hence the egocentricity hypothesis predicts an equal difficulty for
the two tasks.

Huttenlocher and Presson (1972) conclude that the child has
difficulty in imagining himself in a new position, but no difficulty
in imagining a new perspective. Unfortunately they do not explain
why there should be such a discrepancy in the mental mobility of
self and display.

The distinction between a self-related code and a landmark code
suggests a possible explanation. When the child moves around the
display of blocks, he changes his position relative to that display
but the display stays still in relation to adjacent landmarks, such
as the door or window of the room, and the edge of the table. The
situation is different when the display is rotated: the display
position is moved relative to the observer, but the display also
moves relative to the landmarks mentioned. Thus rotation is
easier because the child is required to imagine objects moving
relative to a background - something he is not required to do when
he imagines his own movement. Accordingly when the child makes an
egocentric error - copies the display in front of him - he is merely
reproducing those invariant framework/display relations even though
he may be aware of the fact that things would look different if he
were actually on the far side of the table. Harris and Bassett
(1976) recently found that the way children made their egocentric
errors supports this interpretation.

They asked children to use three miniature blocks to build a
model of the display they would see following a perspective shift.
For example, a child might be shown three coloured blocks, one to
his left, one straight ahead of him and one to the right. If the
child were asked to imagine himself moving to face the left-hand
block, he would be expected to use the three miniature blocks to
build a near-to-far display corresponding to this new perspective.
Harris and Bassett (1976) kept a record of the order that these
miniature blocks were placed in position. They found that for
correct responses, the child typically first positioned the block
that would be most salient in the new perspective. Thus if the

new perspective was a near-to-far line of blocks (as opposed to a
left-to-right display) children typically began their model with
the near block not the far block.   They then added the middle block
and the far block respectively.   This finding is similar to the
serial-order strategies found for drawing tasks and memory tasks
(Bassett, 1976: Freeman, 1975; 1976: O'Connor & Hermelin, 1973),
the child reads from his mental representation in terms of an assumed
order of salience - from top-to-bottom or near-to-far.

The critical question we can now ask is this: what order
strategy does the child use when he makes an egocentric error?
Does he begin with the block that is most salient to him from his
actual position?   Piaget and Inhelder (1967) and Huttenlocher and
Presson (1972) both predict this result since, albeit for different
reasons, they claim that the child cannot imagine himself in a new
position with a new perspective.   The results indicated, however,
that even when making an egocentric error the child started with
the block which would be most salient to him in the imagined perspective.   Thus for the example described above, the child would
reproduce a left-to-right display, but began with the left block
when asked to imagine himself facing that block, and conversely
with the right block when asked to imagine himself facing that.

Thus in terms of the dual code account proposed here, the egocentric error is an uneasy compromise.   The order of block placement indicates the child's awareness that the display would be in
a new position relative to self, were he to change his position.
The location of block placement indicates the child's awareness
that the display would be in the same position as before relative
to adjacent landmarks, even if he changed his position relative to
both.

Accordingly egocentric errors can be interpreted not as proof
of the child's lack of awareness of perspective changes but as proof
of his awareness of the invariance of the relations between a display
and adjacent landmarks despite movement of the observer.

COMPLEX SPATIAL TERMS

This same type of analysis can be applied to the child's grasp
of complicated spatial terms such as "in front of" and "to the left
of".   Although most English speakers may not be consciously aware
of it they use "in front of" in two distinct ways.   Imagine that I
ask Norman to stand in front of George.   Imagine too that George
is not facing me when I make this request.   To comply with the
request, Norman would have to stand near to George's front rather
than between George and myself.   If, however, I transform George
into a toadstool, Norman should stand between me and the toadstool.
The toadstool is attributed a tacit front surface which depends
upon the speaker's position.

Which of these two meanings do children grasp first?   A prediction can be made if we notice the consequence of moving the
speaker.   Even if I move around George, Norman remains in front of
George but if George is a toadstool, then when I move to the far
side of the toadstool, Norman ends up behind the toadstool, so far
as I am concerned.

Hence the first meaning specifies a straight forward landmark
relationship which is invariant across different speaker positions.
The second meaning specifies a similar landmark relation but one
which must be restricted to certain speaker positions.   Hence its
correct usage involves a co-ordination of the self-related and the
landmark spatial codes.   Kuczaj and Maratsos (1975) confirm the
prediction that the first usage is acquired by young children
before the second.   (The authors themselves predicted that the
child would find it easier to understand a usage which depended on
the speaker's own position.)

"To the left of" and "to the right of" are usually used in
relation to speaker position, presumably because landmarks with a
distinct left and right side are infrequent.   None the less young
children assume, as the present theory would predict, that such a
usage exists.   Elkind (1963) reports that children who correctly
identify, for example, a penny as being on the left of a match-box,
continue to claim that the penny is to the left when they move 180°
around the objects.   This error is strikingly similar to the egocentric errors described in the discussion of perspective-taking.
The same explanation can be offered in both cases.   The child
specifies the position of objects in terms of their invariant
landmark relations.   Thus having determined the proximity of the
penny to the left side of the match-box from his initial position,
the child is misled by the fact that the penny remains nearest to
that particular side of the match-box even when he moves to the far
side of the two objects.   Elkind (1963) quotes a child who had
just given the incorrect response.   "How did you do it?" he was
asked.   "Easy," he replied, "I remembered where they were before".

CONCLUSIONS

In three situations, search, perspective-taking and language
acquisition, the child makes errors when he concentrates on
invariant relations between objects and landmarks.   To avoid
these, the child must learn to co-ordinate both types of position
code.   A map - which can be seen as a diagrammatic representation
of a set of objects - landmark relations - is quite useless unless
one's current position on that map can be specified.

Thus the child does not replace the self-related code with a
set of allocentric or landmark relations, but learns to co-ordinate

both codes when necessary.   One important goal for future research is to understand how this co-ordination develops.

BIBLIOGRAPHY

ASLIN, R. N. & SALAPATEK, P.,   Saccadic localisation of visual targets by the very young human infant, Perception and Psychophysics, 1975, 17, pp. 293-302

BALL, W. & TRONICK, E.,   Infant responses to impending collision, optical and real, Science, 1971, 171, pp. 818-820

BASSETT, E. M.,   Production strategies in the child's drawing of the human figure: towards an argument for a model of syncretic perception, Chapter 3 in this volume

BOWER, T.G.R.,   Auditory surrogates for vision. Paper presented at 21st International Congress of Psychology, Paris, July 1976

BOWER, T.G.R., BROUGHTON, J. M. & MOORE, M. K.,   Demonstration of intention in reaching behaviour, Nature, 1970, 228, pp. 679-681

BOWER, T.G.R., BROUGHTON, J. M. & MOORE, M. K.,   Development of the object concept as manifested in changes in the tracking behaviour of infants between seven and twenty weeks of age, Journal of Experimental Child Psychology, 1971, 11, pp. 181-193

BRYANT, P. E.,   Perception and understanding in young children, London, Methuen, 1974

BUTTERWORTH, G.,   Perception and cognition: where do we stand in the mid-seventies? in VARMA, V. P. & WILLIAMS, P. (eds.) Piaget, psychology and education: Papers in honour of Jean Piaget, London, Hodder and Stoughton, 1976

ELKIND, D.,   Children's conceptions of left and right: Piaget replication study IV, Journal of Genetic Psychology, 1963, 99, pp. 269-276

FREEMAN, N.,   How young children try to plan drawings.   Chapter 1 in this volume.

FREEMAN, N. & JANIKOUN   Intellectual realism in young children's drawings of a familiar object with distinctive features, Child Development, 1972, 43, pp. 1116-1121

GANZ, L.,   Orientation in visual space by neonates and its modification by visual deprivation, in RIESEN, A. H. (ed.) The developmental neuropsychology of sensory deprivation, New York Academic Press, 1975

HARRIS, P. L.,   Perseverative errors in search by young children, Child Development, 1973, 44, pp. 28-33

HARRIS, P. L., Perseverative search at a visibly empty place by
        young infants, Journal of Experimental Child Psychology, 1974,
        18, pp. 535-542

HARRIS, P. L., Development of search and object permanence during
        infancy, Psychological Bulletin, 1975, 82, pp. 332-344

HARRIS, P. L., Subject, object and framework: a theory of spatial
        development, unpublished manuscript, Free University, Amsterdam,
        1976

HARRIS, P. L. & BASSETT Reconstruction from the mental image,
        Journal of Experimental Child Psychology, 1976, 21, pp. 514-523

HARRIS, P. L., CASSEL, T. Z. & BAMBOROUGH, P., Tracking by young
        infants, British Journal of Psychology, 1974, 65, pp. 345-349

HARRIS, P. L. & MACFARLANE, A., The growth of the effective visual
        field from birth to seven weeks, Journal of Experimental Child
        Psychology, 1974, 18, pp. 340-348

HUTTENLOCHER, J. & PRESSON, C., Mental rotation and the perspective
        problem, Cognitive Psychology, 1973, 4, pp. 277-299

KUCZAJ, S. A. & MARATSOS, M. P., On the acquisition of "front",
        "back" and "side", Child Development, 1975, 46, pp. 202-210

LUCAS, T. C., Spatial factors in the development of the object
        concept, Master's thesis, Department of Psychology, Clark
        University, U.S.A., 1975

MACFARLANE, A., HARRIS, P. L. & BARNES, I., Central and peripheral
        vision in the neonate, Journal of Experimental Child
        Psychology, 1976, 21, pp. 532-538

MCLAUGHLAND, D., A second cup? A re-examination of young children's
        drawings of a familiar object, Final Honours thesis, Department
        of Psychology, University of Lancaster, U.K., 1976

O'CONNOR, N. & HERMELIN, B., The spatial or temporal organization
        of short term memory, Quarterly Journal of Experimental
        Psychology, 1973, 25, pp. 335-343

PIAGET, J., The construction of reality in the child, New York,
        International Universities Press, 1952

PIAGET, J. & INHELDER, B., The child's conception of space, London,
        Routledge, 1956

TAUBER, E. & KOFFLER, S., Optomotor response in human infants to
        apparent motion: evidence of innateness, Science, 1966, 156,
        pp. 382-383

TRONICK, E. & CLANTON, C., Infant looking patterns, Vision Research,
        1971, 11, 1479-1486

WHITE, B. L., CASTLE, P. & HELD, R. M., Observations on the
    development of visually-directed reaching, Child Development,
    1964, 35, pp. 349-364

WILLATS, J., How children learn to draw realistic pictures,
    Chapter 13 in this volume

TRAINING   PERSPECTIVE   ABILITY

IN   YOUNG   CHILDREN

M. V. Cox

Perspective ability involves the ability to imagine or to represent how objects look relative to one another from another person's point of view.   The best known method of studying this is probably Piaget and Inhelder's three-mountains task (see Figure 1).   The child is seated before a model of three mountains.   A doll is produced and is positioned at various points around the model;   the child is asked to represent what the doll can see from each position.   Various methods of response can be used, but the most common has come to be presenting the child with a selection of pictures and asking him to pick out the one that matches the doll's view.

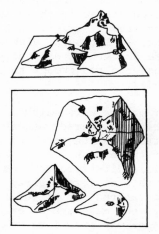

Figure 1.   The three-mountain model used by Piaget and Inhelder (1956).

From their study, Piaget and Inhelder concluded that the pre-operational child (up to about seven years) cannot do this task. He is egocentric; he cannot imagine what the view looks like from another person's position and, generally, he chooses his own view and says that it represents the doll's view. After age seven, the child is gradually able to represent other views, getting the objects in the before-behind dimension correct first of all and, later, the objects in the left-right dimension.

Piaget and Inhelder say that occupation by the child of other people's positions is the key to his acquiring perspective ability. When I thought about this, it did not seem very likely. If you send a child from his own position round to the doll's position, he is not experiencing the doll's view, he is experiencing his own view. It is a different view from his original one, yes, but it is still his own. He has been moving about all his life seeing different views of things, but he is still unable to represent another person's view when that person is in a different position from his own. I felt that a better way of provoking a change in the child was to confront him more directly with the two views - his own and the other person's. I did this by having the child stay in his own place confronted by his own view, while the experimenter, who acted as the other observer, gave him information about her view.

In order to find out which condition would be better in helping the child to acquire perspective ability I conducted a training experiment in which five-year-old children who could not do the task initially were trained to perform like normal ten- or eleven-year-olds. There were four conditions in training: a movement group, a verbal group, a visual group, and a control group. Children in the movement group occupied the other observer's position, as Piaget and Inhelder had suggested. In the verbal and visual groups the children stayed in their own place and received feedback about the other view. I felt that the task was a visual rather than a verbal one, so I thought visual feedback would be more important than verbal feedback. I was not sure about this, how-ever, so I decided to use the two groups to find out. Finally, a control group was included.

Initially the four groups were matched on pre-test scores (see Overall Plan). All children scored between 0 and 2 out of 10 in both the perspectives task and the intersection task (see Figures 2 and 3 for examples of these tasks). In each task, there were always two practice trials with feedback and then ten test trials without feedback and with a different array of objects for each trial; so each test was scored out of 10. There were nine children in each group; the mean age of each group was five years three months and the range was from five years one month to five years four months.

OVERALL PLAN OF TRAINING EXPERIMENT

PRE-TEST

        Perspectives task (two pictures)
        Intersections task

        Raven's Coloured Progressive Matrices
        English Picture Vocabulary Test

           1 week

TRAINING - 20 sessions, 15 minutes each,
              3 - 4 school days apart

1) Visual Group   2) Verbal Group   3) Movement Group
              4) Control Group

           5 days

POST-TEST

        Perspectives task (two pictures)

        Perspectives task (five pictures)
        Perspectives transfer task (different object
           arrangement; two pictures)
        Perspectives transfer task (different object
           arrangement; five pictures)
        Perspectives transfer task (different positions
           occupied by the experimenter)

        Intersections task

           12 weeks

RETENTION TEST

        administered by an independent experimenter

        Repeat of post-test

Experimenter

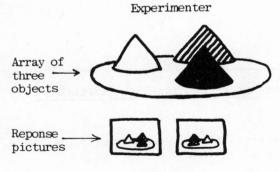

Array of
three ⟶
objects

Reponse ⟶
pictures

Child

Each child is give two practice trials with
feedback using an array of three regularly-
shaped objects of different colours. A
different array of objects (e.g. balls,
bottles, etc.) is presented in each of ten
best trials.

Figure 2.   Arrangement of the perspectives task.

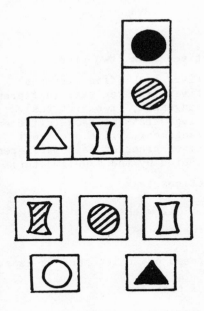

The child is asked to select the
correct card for the bottom right-
hand corner of the intersection.

Figure 3.   The intersection task.

The training consisted of twenty sessions, fifteen minutes each over a period of about nine weeks.   Each child was tested and trained individually.   The training was in small, structured steps, starting very simply and gradually getting more complex; the order of introducing new elements into the training was based on the results of some previous experiments I had done.   Briefly, the child first learned to represent objects in a before-behind relationship as seen from another person's position, then a left-right relationship, and finally he learned to put the two together so that he could deal with the three-mountains task which contains both of these relationships.   By the end of the training, children were choosing from a selection of five pictures which included various confusions of the before-behind and left-right relationships.

I will explain a little more about the differences among the conditions of training.   Children in the <u>movement</u> group, when presented with the response pictures and asked to choose the one which matched the experimenter's view, took the picture round to the experimenter's position to check.   If this was wrong they tried again until they got the right one.   In the <u>verbal</u> group, the children chose a picture and handed it to the experimenter; she held it in front of her so that the child could not see the picture.   She told the child whether his choice was right or wrong;   if it was incorrect, she told him what was wrong with it, and he tried again.   The children in the <u>visual</u> group handed the picture to the experimenter who held it in front of her so that the picture was visible to the child (although it was upside down to him);   he could see whether or not the objects in the picture were in the correct positions to match those in the array.   He judged whether or not it was correct;   if it was incorrect, he tried again. Children in the <u>control</u> group played a ten questions classification game with the experimenter, so each child had the same amount of time spent on him.

After training, the children were given the same perspectives task again that they had had in the pre-testing, that is using two pictures as in Figure 2.   In addition, they had a number of varia-tions on the task (these can be seen in the Overall Plan).   Giving the children five pictures (which included confusions of the before-behind and left-right relationships) meant that, to consistently choose the correct picture, the child would have to attend to both the before-behind and left-right dimensions.   The other variations included reversing the object array and having the experimenter positioned at the sides instead of opposite the child.   All these variations were regarded as 'near' transfer tasks, as they all involved basically the same idea;   the intersection task was regarded as a 'far' transfer task because it did not involve taking someone else's point of view.   I wanted to see how much transfer there would be from each of the trained groups compared with the

controls.   This whole set of tasks after training was called the
post-test and was given five days after the end of training.   The
whole lot was given again after a further twelve weeks, and this
testing was called the retention test.   (See Overall Plan.)

After training, the children in the three perspectives-trained
groups improved their performance compared with controls on the
first task, that is the task using two pictures (see Figure 4);
this was still the case after twelve weeks.   When five pictures
were used (see Figure 5), that is when the child was forced to
consider both the before-behind and the left-right relationships
to get the correct response, all three groups were better than the
controls at the post-test, but the movement group was not significantly better than the control group at the retention test.   On
the whole, the visual and verbal groups transferred their learning
to the 'near' transfer tasks and maintained their superiority over
both the control group and the movement group after twelve weeks
(see Figures 5, 6, 7 and 8).   There was no transfer, however, to
the 'far' transfer task (see Figure 9);   all groups improved.   (I
have my suspicions that the children were doing something very
similar to the intersection task in the classroom.)

There was no significant difference between the verbal and
visual groups;   so, providing information about another view while
the child remains in his own place whether it be verbal or visual
appears to be equally effective in provoking change.   Piaget and
Inhelder's notion that the most effective way for the child to
acquire perspective ability is through occupation of other positions
does not appear correct.

Conceptual conflict or disequilibrium is fundamental to Piaget's
theory of cognitive development and to Berlyne's neo-associationist
account of the dynamics of problem-solving.   These both suggest
that when the child becomes aware of the contradictions which occur
as a result of his use of inappropriate problem-solving strategies,
he re-organizes his thinking to resolve the conflict.

I considered that the training given to the visual and verbal
groups would have greater potential for provoking conflict than the
training given to the movement group.   Because the comparison of
the two opposing views was presented more directly in these groups
than in the movement group, it seemed to me that the children in
the visual and verbal groups would therefore be more aware than
those in the movement group that another's view is different from
their own.   Thus, the greater success of the visual and verbal
training suggests that changes in cognition are promoted by
experiences which create conceptual conflict in the child.

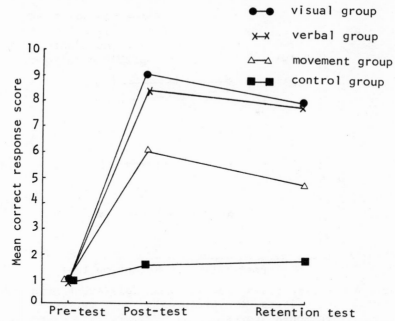

Figure 4. Perspectives task (two pictures): mean correct response scores.

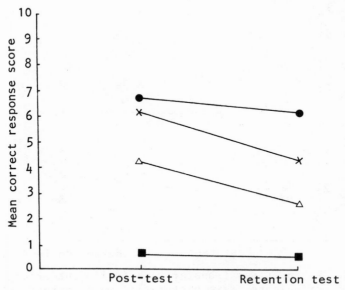

Figure 5. Perspectives task (five pictures): mean correct response scores.

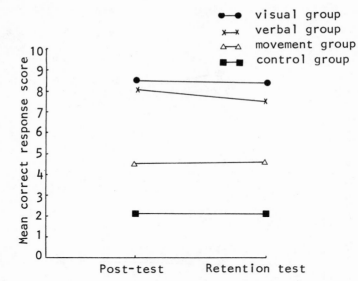

Figure 6.   Perspectives transfer task (different arrangement
of objects, two pictures):   mean correct
response scores.

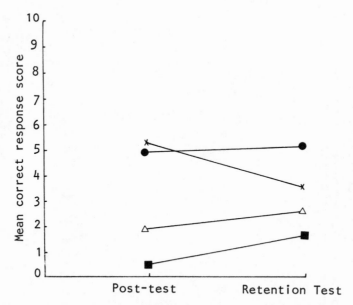

Figure 7.   Perspectives transfer task (different arrangement
of objects, five pictures):   mean correct
response scores.

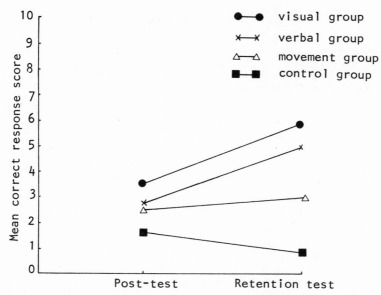

Figure 8. Perspectives transfer task (different positions occupied by the experimenter): mean correct response scores.

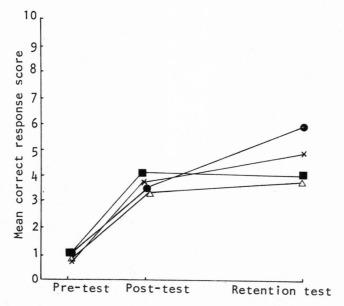

Figure 9. Intersections task: mean correct response scores.

BIBLIOGRAPHY

BERLYNE, D. E.,   Conflict, arousal and curiosity, New York, McGraw
    Hill, 1960

PIAGET, J. & INHELDER, B.,   The child's conception of space, London,
    Routledge and Kegan Paul, 1956

DISCUSSION OF THE PAPER BY COX

McGurk (Surrey). We find that picture selection is a very
conservative estimate of children's ability to take a perspective.
Invariably this method gives a much lower level of performance
than verbal description of the other's view or building the other's
view.

Cox. I think you are right and most other research would
support this argument. I made it as hard as possible for the
children in that I had the experimenter sitting opposite the child.
Another experiment of my own shows that the task is much harder
when the experimenter is sitting opposite the child than at the
side (Journal of Experimental Child Psychology, 1977 (in press)).

Butterworth. Did you discover first of all whether the
children could select their own view?

Cox. Yes. I know there has been some research which
suggests that it is difficult for a child to pick out his own view
but in my experiments they found it easy. They may have made a
mistake on the first go but that is all.

Harris. You want to argue that you have been training perspective ability but it is possible that your procedure just allows
the child to understand what you want him to do and that the perspective ability actually remains quite unaltered.

Freeman. I would like to take this point up. It is not
only that children get a better understanding of what one wants
them to do but get better at employing the optimal strategies for

doing it.   If you look at non-inferential versions of perspective
tasks, like the experiment by Mazangkay et al. (1971), where
experimenter and child sit opposite one another and look at cards,
even three-and-a-half-year-olds know that you can see what is on
your side and not what is on their side.   We ought to analyse the
task demands of switching in a strategy for reporting views.

We used Neil O'Connor's (1973) excellent "three card trick"
(Freeman 1975) where you put down three cards so that the temporal
order of presentation doesn't correspond to the final spatial
order.   What we find is that children who spontaneously pick out
the spatial order are better at a perspective task than those who
are picking out the temporal order.   These children are throwing
away some of the sequential temporal information and casting it
into a spatial mode.   If we were to study the strategies children
use we would be better able to understand whether supposedly
inferential problems are inferential or not.

BIBLIOGRAPHY

FREEMAN, N. H.,   Temporal and spatial ordering in recall by five to
    eight-year-old children, Child Development, 1975, 46,
    pp. 237-239

MAZANGKAY, Z. S., FEENSTRA, H. J. & TAYAG, A. H.,   Co-ordination of
    perspectives among Filipino children. Occasional paper No 10,
    Language Study Centre, Philippine Normal College, Manila, D.406

O'CONNOR, N. & HERMELIN, B.,   The spatial or temporal organisation
    of short term memory, Quarterly Journal of Experimental
    Psychology, 1973, 25, pp. 335-343

SCANNING STRATEGIES OF CHILDREN AND ADULTS

Peter Coles, Marian Sigman and Karen Chessel

ABSTRACT

This paper describes the rationale and design of an investigation of eye movement scanning strategies during familiarisation with and subsequent recognition of two-dimensional geometric patterns. Subjects were preschool children aged from 3:5 to 6:5 years, and adults. Eye movements were recorded using a remote, on-line T.V. oculometer. The main aim of the experiment was to investigate the conflicting claims about the development and function of saccadic eye movements during the process of initial familiarisation with a pattern and its subsequent identification, as put forward by Zinchenko, Vurpillot and by Mackworth and Bruner. Although data collection is complete, analysis has only just begun. Consequently, samples of data will be presented for illustrative purposes only. Some of the theoretical problems for studies of eye movements will be discussed.

Over the past four years we have been developing a relatively new technique for recording eye movements using infra-red T.V. Unlike many earlier systems, this technique does not require the use of bite-bar or rigid head restraint and therefore makes it possible to carry out longer studies with less discomfort. Also data analysis is carried out partly on-line by mini-computer, with cleaning-up and statistical analyses being carried out off-line. These developments make it much more suitable for working with children and even infants, and reduces considerably the gargantuan task of data reduction which so often dissuades people from looking at eye movements. As a description of our technique is to be available elsewhere (Albutt et al., unpublished) we will not enter into details here. Although we have now completed a number of

107

studies with infants, children and adults we are only just beginning
the task of data analysis. Consequently, this paper will be
concerned mainly with a discussion of what we feel are some of the
major theoretical problems that have influenced our own work. We
will present some new data for illustrative purposes towards the
end of our discussion.

Anyone recording eye movements to study visual scanning makes
a number of assumptions about the relationship between eye movements
and information processing. Because these assumptions are rarely
made explicit, we feel that it is important for an understanding of
work on scanning that some of them at least should be pointed out.
During the visual exploration of, say, a static two-dimensional
display, the eye will be observed to make a series of rapid,
ballistic, jerky movements called saccades interrupted by pauses
or fixations. During the pauses the eye is still very active but
it is an open issue what the function of the drifts and microsaccades
that occur might be (Steinman, 1973; Gaarder, 1967; Ditchburn,
1973). The commonest assumption is that fixations are the periods
of information intake. During these periods a small part of the
stimulus, subtending about 2-3° of visual angle, is inspected with
the high resolution of foveal vision. At the same time, but by an
unknown mechanism, areas of the stimulus falling on the peripheral
retina are thought to be singled out for subsequent foveal inspection, the change of fixation being effected by a saccade. This
assumption about the nature of saccadic eye movements may prove to
be too simplistic but, for the time being, it is the model we will
adopt. The practical implication of adopting this model is that
many researchers have restricted their analyses to the distribution
of fixations rather than the saccades although this is not universally true.

Taking this latter approach to the study of visual scanning,
Vurpillot (1976) concentrated on three characteristics of her child
subjects' eye movements - locus of fixation within a stimulus,
duration of fixation and sequence of fixations. The areas of the
stimulus fixated would indicate the information that is sampled,
the sequence of fixations would indicate the strategy the subject
is using and the duration of the fixation would correspond to the
time the observer needs to register the information contained in
the area fixated.

In her experiments with children, Vurpillot found a clear
developmental trend from age three to eight years on these measures.
The subjects' task was to say whether two schematic houses were the
same or not the same. Identity or difference was established by
manipulating the contents of the six windows in each house by means
of permutation (where the same contents appeared in different
windows in the two houses) and substitution (where one or more
windows contained objects not present in any of the windows of the
other house).

Children under five-and-a-half years typically made fewer eye movements, fixated for longer periods of time, did not sample information systematically by point-to-point checks between the houses, and looked at insufficient details before making their decisions. By age six-and-a-half years, fixations were shorter and inspection was relatively systematic and comprehensive. Vurpillot did not, unfortunately, include any adult subjects as controls. The implicit assumption seemed to be that by age eight years there would be no significant differences between the child and the adult.

This, however, was not the picture presented by Mackworth and Bruner (1970). In their experiment, six-year-olds and adults were shown blurred or sharp colour photographs of relatively familiar objects, such as a fire hydrant. With the sharp pictures and instructions to "simply look at the pictures", there were few significant differences on any eye movement measure between adults and children. This lack of a developmental difference for pictorial material was also found by Zinchenko, van Chsi-Tsin and Tarakanov (1963) with children as young as three-and-a-half years, their explanation being that even for the three-year-old, looking at pictures is a familiar activity.

With the blurred pictures the task was to identify what the picture was. On the basis of the adult eye movement records a measure of informativeness was assigned to each 2° square of the 20° X 16° stimuli using a similar criterion to that adopted by Mackworth and Morandi (1967). The six-year-olds typically spent less time fixating informative areas than the adults and made fewer large eye movements (i.e. over 6°) or what Mackworth and Bruner called "leaps", but made many more short eye movements, or "steps", concentrating on apparently 'irrelevant' details. Fixation times were shorter for the adults than for the children as predicted by the developmental trend found by Vurpillot (1976).

Two interesting issues arise out of the studies of Vurpillot and Mackworth and Bruner. The first is that in Vurpillot's experiment the six-year-old is portrayed as being systematic and mature in his exploration. With the different kind of task in Mackworth and Bruner's study, the six-year-old seems to concentrate on irrelevant details and shows few attempts at a systematic integration of all the parts of a stimulus. As many Soviet writers, such as Vygotsky (1962), Luria (1961), Zaporozhets (1965) and Zinchenko et al. (1963) have pointed out, discussions of competence in young children are notoriously context-specific. In fact, because of this we have carried out a study to see just how much a variation in context will affect a child's scanning strategies.

The child taking part in a problem-solving experiment has a double task. On the one hand he has to form a model of the problem and on the other, he must formulate an adequate strategy

for its solution.   Even with training periods and comprehension
tests, it is very difficult to establish whether the child and the
experimenter have the same model of the experimental task, and it
should never be simply assumed that they do.

Also, by their very nature, most eye movement studies with
young children deny them two important strategies for problem-
solving.   The first involves the sensori-motor "prop" of using
the hand or finger to assist scanning, as young children apparently
have difficulty in maintaining fixation without aid (Lesèvre, 1968).
Vurpillot (1976) was aware of this limitation in her procedure and
did, in fact, find improved performance when she repeated the study
without eye movements being recorded and allowing the children to
handle the pictures.

Secondly, children, as Vygotsky emphasised, rely heavily on a
dialogue with adults in order to solve problems, the difference in
their performance with and without help of adults being called the
"zone of potential development".   It would be interesting to see
just how much a young child's scanning can be modified when given
assistance by an adult.

In an interesting variant of Vurpillot's experiment, Olson
(1970) suggested that the young child's poorer performance may in
part be due to his expectation about the criteria of identity or
difference.   When judging houses, as any estate agent knows, there
are "big differences", such as between barns and castles, and "small
differences" such as the contents of the windows.   By showing the
child what the range of choices was to be Olson did manage to
improve the performance of young children on a "same-different" task.

The other issue which arises from Mackworth and Bruner's study
concerns the length of eye movements.   It will be recalled that the
six-year-old made few eye movements greater than 6°.   The authors
suggested that the young child may have a limited capacity for processing information in the visual periphery.   In this respect he
may resemble an adult with "tunnel vision" (Tyler, 1968;   Luria,
Karpov and Yarbus, 1966) where adequate visual search is impossible
without an awareness of potentially interesting features around the
point being fixated.   Piaget and Vinh-Bangh (1961) reported a
similar collapsing of the effective visual field in the young child,
which they termed "centration".   Again this had the effect of
reducing large eye movements, but for Piaget this was less the
result of inadequate peripheral vision than that the young child
does not yet appreciate that parts of a visual stimulus may be
related together by means of a system of Cartesian co-ordinates.

Indeed as Whiteside (1974) suggested, poor ability to process
information in the periphery could predict an _increase_ in large eye

movements.   In a test involving familiarisation with and subsequent
recognition of dot patterns, Whiteside found that both elderly
subjects and children showed more extensive eye movements than
college students, possibly because they had poorer peripheral vision
and therefore had to process information foveally.   It does seem,
however, that this apparent contradiction arises out of a confusion
between foveal and peripheral vision and what Neisser (1967) called
"global" and "focal" attention.   To say that the child is relatively
poor at attending "globally" or shifting attention internally, does
not necessarily imply that he has poorly developed peripheral vision.

This confusion was appreciated by Zinchenko at al. (1963) who
also presented a somewhat different approach to the study of eye
movements to that of the authors discussed earlier.   For Zinchenko
et al. not only fixations, but the saccadic eye movements themselves
are thought to be involved in information processing.   For many
Soviet psychologists, visual inspection is considered to be analogous
to, although developmentally it matures later than manipulatory,
haptic exploration, whereby an internal "motor copy" of the stimulus
is built up using the actions of exploration.   Zinchenko et al.
would predict that, with experience, exploration tends to be more
isomorphic with the stimulus, but that an internal scan may be
substituted for overt exploration during the recognition of familiar
objects.   In other words, motor-copy theorists like Zinchenko seem
to be more interested in the pattern of eye movements than in
fixations.

This position contrasts sharply with another model of saccadic
eye movements put forward by Noton and Stark (1971).   For them,
patterns are thought to consist of features which have to be
sampled and stored in a particular sequence - a "scan path" - in
order to be represented in memory.   Scan paths were thought to
vary between, but not within individuals for both familiarisation
with and subsequent recognition of a particular stimulus.   However,
the notion of the stimulus will surely change according to the task
in hand and as Yarbus (1967) has demonstrated the pattern of fixations of a given subject scanning a given picture does change
markedly with a variation in the instructions to the subject.

For Zinchenko et al., the sequence of fixations was not
particularly important.   In fact foveal fixations were also not
always felt to be necessary in order to scan a picture.   In a
study using stabilised images - where shifts of foveal fixation
with respect to the stimulus are impossible, Zinchenko and Vergiles
(1972) found subjects able to solve quite complex problems.   They
did, however, find small eye movements that were spatially congruent with the stimulus, but were not of the same scale as the
stimulus.   They called these small movements "vicarious perceptual
actions" and found in them further support for their motor-copy
theory of representation.

Not everyone would agree with the materialistic view of perception and representation put forward by Soviet psychologists. However, the particular findings of Zinchenko et al. (1963) with preschool children during a familiarisation and recognition task using geometric shapes are important.

Like Vurpillot (1976) and Piaget and Vinh-Bangh (1961), Zinchenko et al. found a developmental trend between the ages of three-and-a-half and six-and-a-half years. If unfamiliar geometric shapes were to be learned, the younger children made very few and tightly clustered eye movements around inessential parts of the patterns. By five-and-a-half to six-and-a-half years eye movements were much more dispersed and concentrated on the contour. In this sense they were considered to be more isomorphic with the stimuli. During a later recognition task with the same stimulus a reverse trend was found. The older children made very few eye movements and concentrated on a few details only, whilst the younger children showed large, almost exploratory eye movements. Zinchenko et al. suggested that it was only during the act of recognition that the younger child realised what the task of familiarisation implied. This is reminiscent of Olson's point of view in his version of Vurpillot's experiment, and was something that we have looked at in our own studies to be described shortly. The fact that large eye movements are found in the young child would seem to make the arguments about centration and peripheral processing specific to certain contexts.

In planning our own experiments we have tried to make use of the conflicts and questions raised by the various studies we have described. In particular, we were interested to see if the young child's strategies for familiarisation would become more systematic with practice on the recognition tasks as Zinchenko and Olson suggested. After some deliberation, we decided to use geometrical patterns - matrices of crosses and tranges, rather than familiar, representational material (see Figures 1a - 1d). It is true that although geometrical material does not have the "ecological validity" of representational material, it cannot be considered to be meaningless for the child although we may not know what particular associations the material has for him. On the other hand, geometrical material allowed us greater experimental control and, being unfamiliar for both children and adults, would possibly be more likely to show up any developmental differences.

There were four groups of six subjects (three male and three female) - three-and-a-half to four-and-a-half-year-olds, four-and-a-half to five-and-a-half-year-olds, five-and-a-half to six-and-a-half-year-olds and adults. Each subject was presented with a 4 X 4 matrix containing a particular configuration of crosses and triangles (Figure 1a) and was asked to look at it carefully. After twenty seconds he was shown a pair of matrices (Figures 1b, 1c, 1d), one

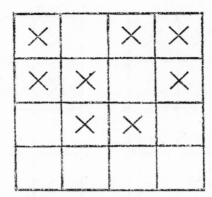

Figure 1a.   'Target' or familiarisation matrix from the
              second more difficult series

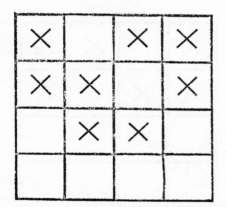 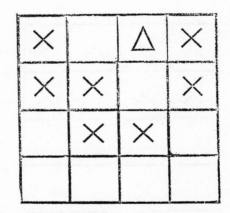

Figure 1b.   'Target' and comparison matrix

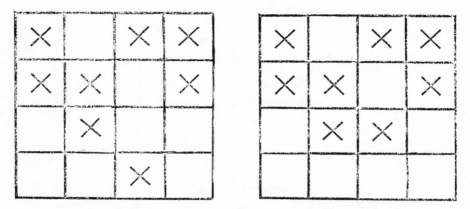

Figure 1c.   'Target' and comparison matrix

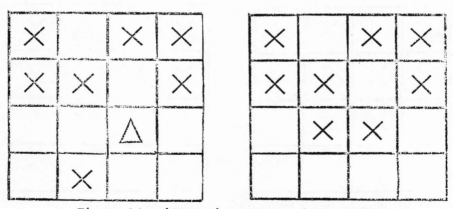

Figure 1d.   'Target' and comparison matrix

of which matched the familiarisation pattern, or "target".   The
subject was asked to indicate which of the two was exactly like
the one he had just seen, by pressing one of two buttons situated
to his right and left respectively and thus corresponding to the
picture on the right or left.   The subject was then shown the
target pattern again for a further twenty seconds and then a
different pair for identification.   This procedure was repeated
once more, the left-right position of the matching pattern being
alternated.

In order to familiarise subjects with the task they were
presented with a series of matrices similar to the experimental
sets, but in a booklet which could be handled.   When the
experimenter was sure that the child understood the task, on the
basis of his performance with the practice series, a similar series
was presented with slides, using the eye movement apparatus, again
for practice.   Only then would we proceed to the experimental
series where eye movements were recorded.

The three comparison pairs for each of the two experimental
series were of differing difficulty as determined by the number of
discrepancies between the correct and incorrect version.   In one
instance the pattern of elements would be the same for the matching
and discrepant versions (Figure 1b) but, instead of, say, a cross
in one cell, the incorrect one would have a triangle in the corresponding cell.   In another pair (Figure 1c) the overall pattern
would differ in the incorrect version whilst in the third pair
(Figure 1d) both the pattern and the elements would differ in the
incorrect version.   Two series were used, the first being relatively
easy and the second more difficult.

So far we have analysed the data from one adult, one three-and-
a-half-year-old and one five-and-a-half-year-old for the same
experimental condition, and so the following results should be seen
as tentative only.   For illustrative purposes, we chose the most
difficult series for presentation here.   In an effort to use as
much of our data as possible we have analysed the records in a
number of ways.

1.   Initial Familiarisation

When shown the 'target' pattern (Figure 1a) for the first time,
there seemed to be marked differences in the pattern and characteristics of the fixations of the adult and the children (Figures
2a – 2c).   As was expected from the results of Vurpillot (1975),
Zinchenko et al. (1963) and Mackworth and Bruner (1970), the
children's fixations were much longer than those of the adult and
the younger child's longer than the older child's.   As a corollary,

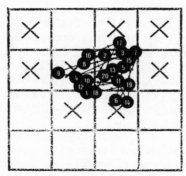

Figure 2a. Subject MK (adult).   Plot of first twenty
fixations during initial inspection of 'target'

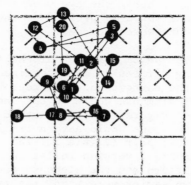

Figure 2b. Subject RH (5:4 years). Plot of first twenty
fixations during initial inspection of 'target'

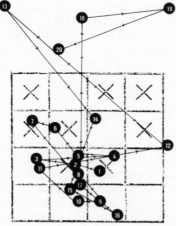

Figure 2c. Subject NC (3:4 years).   Plot of first twenty
fixations during initial familiarisation with 'target'

the children made fewer eye movements in the time available than
the adult.   However, although the adult made more fixations than
the children, they were concentrated on fewer of the cells of the
matrix than for the children.   Figures 2a, 2b and 2c show the
first twenty fixations of each of the three subjects.   It will be
seen from Figures 2b and 2c that the children's fixations are much
more dispersed than the adult's, especially the three-and-a-half-
year-old's.   It will also be noticed that this child, unlike the
other, older subjects, spent some time looking off-target altogether.
You may recall that Whiteside (1974) also found adults' eye movements
to be less extensive than children's.   This might be interpreted as
showing a greater capacity for "global" processing in the adult than
in the child, or it may be, as Zinchenko et al. (1963) suggested,
that attention shifts in the adult are often carried out internally.

    A closer inspection of the initial familiarisation data
(Figures 2a - 2c) reveals that the adult's scanning is not only
more constricted than the children's, but is also more organised or
systematic.   Apart from using the 'conventional' measures for
analysing our data - such as fixation duration, dispersion, etc. -
we decided to calculate transition probabilities for a number of
measures, such as locus of fixation, duration of fixation, saccade
size, saccade vector, and, for locus at least, have found some very
interesting results.   The analysis of transition probabilities in
this case suggested that, for a given locus of fixation in the adult
subject, all other possible loci were not equiprobable.   For pre-
liminary analysis, we treated all fixations within a single 'cell'
of the matrix - about $2\frac{1}{2}^{o}$ square - as equivalent, and calculated
the transition probabilities of fixating any cell given a fixation
in any cell.   This analysis revealed that some cells were paired
together such that a fixation in cell 'x' was followed by a fixation
in cell 'y'.   We then looked to see, given 'x' then 'y', what was
the probability of fixating any other cell?   This process was
carried further until a limit was found where all subsequent fixations were equiprobable.   This analysis revealed a complex 'chain'
of between five and seven cells that was repeated twice within the
same trial and again on a subsequent trial.   In other words, the
adult tended to fixate certain cells in a particular sequence and
that this whole sequence appeared three times.   This is shown in
Figures 3a - 3e.   In Figure 3a are two almost identical sequences
taken from the adult's initial familiarisation pattern.   Fixations
3 - 8 represent the first sequence and 11 - 16 the second sequence.
Figure 3b shows an abbreviated version of the same sequence which
appeared in the final (third) inspection of the 'target' pattern,
and Figure 3c shows a schematised representation of the sequence.

    There are obvious similarities between these sequences and
Noton and Stark's (1971) 'scan paths', but the sequences have a
more formal basis, as defined by transition probabilities.

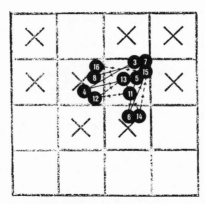

Figure 3a. Two similar sequences of eye movements during
initial familiarisation with the target.   (Subject MK.)
Sequence (a) 3-8 (b) 11-16

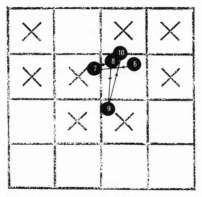

Figure 3b. Almost identical sequence to Figure 3a, occurring
in final inspection of figure.   (Subject MK.)

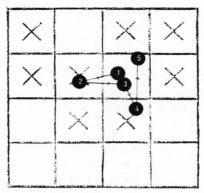

Figure 3c. Schematic representation of the sequence of
fixations for subject MK

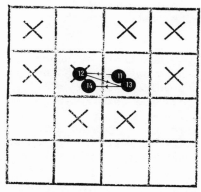

Figure 3d. Subject RH (5:4 years).   Sequence of fixations
between adjacent cells during second inspection of 'target'

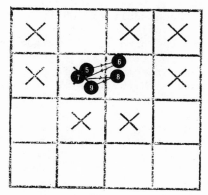

Figure 3e. Subject RH (5:4 years).   Sequence of fixations
between adjacent cells during final inspection of 'target'

At this stage we do not endorse the theoretical view of Noton and
Stark that 'scan paths' are unique for a given subject and picture
nor that they are necessary for recognition as implied by their
notion of a 'feature ring'.   A more parsimonious explanation would
be that the sequence does represent some external analogue of an
attempt to memorise the pattern and that the repetitions are
'rehearsals'.

    It is interesting that these sequences did not emerge in either
of the children, to the same extent.   The five-and-a-half-year-old
did show, however, a predilection for passing from one particular
cell to an adjacent cell and back again, as shown in Figure 3d,
which was taken from the second presentation of the target and 3e,
which was taken from the third presentation.   The analysis of
transition probabilities has not, to our knowledge, been used before
in analysing eye movement data, but seems to be potentially very
exciting.

                2. Subsequent Inspection of the 'Target'

    Part of the rationale for our particular experimental design,
it will be recalled, was to see whether subjects, especially the
younger children, would organise their inspection of the target in
a more defined manner once they had had experience of the recognition task.   This information would be shown in the scanning of
the second and third presentations of the target after the recognition, forced-choice trials.   The patterns of fixation and eye
movements are shown in Figures 4a - 4c and Figures 5a - 5c.
Looking at Figures 4a - 4c reveals few obvious differences between
the three subjects.   Both adult and child patterns are relatively
dispersed and all three subjects spent an early part of their
scanning investigating the area of the target that had been changed
in the previous comparison trial (see Figure 1b).   Superficially
it would seem that the three-and-a-half-year-old had made use of
her previous experience with the task to organise her current
search, although this is only a tentative suggestion.   This does
not seem to be true for the final inspection of the target (Figure
5c).   By this time the young child was bored by the task and would
not use the twenty seconds to get information which would help her
in the subsequent recognition trial.   This is shown by the large
number of off-target fixations.   The older child and adult were
probably also bored by the task, but tended to keep their scanning
to a relatively constricted area of the matrix, again focussing on
the area that had been altered in the previous 'incorrect' version
(see Figures 5a, 5b and 1c).   Also the adult, unlike the child,
spent time apparently following a preferred sequence of fixations
or eye movements (Figure 3b).

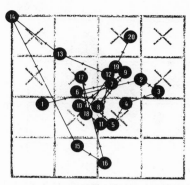

Figure 4a. Subject MK (adult).   Second inspection of
'target' - first twenty fixations only

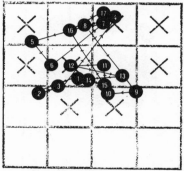

Figure 4b. Subject RH (5:4 years).   Plot of all fixations
during second inspection of 'target'

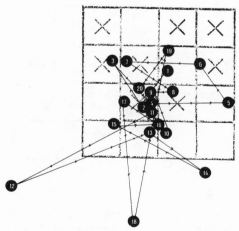

Figure 4c. Subject NC (3:4 years).   Plot of first twenty
fixations during second inspection of 'target'

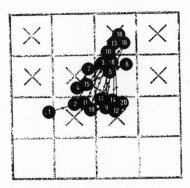

Figure 5a.   Subject MK (adult).   Plot of first twenty
fixations during third inspection of 'target'

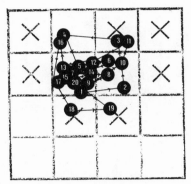

Figure 5b.   Subject RH (5:4 years).   Plot of first twenty
fixations during third inspection of 'target'

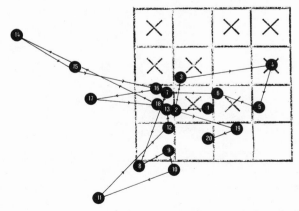

Figure 5c.   Subject NC (3:4 years).   Plot of first twenty
fixations during third inspection of 'target'

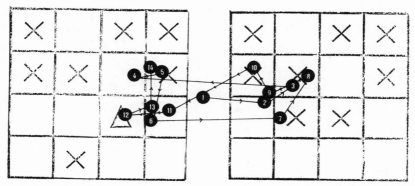

Figure 6a. Subject MK (adult).   Plot of fixations up to decision
during first identification trial. (Time taken - approx. 5.06 secs.)

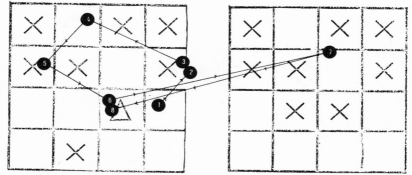

Figure 6b.   Subject RH (5:4 years).   Plot of fixations up to
decision during first identification trial. (Decision time -
approx. 9 secs.)

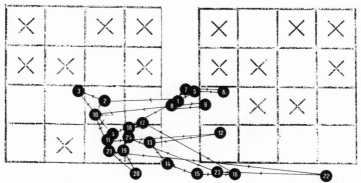

Figure 6c.   Subject NC (3:4 years).   Plot of fixations up to
decision during first identification trial. (Decision time -
approx. 10 secs.)

124 P. COLES ET AL.

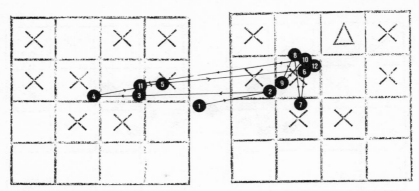

Figure 7a. Subject MK (adult).   Plot of fixations up to decision
during second identification trial. (Decision time –
approx. 3.78 secs.)

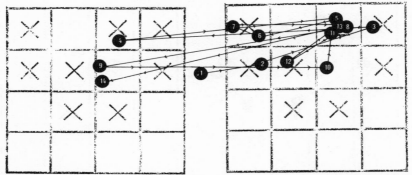

Figure 7b. Subject RH (5:4 years).   Plot of fixations up to
decision during second identification series. (Decision time
– approx. 7.86 secs.)

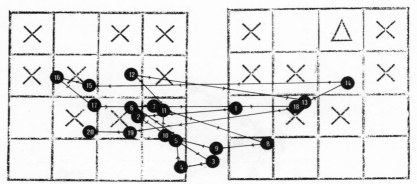

Figure 7c. Subject NC (3:4 years).   Plot of fixations up to
decision during second identification trial. (Decision
time – approx. 10 secs.)

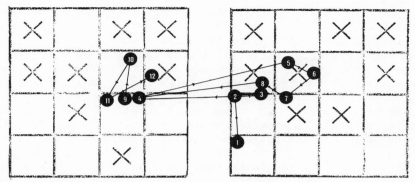

Figure 8a. Subject MK (adult). Plot of fixations up to decision
during third identification trial. (Decision time
- approx. 4.20 secs.)

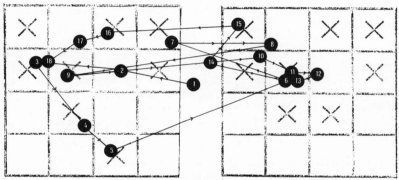

Figure 8b. Subject RH (5:4 years). Plot of fixations up to
decision during third identification trial. (Decision time -
approx. 8.30 secs.)

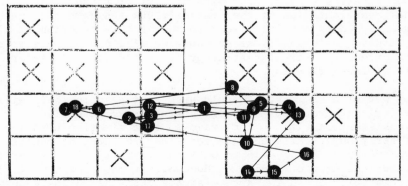

Ficture 8c. Subject NC (3:4 years). Plot of fixations up to
decision during third identification series. (Decision time -
approx. 9.35 secs.)

3. Scanning during Identifications

It is almost meaningless to take the inspection series of these three subjects in isolation from the experiment as a whole, because of the effects of order and side preference, etc. that are only controlled for between subjects. So, at this stage of analysis, we feel it would be unwise and potentially misleading to try to interpret the scanning during these trials. It can be said, however, as would be expected, that the adult made her decision more quickly than the children - taking about five seconds as opposed to six to eight seconds for the five-and-a-half-year-old and ten seconds for the three-and-a-half-year-old. The patterns of fixations up to the point of decision for each stimulus are shown in Figures 6a - 6c, 7a - 7c and 8a - 8c. Perhaps the most noticeable result for these trials is the apparently orderly and economical scanning of the stimuli by the five-and-a-half-year-old and the (superficially at least) similarity of strategy used by this child during the first and third identification trials (Figures 6b and 8b).

It is not clear whether a fixation on the discrepant element is necessary for correct identification of the 'target'. This issue is complicated by the problem faced by anyone plotting eye movement data, namely that of the area that should be ascribed to a given fixation. Our figures show areas of about 1° diameter but it would be more reasonable and less misleading to show areas of foveal fixation as $2^{\circ} - 3^{\circ}$.

The only other comment that we feel we can make on the results of the identification series concerns the number of eye movements from one pattern to the other. The three-and-a-half-year-old seemed in every case to make many more "inter-figural" eye movements than the older subjects. It may be that the three-and-a-half-year-old was comparing the patterns with each other rather than with an internal representation of the 'target', but the data that we have so far analysed is not sufficient to answer this question. Also, until we have analysed all of our data we will not be able to say to what extent a particular strategy is related to success or failure of identification.

By way of a summary, it would seem that despite their different theoretical backgrounds, the various studies we have discussed show some consistent results. For example, that fixation durations are longer for younger children than for older children or adults. Also the younger child seems to be less systematic in his exploration than older children or adults. However, it may be that this lack of systematicity could in part be simply that the child is answering a different question to that understood by the adult; or it could be that he is deprived of two important aids - an adult tutor and

his finger!   The question of global versus focal attention seems to
be relatively open.

We do feel that exploration may not be a piecemeal affair of
foveal fixations being guided one at a time by peripheral information.   It may turn out that for adults at least whole strings of
fixations are programmed in advance after some kind of overall or
global analysis (Heywood, personal communication).   We hope that
by analysing transition probabilities we may be able to gain some
insight into this problem.   It is not yet clear whether our
experiments will actually solve any of the problems that we have
discussed.   What is clear, however, is that as more data is
analysed the number of new questions seems to multiply too, but
perhaps this is the mark of progress in science.

ACKNOWLEDGEMENTS

The experimental work described in this paper was supported by
a Medical Research Council Grant, No. G974/236/C, to Professor J.
S. Bruner.   The authors would like to acknowledge their debt to
Dr Simon Heywood, John Churcher and Paul Bamborough for developing
the eye movement recording apparatus and to Stephen Fearnley for
help with computer programming.   We would also like to thank Dr
Mike Scaife for commenting on an earlier manuscript.

BIBLIOGRAPHY

ALBUTT, M.G.V., BAMBOROUGH, P., CHURCHER, J., HEYWOOD, S. P.,
RICE, P. D. & SALTER, S. H.,   Eye movement recording by on-line
     analysis of television, unpublished typescript, Department of
     Experimental Psychology, University of Oxford

DITCHBURN, R. W.,   Eye movements and visual perception, Oxford,
     Clarendon Press, 1973

GAARDER, K.,   Mechanisms in fixation eye movements, British Journal
     of Physiological Optics, 1967, 24, pp. 28-44

LESEVRE, N.,   L'organisation du regard chez les enfants d'age
     scolaire, lecteurs normaux et dyslexiques (étude electro-
     oculographique), Revue Neuropsychiatrique Infantile, 1968,
     16, pp. 323-349

LURIA, A. R., KARPOV, A. & YARBUS, A. L.,   Disturbances of active
     visual perception with lesions of the frontal lobes, Cortex,
     1966, 2, pp. 202-212

LURIA, A. R.,   Speech and the regulation of normal and abnormal
     behaviour, London, Pergamon Press, 1961

MACKWORTH, N. H. & BRUNER, J. S., How adults and children search and recognise pictures, Human Development, 1970, 13, pp. 149-172

MACKWORTH, N. H. & MORANDI, A. J., The gaze selects informative details within pictures, Perception & Psychophysics, 1967, 2, pp. 547-552

NEISSER, U., Cognitive Psychology, New York, Appleton-Century-Crofts, 1967

NOTON, D. & STARK, L., Scan paths in saccadic eye movements while viewing and recognising patterns, Vision Research, 1971, 11, pp. 929-942

OLSON, D., Cognitive Development, New York and London, Academic Press, 1970

PIAGET, J. & VINH-BANGH, Comparaisons des mouvements oculaires et des centrations du regard chez l'enfant et chez l'adult, Archives de Psychologie, (Genève) 1961, 38, pp. 167-200

STEINMAN, R. M. ET AL., Miniature eye movements, Science, 1973, 181, (4102), pp. 810-819

TYLER, H. R., Abnormalities of perception with defective eye movements (Balint's syndrome), Cortex, 1968, 4, pp. 154-171

VURPILLOT, E., The visual world of the child, London, George Allen & Unwin, 1976

VYGOTSKY, L. S., Thought and language, Cambridge, M.I.T. Press, 1962

WHITESIDE, J. A., Eye movements of children, adults and elderly persons during inspection of dot patterns, Journal of Experimental Child Psychology, 1974, 18, pp. 313-332

YARBUS, A. L., Eye movements and vision, New York, Plenum, 1969

ZAPOROZHETS, A. V., The development of perception in the preschool child, in MUSSEN, P. H. (ed.) European Research in Child Development, S.R.C.D. Monograph, 1965, 30 (100), pp. 85-105

ZINCHENKO, V. P., Chzhi-Tsin, V. & Tarakanov, V. V., The formation and development of perceptual activity, Soviet Psychology & Psychiatry, 1963, 1, pp. 3-12

ZINCHENKO, V. P. & VERGILES, N. Yu., Formation of visual images, New York & London, Consultants' Bureau, 1972

SPATIAL REPRESENTATION BY BLIND AND SIGHTED CHILDREN

Susanna Millar

The problem I want to consider is how the mode and level of experience affects children's spatial thinking. To the non-psychologist spatial and visual experience are almost synonymous. Congenitally and early blind children lack such experience. Of course, other sense modalities also provide spatial information. We can, for instance, locate sounds, although this is not always very accurate; and hearing does not inform us about physical expanse, planes and surfaces. But this information can be derived from touch and movement as well as from vision. Some major theories of children's spatial representation regard the source of information as largely irrelevant. For instance, Gibson (1969) assumes that spatial representation depends upon the progressive detection of invariant amodal features and relations in the external world. Piaget's (1956, 1971) view is very different. He considers the process one of intellectual construction, derived from internalized sensori-motor activity. It is not perhaps entirely accidental that the bulk of Eleanor Gibson's work is concerned with vision; while initial evidence for Piaget's view depended more on observations on active touch. Also many of the tasks he so ingeniously devised are intellectual problems that can be solved most economically by con-siderations of logical implication. I do not wish to take issue with either of these theories here. In my view, both stress factors - detecting spatial relations, sensori-motor and intellectual activity - that are indeed important in spatial thinking. But these factors are not mutually exclusive. Nor do they exhaust the parameters that are involved. Gibson's and Piaget's arguments against regarding the mode of experience as important are very different. However, the views they consider are indeed unlikely. One would certainly agree that perception is not a mosaic of sense

data, and that spatial thinking cannot be described as a photo-copy
of visual perception.   But it is not necessary to assume either in
order to ask the question what effects the mode and level of
experience do have.

THE   MODALITY   OF   SPATIAL   EXPERIENCE

I shall argue firstly that the modality of spatial experience
can affect efficiency and the manner of processing.   For this, I
shall briefly review some evidence from my own studies that has led
me to this view.   Secondly, I shall discuss some findings which
show how processing can change with the level of practice in one
modality - the kinaesthetic.

My concern is with the representation of geographical space.
By this I mean the physical expanse, planes or surfaces in which
the child has to:

a) discriminate spatial objects or shapes;
b) locate objects in relation to himself; and
c) locate objects in relation to each other.

To understand this we need to look at the processes on which memory
for spatial inputs depends.

About memory for shapes, the following points seem to me to be
important.   Memory for visual shapes is clearly better than for
tactual shapes even by preschoolers.   Indeed three-year-olds are
even worse than four-year-olds, and neither have any particular
difficulty with visual recognition (Millar, 1971).   This seems to
be not solely a question of discrimination difficulty, but depends
also on the features on which children rely in memory.   These have
effects on which strategies are possible.   For instance, in visual
tasks it is possible to instruct preschoolers to try to "see shapes
in their heads" during delays.   This improves visual recognition,
even if they cannot name the shapes (Millar, 1972).   By contrast,
instruction to mentally "trace around" tactual shapes during delays
has little or no effect on tactual recognition (Millar, 1974).
Moreover, similarity in the feel of successive items disturbs recall
of tactual objects or letters, even though the children can discriminate the shapes, if they are slow in naming them.   Such subjects
seem to rely on tactual features in memory.   This is associated
with relatively poor recall.   If the shapes can be named quickly,
recall of successive items is disturbed only by similarity in the
name sounds (Millar, 1975a, b).   Recall is not only much better,
but suggests that subjects relied on name sounds in memory.   The
features on which subjects rely in memory thus have effects on
processing and strategies.

A further point is that memory strategies are not necessarily
fixed or invariable.   Children do not always use either all the
information, or use all the strategies that are available to them.
This can depend on the material, the task, and familiarity.   Thus,
young children have no difficulty, in principle, in using visual
information (that is information from another modality) in tactual
tasks: added visual information at input improves their tactual
shape recognition (Millar, 1971).   Nevertheless, they do not
necessarily re-code tactual shapes into some "visual" form.   Thus,
there is not only frequently no difference between the blind and
blindfolded sighted children in recognizing tactual shapes;   more
importantly, they can be affected in the same way by distractors
(Millar, 1974).   This suggests that they may rely on the same
features (either modality specific or verbal) in memory.   This
appears to be the case for tactual shapes, and as we shall see
later, for remembering distances from simple movements.   There
are, however, spatial tasks on which blind and blindfolded sighted
children do differ.

I am turning here to the question of locating objects in
relation to each other.   The tasks on which blind and blindfolded
sighted children typically differ are those in which a location, a
direction, or a distance needs to be specified in relation to more
than one reference axis or lines in a spatial lay-out;   and when
such reference lines or lay-outs are not available for inspection
at the time;   in other words, when dual references have to be made
mentally.   This does not mean that the sighted have access to
accurate mental pictures.   They make far too many mistakes for
that.   But blind children find such tasks particularly difficult.
There are good reasons why this should be so, if spatial thinking
is affected by the mode of experience.

Let me briefly look at some of these modality differences.
Vision is specialized for detecting spatial features.   It typically
provides information about features in relation to each other in one
global look.   Scanning is, of course, involved, especially in larger
visual fields.   But any one feature can be assessed more or less
randomly in relation to others and to boundaries.   (I am not
talking here of learned scanning directions as in left-right
Western, or right-left Hebrew reading.)   If processing reflects
such access to spatial features in relation to each other, this
would have advantages particularly in tasks in which a location or
direction has to be specified with reference to a spatial lay-out
or more than one mental reference axis.   Back and forth scanning
is possible also in tactual exploration.   But touch is specialized
for texture, and has a smaller range.   This means that to refer to
a distant boundary is not easy without moving;   that is, changing
position and so losing your initial anchor point.   Movement in
real space is essential.   However, kinaesthesis is specialized for

information about the position and movement of the body and body
parts.   It provides cues to the important gravitational vertical,
and (across the body) horizontal directions.   We live in a
gravitationally oriented environment.   It is therefore not
accidental that the vertical and horizontal directions are the
important reference axes.   As soon as we are upright, self-
referent cues are normally congruent and relatively invariant
with external information about these orthogonal directions.   And
this is so whether the feedback or correlation is with vision or
touch.   Since coding orthogonal directions requires only one to
one mapping with self-referent cues (or one description 'far', or
'across' (Pufall & Shaw, 1973), the blind should be able to code
these.   However, if subjects rely on memory for movements, they
are relying on largely uni-directional information in which anchor
points have to be recalled as past positions.   Moreover, there is
evidence to which I shall return later, that memory for movements
deteriorates with delay and further movements.   Nor is it always
under attentional control.   This means that active strategies of
the kind that are easy with verbal material, would not always be
possible.   Thus, if subjects rely on memory for movements this
would make it more difficult to:

    a) remember more than a relatively short sequence;
    b) more difficult to determine directions and locations that
       require reference to more than one axis in memory;   and
    c) backward spatial recall would be more difficult.

    Evidence for differences in strategy between the blind and
sighted in such tasks comes from a study (Millar, 1976) in which
I used mental rotation of a straight line.   The line was drawn by
subjects through a straight slot in a plastic square placed on a
table.   Subjects then walked around the table in a clockwise
direction to the corners and to the sides of the table.   From each
of these they had to reproduce the direction of the line as it would
appear from that position.   In another task, the subject remained
stationary while the square was rotated between the palms of his
hands, and stopped at the same points.   Blindfolded sighted
children aged between six and ten years were by no means perfect
or even very accurate.   But their errors did not differ very much
as a function of the test position.   This would be expected if
they could make use of some mental spatial lay-out from the stopping
point.   (Indeed many of them said that they were trying to do just
that.)   No matter how inaccurate this lay-out would be, it would
not greatly matter where at the table the test position was;   and
it would also help with directions from the corners.   These would
be diagonals, i.e. complex directions (Pufall & Shaw, 1973) in that
they require two references (e.g. far and left to near and right).
The blind showed a different pattern of performance.   They had no
greater difficulty than the sighted with the first two right-angled
positions (i.e. orthogonals).   But they could not cope with

rotating to the complex diagonal directions at all, and had difficulty also at the furthest orthogonal stopping point.   This is consistent with the assumption that they relied on memory for the movement sequence.   Only a short sequence would be remembered (the first two right turns), and it would be difficult to access more than one reference direction concomitantly to determine the complex direction from the corners.   (It is, of course, difficult to imagine oneself moving in more than one direction at the same time.)

Further evidence for this strategy difference between blind and blindfolded sighted children was obtained in a study in which I used recall of a location in relation to a spatial lay-out presented kinaesthetically (Millar, 1975c).   On the assumption that the sighted can image a spatial lay-out - although not necessarily accurately - they should have no more difficulty in recalling a location on it from the end point than from the starting point.   That is, backward recall would not be more difficult than forward recall.   Subjects who rely on memory for movement inputs should find backward recall much more difficult, and particularly so for the location that is the longest distance and takes the longest time from input to recall.   Kinaesthetic inputs were movements through a spatial display from start to end point, with a stop on the way either near the starting point (primacy position) or near the end point of the display (recency position).   Recall of the two locations was either forward, from the starting point, or backward, from the end point of the spatial display.   Blindfolded sighted children were no worse at backward than forward recall.   Indeed, if anything, they were slightly better.   This is consistent with the assumption that they constructed some form of mental spatial lay-out from the stopping point. The blind were differentially worse on backward recall and more so in recall of the first location (primary position).   This point was the furthest in distance and required the longest time from input to recall.   This was again consistent with the hypothesis that they relied on memory for the movement inputs.

The findings in relation to age are of some interest.   In all spatial tasks older children were much better.   But there was no sort of interaction between age and sighted status.   This is important.   It suggests that improvements with age take place within the strategies that are elicited by a given modality.   Age did interact to a small but significant degree with pre-cuing (Millar, 1975);   that is telling children in advance whether recall would be forward or backward.   Older children, whether blind or sighted, benefited from such cuing, especially for the primacy position.   The youngest were not affected either way;   and the middle group actually found it slightly more difficult to cope with the additional information.   Clearly, intelligence - in the sense

of increasing ability to utilize relational and additional
information, is a factor in improved performance.   Intellectual
and modality effects thus seem to be independent.   But both are
involved in spatial representation.

PROCESSING   AND   THE   LEVEL   OF   PRACTICE

        I should now like to turn to the second problem.   This is the
question how processing may change with the level of practice.
The concern here is with memory for a simple kinaesthetic distance
- moving from a fixed point to a stop.   The task does not require
mental reference to more than one axis.   No differences in strategy
between the blind and blindfolded sighted were therefore expected,
or indeed found.   The question is rather whether children's
memory for movements requires processing capacity.   This is, of
course, particularly important in understanding spatial thinking
by the blind who tend to rely on movement information in spatial
memory tasks, as we saw earlier.   The evidence from adults is
somewhat equivocal.   Indeed, some writers have suggested that
only peripheral processes are involved (Craft, 1973).   Certainly,
kinaesthetic memory seems to be affected by delay and subsequent
movements (e.g. Posner, 1967;   Boswell & Bilodeau, 1964) but this
could depend on central programmes (Keele, 1975).

        Some of my findings in the analogous case of tactual memory
suggested that the involvement of processing capacity may depend
on the level of practice (Millar, 1974).   The finding I want to
discuss implies that this is indeed the case for children's
memory for movements.   To tap processing capacity, I used
difficult verbal tasks during delays, analogous to the Peterson
distractor (Peterson & Peterson, 1959) design.   Kinaesthetic
coding was tested by a simple rotary movement interpolated in
delays.   These conditions were compared to unfilled delays and
immediate recall.   Recall of a repeated movement was compared with
recall of continually new inputs (as in the Hebb, 1961, paradigm),
and further with a movement that had been previously practiced at
a lag of a day or more.   Very briefly, the results showed that
difficult verbal tasks in delays disturbed kinaesthetic memory;
but the effect was specific to recall of the repeated new movement.
Neither recall of continually new inputs or of the previously
practiced one were affected by difficult verbal tasks.   By contrast,
there were large effects of delay especially in a first task;   and
the movement distractor had some effects at all levels of practice
or repetition.   The findings for eight and four-year-old sighted
children, tested under blind conditions, were similar to those of
the blind.   The only difference between older and younger children
was that the latter required more practice and "warm-up".

The results seem to imply that central capacity is involved particularly in laying down longer term movement programmes. Recall of continually new inputs may depend on more peripheral processes; while recall of motor commands from an established programme may be sufficiently "automatic" not to require further attentive monitoring. However, more important for the question here are two implications. Firstly, in our concern with children's performance levels we may be missing the fact that practice may affect not merely efficiency (this is sufficiently obvious), but can evidently also produce 'qualitative' changes in processing. Secondly, children's memory for movements does seem to be subject to attentional controls, even if only at given levels of practice. This implies that it should be possible, in principle, to train blind children to use some form of active attentional strategy, so that memory for movements can be used in tasks requiring mental reference to other directions. Feedback from small scale two dimensional tactual materials may be needed for this. Blind children seem to be quite capable of the translation from three dimensional experience to two dimensional representation which this involves (Millar, 1975d).

The practical problems in training young blind children to utilize attentional strategies in memory for movements require a good deal of further study. But the theoretical implications are fairly clear. They suggest that it should, in principle, be possible for spatial thinking based on memory for movements (possibly in conjunction with other information) to equal performance based on visual experience. There is no reason to suppose that the formal or logical description of such spatial performances would differ (both are likely to be inferior to geometric calculation). Nor need it be supposed that different "spaces" are constructed on the basis of differences in experience. On the contrary, the fact that we all live in gravitationally oriented environment makes this unlikely. Nevertheless, although the formal description of the level of performance would be the same, it is clear from the evidence here, that the route by which this is achieved, - the processes and strategies that underly spatial memory and representation, - differ both with the mode of experience and the level of practice.

At the beginning of my talk I implied that some major theories of spatial representation (although by no means all developmental psychologists) have perhaps rather neglected the problems studied here. This is probably because the emphasis has to a large extent been on logical descriptions of spatial performances at different ages. "Mental structures", for instance, are essentially logical descriptions of performance levels. Formal descriptions are both necessary and illuminating. But if we want to understand how children actually go about spatial memory tasks, we must also be

concerned with the parameters that determine the strategies they
use.   I am not suggesting that the variables with which I have
been mainly concerned here are the sole, or even necessarily the
most important factors.   Nevertheless, both the modality of
experience and the level of practice seem to have quite specific
effects.   The effects of the mode of experience are, I think, two-
fold.   Firstly, it affects the amount and type of spatial information that is available; and secondly, it affects the features that
are utilized in memory, and these determine, at least to some extent,
the type of strategies that are possible.   Memory for visual
experience does not consist of accurate photographic copies.   But
it does seem to permit quasi-random access in memory to more than
one spatial feature in relation to others.   Information about
spatial features is less easily gained from movement and touch.
Moreover, the susceptibility of kinaesthetic memory to the effects
of delay and of further movements explains some of the difficulties
by the blind in tasks that require more than one concomitant spatial
reference.   Such differences are both of theoretical and practical
interest.   The other factor which may require more emphasis is the
effect of practice and repetition in producing qualitative changes
in processing.   The findings suggest that attentional strategies
in kinaesthetic memory may crucially depend on this.

        To sum up.   The codes on which children rely in spatial
memory are not fixed or invariable.   They depend on the material,
familiarity and on the task.   In memory for tactual shapes both
blind and sighted children under blind conditions seem to rely
mainly on tactual and verbal codes.   But the blind and sighted do
differ if spatial tasks require concomitant mental reference to
more than one spatial feature.   The evidence suggests that this
is because the sighted can use some (not necessarily accurate) form
of mental spatial lay-out.   Blind children have difficulties with
this.   They tend to rely on memory for movement sequences.   These
are susceptible to effects of delay and further movements, and are
not always under attentional control.   The modality of experience
thus seems to affect children's spatial representation through the
features they utilize in memory and the strategies these elicit.
In considering memory for movements further, I referred briefly to
a finding which suggests that the level of practice can change kinaesthetic processing.   In principle, memory for movements could
thus be used for spatial reference.   The formal descriptions of
performance levels would then be the same, but the strategies by
which these are achieved would differ nevertheless.   I have argued,
therefore, that effects of modality differences on strategies, and
of the level of practice on changes in processing, are among the
factors that should be taken into account in theories of children's
spatial representation.

BIBLIOGRAPHY

BOSWELL, J. J. & BILODEAU, E. A., Short-term retention of a simple motor task as a function of interpolated activity, Perceptual and Motor Skills, 1964, 18, pp. 227-230

CRAFT, L., A two-process theory for the short-term retention of motor responses, Journal of Experimental Psychology, 1973, 98, pp. 196-202

GIBSON, E., Principles of Perceptual Learning and Development, Appleton-Century - Crofts, 1969

HEBB, D. O., in J. F. DELAFRESNAYE (ed.) Brain Mechanisms and Learning, Oxford University Press, 1961

KEELE, S. W., The representation of motor programmes, in P.M.A. RABBITT & S. DORNIC (eds.) Attention and Performance, Academic Press, 1975

MILLAR, S., Visual and haptic cue utilization by preschool children, Journal of Experimental Child Psychology, 1971, 12, pp. 88-94

MILLAR, S., Effects of instructions to visualize stimuli during delay on visual recognition by preschool children, Child Development, 1972, 143, pp. 1073-1075

MILLAR, S., Tactile short term memory by blind and sighted children, British Journal of Psychology, 1974, 65, pp. 253-263

MILLAR, S., Effects of phonological and tactual similarity on serial object recall by blind and sighted children, Cortex, 1975a, XI, pp. 170-180

MILLAR, S., Effects of tactual and phonological similarity on the recall of Braille letters by blind children, British Journal of Psychology, 1975b, 66, pp. 193-201

MILLAR, S., Spatial memory by blind and sighted children, British Journal of Psychology, 1975c, 66, pp. 449-459

MILLAR, S., Visual experience or translation rules. Drawing the human figure by blind and sighted children, Perception, 1975d, 4, pp. 363-371

MILLAR, S., Spatial representation by blind and sighted children, Journal of Experimental Child Psychology, 1976, 21, pp. 460-479

PETERSON, L. R. & PETERSON, M. J., Short term retention of individual verbal items, Journal of Experimental Psychology, 1959, 58, pp. 193-198

PIAGET, J. & INHELDER, B., The child's conception of space, Routledge & Kegan Paul, 1956

PIAGET, J. & INHELDER, B., <u>Mental imagery in the child</u>, Routledge
    & Kegan Paul, 1971

PUFALL, P. B. & SHAW, R. E., Analysis of the development of
    children's spatial reference systems, <u>Cognitive Psychology</u>,
    1973, 5, pp. 151-175

"I'M COMING TO GET YOU: READY! STEADY! GO!"

THE DEVELOPMENT OF COMMUNICATION BETWEEN

A BLIND INFANT AND HIS PARENTS

Cathy Urwin

"To learn to speak is to learn to play a series of roles."

> M Merleau-Ponty – The Child's
> Relations With Others, The Primacy
> of Perception, North-Western
> University Press, U.S.A., pp. 96-158

SUMMARY

While the previous paper was concerned with blind children, this paper is about the implications of blindness in infancy. It highlights some of the constraints on the development of communication between blind infants and their parents, with particular reference to their implications for early language development. Taking a particular child as an example, it describes how the parents found ways of adjusting to these constraints, and the consequences for the development of reciprocal interaction between them. During the conference proceedings, a video tape was shown to illustrate the evolution of particular play routines over the seven to twenty-month period, during which time the child was observed at home at fortnightly intervals. Characteristics of his early language development and symbolic play are summarised and discussed in relation to the history of social interaction. Concluding discussion suggests that changes in the child's representation of self in relation to others occurring at the end of the sensori-motor period may indicate changes crucially important for further developments in language usage. This directs attention towards the underlying transactional processes developing in the infancy period preceding it.

EARLY   LANGUAGE   DEVELOPMENT   IN   BLIND   CHILDREN

Perhaps it is unnecessary to emphasise the importance of language to the developing blind child.   It allows for greater participation in events with other people, and makes available or extends many opportunities for learning.   It provides a medium for consolidating sense impressions and for the expression and control of emotions.   In acquiring language the blind child acquires a means of representing his world which will increase his ability to interact and act effectively within it.

But the importance of language to the blind child by no means guarantees the ease with which he acquires it.   Differences from sighted children in course and rate of development are most evident in the early stages.   While individual differences are particularly marked at this time, characteristic anomalies appear fairly frequently and are often severe enough to cause concern (Urwin 1976a).

While many blind children are slow to start speaking in the first place, their speech is often restricted to their own body movement or is closely tied to familiar routines.   The propensity to imitate is particularly marked, as both parents and children rely on this to maintain social contact.   This is partly responsible for many blind children's early language consisting entirely of ready-made phrases which they may or may not use appropriately to context. More extreme cases of echolalia are not uncommon among blind children with no other neurological damage.   While sighted children vary in the kinds of words which dominate their early vocabularies (Nelson 1973), few blind children begin to acquire nominals until comparatively late in development, and it is extremely rare to find a blind toddler "delighting in naming for naming's sake".   If development is proceeding well in other areas, once begun, the development of language for talking about objects and events may move forward rapidly: "And it is amongst their achievements that, by the time they reach nursery school age, they may even outdo the seeing in this respect" (Burlingham 1961).   However, a particular delay which is apparently universal is the acquisition of appropriate usage of the I-You pronoun distinction (Adelson and Fraiberg 1973).

Since it is in the early stages that many difficulties are most marked, this implies that preconditions essential to the development of linguistic communication as a generative system may not have been fulfilled, and that many of the difficulties of early language development are related to the severe constraints which blindness poses for the development of social relations and the child's understanding of his environment in the infancy period.

BLINDNESS IN INFANCY

It is in the infancy period, prior to the emergence of speech, when many of the constraints to development which lack of vision poses are most evident. Establishing co-ordinated reaching, active search and mobility is crucial to the blind child's developing understanding of his environment. However, where sound gives shifting and disparate information as to the existence of objects, their properties and their location, co-ordinated reaching to sound-making objects is a more complex operation than visually guided reaching, and does not emerge before nine to ten months (Bower 1974, Fraiberg 1968). Clinical literature highlights the period prior to its emergence as one in which the blind infant is particularly vulnerable to deviant development (Wills 1971) and the importance of the steps taken by the parents at this time. It is also, of course, the time when, coping with the implications of the diagnosis, their own resources are likely to be particularly low. Since the baby shows few signs of attempting to obtain objects, or active interest in the environment, it is all too easy to leave the baby on his own, to revel in a bevy of sounds. Complications for the development of manipulatory skills and motor co-ordination are likely to ensue, delaying further developments in exploratory activity and mobility (Burlingham 1961, Fraiberg 1968, 1971, Wills 1971).

Many of the early language difficulties may be related to delays in cognitive functioning consequent on restricted opportunities for active exploration. But language development cannot be explained in terms of cognitive development alone. The child's developments in language usage may promote developmental change in other spheres, and adds new dimensions to communicative exchange itself. And his knowledge of objects and events is not, per se, sufficient to account for the child's acquiring 'words' to represent this experience and to communicate it. Theoretical and philosophical critiques abound to demonstrate the inadequacy of associationist principles for explaining the productivity of language, how it is acquired, how it is used, and the 'meaning' of words themselves. The meaning of words is not given by a one to one correspondence between 'sign' and 'thing signified'. Developments in creative language depend on the use of symbols which bear an arbitrary relation to reality, owing their power to the capacity to "bring other realities to mind" (Reynolds 1975). At the same time, taking 'identity of meanings' as an ideal fundamental to all communication (Habermas 1970), successful communication depends on the speaker's comprehending and identifying the meaning of the symbol from his own position and from that of the other at the same time. This requires us to see the child's developments in word usage in the context of evolving negotiatory processes and shared experiences already established between himself and others prior to the emergence of speech. From this viewpoint, the inter-personal nexus underlies the 'meanings'

realised in the child's early words; it also predicts that the
history of social relations between the infant and his family may
bias the child towards acquiring particular arbitrary signs rather
than others in the early stages, and at the same time provides the
conditions in which he may learn how they are used (Urwin 1976b).

THE DEVELOPMENT OF COMMUNICATION BETWEEN
THE BLIND INFANT AND HIS PARENTS

With respect to the elaboration of communication between parent
and child in the pre-verbal period, the implications of the baby's
blindness are severe. A great deal is demanded of the parents at
this time; but they are not helped by the restricted opportunities
for social exchange consequent on the infant's lack of vision. He
does not return their gaze, must be coaxed to smile, and in many
ways lacks means for initiating social contact (Burlingham 1961,
Fraiberg 1968). While looking towards the mother is one of the
most irresistible means for initiating interaction the sighted
infant has available to him (Dunn forthcoming), the blind infant
does not turn towards the mother with a smile of greeting as she
enters, or lift up his arms to be picked up, or follow after her
as she goes. And while lack of vision poses constraints on the
child's understanding of the world, his access to it will be different in kind from those who can see. Different sensory cues
will tell him of the significance of particular events and
different aspects of the same event will be significant to him.
While his parents' access to the world will be largely dominated
by vision, they will lack cues to the object of the child's attention and involvement of the moment, and reciprocally he to theirs.
Broadly speaking, for the sighted infant the impact of developmental change in the infant influences the form and occasion of the
mother's participation in interaction (Blount 1971, Escalona 1971)
as she must adjust to the baby's developing interests in objects
(Trevarthen et al. 1975) and the implications of developing mobility.
Crucial changes occur towards the end of the first year as the baby
begins to co-ordinate interaction with people with actions towards
objects (Sugarman 1976). Gesturing towards objects and events in
the more distal environment, showing and offering objects to gain
attention (Bates et al. 1975), and drawing adults into his own
object projects may allow "the incorporation of topical content
into his communications" (Trevarthen and Sylvestra-Bradley 1975).

From the earliest established means of regulating social contact and reciprocal exchange, to establishing mutual attention to
events in the more distal environment (Scaife and Churcher forthcoming, Schaffer, Collis and Parsons 1975), the baby's lack of
vision may markedly influence the form of social exchange between
himself and his parents, and the occasions in which it occurs.

At the same time, the later emergence of reaching, active search, and the typical delays in mobility may also influence how and when the parents participate in interaction with the child.   Under such conditions the emergence of speech becomes particularly important to the parents, "providing a form of longed for contact which they have missed" (Burlingham 1961).   But difficulties in establishing communicative exchange and reciprocity of perspectives within and across physical space may result in biases in the history of social interaction through which the child's early word usage is realised.

A LONGITUDINAL INVESTIGATION

To illustrate the implications of some of these factors, the following account concerns the development of social interaction between a particular child and his parents.   It aims to highlight the mutual discoveries made by parents and child, describes the evolution of particular forms of reciprocal exchange, and indicates ways in which the history of interaction relates to the child's early language and how he uses it.

The child's family was visited at fortnightly intervals, from seven to twenty months, and informally thereafter.   Audio and observational records were taken at each session, and he was video-taped at monthly intervals in interaction with one or another of his parents.

JERRY

Jerry is completely blind, with a form of optic atrophy.   He is first born, an extremely attractive child, with well formed eyes, and is normal in all other respects.   Diagnosis was made at three months.   Although his mother has been through several periods of relatively severe depression, in many respects Jerry's development has progressed extremely well.

OUTLINES OF DEVELOPMENT

Unlike the majority of blind children, Jerry's becoming mobile has not been delayed.   From very early in the first year his parents discovered that one of the most successful ways of making him laugh was to stand him on his feet, bouncing him up and down. By seven-and-a-half months he would stand with support and take a few steps when held.   He was taking steps unaided by the end of the first year, and though initially likely to topple over, he would walk across the room on his own by fifteen months.

Reaching for sound-making objects, however, was not consolidated before nine-and-a-half months (within the age range typical for blind infants, Fraiberg 1968). Active search for objects which he could no longer feel or hear began towards the end of the eleventh month.

CHARACTERISTICS OF SOCIAL INTERACTION

In the beginning months of the study, Jerry had few toys, and his mother felt he had little or no interest in them. She herself spent little time encouraging this, though she left toys with him in his cot. As the time Jerry spent in active exploration increased (the furniture becoming particularly important as his mobility got going) his mother left him to his own devices, pleased that he could keep himself occupied while she got on with the housework. Little of their interaction involved both mother and child acting jointly on particular objects. An important exception occurred between twelve and seventeen months with the evolution of their own version of "give and take" (Bruner 1974), or more properly "drop and retrieve". This had been preceded by forms of teasing involving the mother's tickling him with objects and coaxing him to give them up. The routine flowered as Jerry began experimenting with dropping and retrieving objects in his own play. During its peak period, successive turns of the routine were under the baby's control as he would deliberately drop an object for his mother to retrieve and return with a climax of excited tickling. However, initiating the routine in the first place depended on the mother's decisions, and it was not reversible in the sense that the baby would not offer or return objects to the mother. By seventeen months the child became, again, more resistant to giving up objects. At this time various forms of combinatorial activities were dominating his own investigations. To some extent these new interests competed with his involvement with the parents.

Having to get on with her own work, the mother's beliefs about what toys are for certainly influenced the relatively limited extent to which she attempted to encourage his interest in them. However, like many mothers of blind children, she found that the relatively bizarre nature of some of his investigatory strategies, tapping things with his teeth, repetitive flicking and banging, and so on, effectively excluded her. And, at the same time, no invitations were likely to come from the baby. He could not look up towards her, to invite her participation; and no clearly unambiguous equivalents to his "showing" or offering objects, or using them to call attention to himself, or appealing to the adult for help, emerged. As to establishing communication about objects and events in the more distal environment, there were no equivalents to the baby's pointing, reaching or demand gestures through which mutual attention to objects outside their immediate sphere of action could

be achieved.   Vision, of course, may give instantaneous information
as to the direction of another's attention;   in contrast, cues
associated with listening are ambiguous.   Although the parents
could sometimes detect what the child was listening to, and would
comment on it, in general this depended on their attention already
being involved.   That the child's access to other people's
activities was similarly restricted is obvious.

While Jerry's parents found it difficult or irrelevant to
encourage his interest in toys, and little interaction centred on
the more distal environment, there were other arenas in which the
extent of their active participation was quite the opposite.
Within the dimensions of social play, the parents found ways of
using touching and speaking to sustain and prolong heightened
exchange.   But one of the most crucial characteristics of their
interaction repertoire depended on the fact that once the parents
discovered particular devices which "worked", they would use them
again and again.   Many forms of play exchange became ritualised,
giving rise to play routines which persisted to evolve over several
months.

Some of these involved vocal interchange, the parents
capitalising on the child's willingness to imitate, building rituals
around his current productions.   As consonantal sounds appeared in
his verbal repertoire, "Where's Dadda?" "Where's the babba?" and
later, "Logger logger ligger lugger", served to promote extended
bursts of mutual imitation.   Other routines based on varying
intonation patterns, particularly rising and falling contrasts,
were incorporated as the mother capitalised on the child's developing vocal differentiation.   Such devices are not uncommon amongst
mothers and sighted infants.   But particularly when Jerry was
distressed, his mother would use such frames to "carry on a conversation like" with him, from next door.   And, by the beginning
of the second year, such dialogues might last up to fifteen minutes
at a time, the child dictating the lead within the set of alternative
forms available.   Although the child's willingness to imitate fluc-
tuated (perhaps in relation to phonological or receptive developments,
or competing interests), vocal exchange set apart from ongoing action
or physical events persisted as a dominant form of exchange;   eventually imitation frames provided a vehicle for encouraging the child
to repeat standard words and routine phrases.

But in addition, play periods involved a large amount of body
play.   The parents made use of well-known nursery games, with
subtle adjustments to the fact that Jerry could not see.   This is
not surprising since games such as "Pat-a-Cake" and "Round and
Round the Garden", "Ring-a-Roses" and "This Little Piggy" involve
a large amount of touching, body activity and predictable speech to
build up the climax.   It is, perhaps, more surprising that they
should find ways of playing "Peek-a-Boo" with him.

At the same time both parents discovered their own modes of play, and here there were differences in their repertoires.   In the first months of the study, Jerry's mother used gentle touching and rhythmic stroking, watching for signs of response in his changing facial expressions and the affectivity of his body movement.   As to his father, "He plays rough with him and Jerry comes back for more".   Initially, perhaps, it was not appropriate for her to play in this way.   "He plays those games with his Dad."   As Jerry got older, she herself teased him more, became more vigorous and took over some of the father's modes of play.

Of those play routines particularly important to Jerry and his father, two I will call, for simplicity's sake, "Don't you do that," and "Are you sure?"   The former was based on mock threats and rebukes to the child as the father taunted him to fight back. "Are you sure?" first emerged in encouraging the child in precarious positions.   He would stand Jerry on the table, with "Jerry!   Are you sure?" and Jerry would answer "Sure Dadda!" and leap off to be caught by his father.

Some of the early established play routines declined in effectiveness or relevance, to disappear from their interactive repertoire.   And with new developments in mobility, new forms of play emerged.   Other routines remained dominant, the exchange formulae themselves carrying with them the conditions allowing or demanding their evolution.   While functioning to maximise heightened social contact in the present context, relying on familiar and pre- dictable routines maximised opportunities for mutual expectancies to become established.   At the same time, from one play episode to another the parents related to find and extend what had already been established between them, epitomising characteristics of a developing relationship.   While the parent appealed to what the child already "knew", she would introduce subtle variations, or flaunt the child's expectations, so that the exchange format might remain interesting to them both.   Since many routines were based on similar properties, an element from one might be used to substitute for another, or familiar forms might be introduced into a new context.   At the same time, the parent had to adjust to broader dimensions of developmental change in the baby.   New developments in mobility and his interest in objects opened new contexts within which a familiar exchange form would find expression.   This both acknow- ledged the new range of interests of the child with particular pertinence, demonstrating their mutual accessibility, and allowed parents and child to make social contact where the baby's new range of interests to some extent competed with his involvement with them.

But some of the most crucial changes occurred within the predic- table interchange frames themselves, as the parent adjusted to evident changes in the baby's anticipation and active control.

She would flaunt the child's expectations and introduce constraints, pushing the child towards making his intentions explicit, and acting as initiator. This entailed the implicit demand that he appreciate her own perspective on the situation, emphasised with differentiation of roles between the participants, and their potential reversibility according to the procedures of the routine.

Two routines exploited throughout the study period by both parents, their own versions of "I'm coming to get you", and "Ready, Steady, Go!" provide examples which must serve to illustrate some of these features.*

"HE'S COMING TO GET YOU! READY, STEADY, GO!"

At seven months, "He's coming to get you!" was one of the most frequently exploited interchange frames with which Jerry's mother would build up Jerry's excitement and signs of anticipation and responsiveness which she could take as confirming his attention towards herself. Using repetitive phrases and dramatising her voice, she would respond to changes in the child's facial expressions and the affectivity of his body movement with further prompts and acknowledgements to sustain the exchange. Although the mother is already appealing to the routine's being familiar to the child, the initiative and control largely rests with her, and sequences terminate as the child's attention can no longer be retained.

    1. Jerry 0.7.2.   Standing supporting Jerry, his mother eases him forward to encourage him to walk.   "Where's yer Da?   He's coming!   He's coming!   Quick!   Here's yer Da!   Yes he is!" Jerry vocalises and smiles.   "He's coming!   Quick!   He'll get yer!"   Jerry vocalises.   "He's going a getcha!   Where is he?"   She swings Jerry around to face her.   "Hello," as they are face to face.   "Where's yer Da?   Call him."   Jerry is pitching badly, so she helps him down to sitting.

With developments in mobility, the child's more explicitly co-ordinated actions alter the phasing of the Mother's speaking to promote it.

    2. Jerry 0.8.9.   Jerry's mother is across the room from him. He has rolled into a crawl position, his head down.   "Dad." Jerry lies still.   "Da-ad.   Here he is.   He's coming.   He's going to getcha!"   Jerry vocalises and smiles and raises his body.   "Yeah?"   Jerry stills.   "Is he at work?   Jerry?

---

* During the conference an edited video tape, compiled from recordings taken at monthly intervals of Jerry in interaction with one or another of his parents was presented.

Where is he?"   Jerry swings into a crawl position.   "Where
is he?"   Jerry begins moving his legs.   "Go and get him."
Jerry vocalises.   "Arr, go."   Jerry vocalises.   "Ta-ah,"
Jerry squeals, and part rolls.   "Bye-bye."   Jerry vocalises,
raises his head and shifts his feet.

By nine months, Jerry is taking steps while held, and his
mother is already letting him go to stand unsupported for a few
seconds.   "Ready, Steady, Go!" as the mother uses her voice in
the anticipation phase to sustain his efforts, and the climactic
"Go!" to catch him as he topples.   Using this action procedure,
"He's coming to get you!" finds a new expression.

3. Jerry 0.9.4.   The mother stands Jerry up again, and lets
him go.   He stands steadily.   "There's a doggie come – and
he's coming to get you!" and she catches him as he falls
forward.

And by ten months, Jerry is standing unsupported for longer
periods.

4. Jerry 0.10.19.   Jerry's mother stands him up, "Ready,"
and lets him go, "Steady," "He's on his own! He's on his
own!"   Jerry vocalises, "Yes," and he stands still for several
seconds.

By the end of the first year, Jerry is taking more active
control over well-established procedures.   The parents introduce
new constraints taking advantage of what the baby knows already so
that the exchange will remain interesting to them both.   They
begin to assert the differentiation of roles between them, extending
the baby's discoveries of the effects of his actions in relation to
theirs.

5. Jerry 0.11.16.   Sitting astride his father's leg, Jerry
can now re-start the simple, repetitive routine based on
synchronised action;   to some extent he can respond to his
father's varying the pace as he teases him to promote responses
from the child which would confirm his active participation.

Jerry's father has been giving him rides, building the climax
with "Ready, Steady, Go!"   He calls a halt, "And no more.
ALL STOP."   Jerry's head is down.   He clenches his fist.
Teasing him, his father jerks his leg three times and pauses.
Jerry bounces three times and pauses.   Jerry then bounces four
times and pauses.   His father does the same.   His father
jerks his foot to make a noise three times, and pauses.
Jerry smacks his legs three times, and lifts his hand out.
His father takes it, and Jerry begins bouncing and vocalising.
His father co-operates in re-starting the procedure.

By the beginning of the second year, Jerry is actively exploiting the rhythm to dominate play sequences when close physical contact with the parent invited new forms of teasing.

6. <u>Jerry 1.0.20</u>.   Jerry now uses prolonged demand-vocalisations to request more play.   Standing holding his father's knee, he whines.   "Do you want to come up?"   Jerry whines.   "Do you want to come up more?"   Jerry whines again.   The father continues in this vein, and apparently gives in to the child's frustration.   "All right then.   Just once more, yeah?" Jerry whines quietly and his father puts his hands around his waist, "Ready?" as if to lift him.   Then he drops his hands, sitting back.   "No, I've decided not to."   Jerry protests vigorously, then shows distress, and laughingly, the father picks him up.

While Jerry's mother's play with him became more vigorous over the following months, both parents began to push the child towards sustaining rhythmic stampings, clapping and body actions through their speaking alone, independent of physical support.   By seventeen months he had come to exploit signs of excitement which previously the parent's initiative had been tailored to promote.   Deliberately he would flap his arms and bounce to build the crescendo of vocalisation and tickling.   He took regularised action patterns out of one play routine context, applying them in another.

7. <u>Jerry 1.5.0</u>.   Jerry's mother has been holding his fingers so he can jump to "Ready, Steady, Go!"   "Ay up!" and she stands him on his feet.   Jerry leans forward deliberately, curls up in a ball on the floor and waits for his mother. She laughs, takes hold of him and turns him over.   "Gotcha!" Jerry pauses, then rolls deliberately on one side.   "Again?" She turns him upside down.   "Gotcha!" and lets him go. Jerry rolls deliberately on his side again.   She turns him upside down.   "Gotcha!"   Jerry rolls onto his side again. The mother turns him upside down.   "Gotcha!"   She turns him all the way around, and puts him down.   "Gotcha!" and Jerry rolls over the other way.

At seventeen months, the parents build up the child's anticipation with "I'm coming to get you," approaching him from across the floor.

8. <u>Jerry 1.5.0</u>.   Jerry is standing some distance away from the mother.   "I comin'.   I comin'!"   Jerry circles in anticipation, and falls.   The mother laughs.   "Ready?   I comin'!"   She steps towards him, and stamps.   Jerry curls his feet up, hunches his body, withdrawing away in anticipation.   "I comin'!"   She steps forward again, and stamps her

feet.   Jerry curls away.   "I comin'!"   She stamps again.
"And he's going a have him!"   She lifts the child up and turns
him upside down.

By twenty months, in action, Jerry will now take the dominant
role.

9. Jerry 1.8.6.   Jerry gets up from the floor, some way from
the father.   "He's coming!" the father says, "He's coming!"
as Jerry speeds up; "Oh, he's got him!   Oh, he's caught his
Daddy!" as Jerry does so.

Jerry now has words for "Ready," "Steady," and "Go".   In play
with his father, his use of words extends his opportunities for
controlling the pace of the routine and building the climax.

10. Jerry 1.8.6.   Jerry is standing by his father.   "Are you
ready?"   His father drops his hands with a thump.   Jerry
takes over.   He pauses before building up the anticipation.
He then produces, "Steady..."   Again Jerry pauses, and with
a climactic "Go!" he leaps at his father.

Though tied to the immediate context, Jerry's use of words
expresses a reversibility of perspectives dependent on the past
history of interaction through which the "meaning" of the words
has been derived.

                        JERRY'S   EARLY   LANGUAGE

Jerry's early language was highly imitative, the child acquiring ready-made phrases rapidly and easily.   His productive vocabulary consisted almost entirely of names of people, family friends
and relations, social phrases, words for his own body movement,
songs and ritualised forms associated with particularly well-
established routines.   By twenty months, Jerry had acquired few
nominals, and rarely used them.   Although his parents might hear
him use the "name" of the thing to accompany his own ramblings and
exploration of the furniture, he never volunteered these words in
interaction with them.   This was in spite of the fact that Jerry's
object play was now quite sophisticated, with the emergence of
combinatorial activities and clear indications of representative
functioning.   The lack of words to refer explicitly to objects
confused the parents.   But in fact they themselves rarely used
names of objects or toys in interaction with him until he was
eighteen months old.   By this time he was speaking, so they began
to teach him to imitate the names of things.   They took his
involvement with toys more seriously, and would now use their
names to draw his attention to particular favourites.   But Jerry's
using nominals himself in initiating communication was very much a
later development.

As such, Jerry's early language shows characteristics apparently common amongst blind children, as previously outlined. However, for a blind child of his age, his early speech was both prolific and relatively articulate. Imitation rituals served as a mode of communication in their own right (McTear 1976), and the child would dictate the mother's response, ringing the changes within the set of alternative forms available, running through the names of friends and relations himself. While this framework for communicating through mutual imitation was established in the pre-verbal period, the body-action games contributed to the build-up of a vocabulary of words and phrases centred around his own body movement. But here we find a generativity of functions and structure which suggests that some of the characteristic develop-mental problems have been avoided (Urwin 1976b). Early acquired forms such as "Up", "Down", and "Sure", were generalised to new contexts of interaction and as accompaniments to his own play, eventually including that involving objects. The evolution within the routinised action frames themselves provided the conditions through which he could use "Clap hands", "Lay there" and "Don't you do that, Daddy!" to initiate, control, and protest at, the actions of the other.

Amongst common language difficulties, I previously mentioned the apparently universal delay in blind children's mastering appro-priate usage of the I-You pronoun distinction. Adelson and Fraiberg (1973) have studied its evolution in a group of congeni-tally blind children whose language and general development was otherwise proceeding well. They found a concomitant delay in the emergence of representation of self in the children's own pretend play. They show no interest in using objects to recreate familiar scenes, or to act out the distinction between self and other, with separate roles, in doll play. Such developments in symbolic repre-sentation emerged later, after the children had been speaking for some time already; and with them, the distinction between "I" and "You" used appropriately in language. The study can be faulted on a number of grounds, and the whole question raises issues which are too complex to be discussed here. But it draws attention to the particular problems to the blind child's developing the capacity to represent himself as an "I" in a universe of "Is", ("I" am an "I" to "Me", "You" are an "I" to "You", "He" is an "I" to "Him", and so on), and in establishing mutuality of perspectives and reversibility of roles prerequisite to mastering appropriate usage of "I" and "You". Secondly, it highlights the marked differences between the fantasy play of blind children from those who can see, imitate and recreate domestic scenes and day to day activities with dolls and other objects.

For Jerry, I could find no examples of symbolic transformations of objects, of his using one object to stand for another, and few,

if any, instances of his recreating non-present events around
particular things.   However, from twelve months onwards, his own
play activities incorporated recognisable elements of well-
established play routines, from clapping and playing "Indians" with
his mouth, to using songs and ritual phrases to accompany his ramblings.   And at eighteen months, the following examples appeared in
the audio record of the observation session.   While his mother has
left the room, Jerry recreates with variations, episodes of play
which had occurred with his mother and father in the previous hour.

Using a low voice for his mother and a "gruff" voice for his
father.

With the mother:

JERRY:	"Don't you do that!"
MOTHER'S VOICE:	"Don't you dare!"
JERRY:	"Don't you do that!"
MOTHER'S VOICE:	"Don't you dare!"

And with the father:

FATHER'S VOICE:	"Are you sure?"
JERRY:	"I sure!"
FATHER'S VOICE:	"Are you sure?"
JERRY:	"I sure!"
FATHER'S VOICE:	"You sure? Jerry? Are you sure?"
JERRY:	"I sure! I sure Dadda!"
	and bursts of hysterical laughter.

DISCUSSION

The emergence of symbolic play at the end of the sensori-motor
period has been taken to indicate changes in representative functioning prerequisite to the use of words in their arbitrary sense (Bates
et al. 1975), and the capacity to produce syntactic combinations
(Morehead and Morehead 1974, Sinclair 1971).   However, no clear
distinction has been made between the significance of symbolic play
involving transformations of objects and the beginnings of role
play, where the child recreates familiar scenes in phantasy, or
acts towards dolls or other people as others have acted towards
himself.

Several lines of evidence are now being cited to question the
"egocentricism" of the very young infant (Scaife and Bruner 1974)
and the basis from which communication evolves.   For example, very
young infants may change their orientation of gaze in response to
an adult's changing the locus of his visual attention in face to
face situations (Scaife and Churcher forthcoming):   two-week-old
infants may imitate mouth movements after the adult model has ceased

to perform (Meltzoff 1976). Many such results demonstrating the capacities of very young infants cast some doubt on the lack of differentiation between self, other, and environment traditionally assumed of them. Nevertheless, demonstrating the appealing range of social acts of which they appear to be capable depends on the subtle adjustments exploited by the adult to sustain the performance (Trevarthen et al. 1975). Developmental questions concern the nature of the transactional processes through which the adult comes to respond to the child as "communicant" rather than acting as "communicant-interpreter" (Sugarman-Bell 1976). Re-interpretations of the significance of the "Attachment Systems" have emphasised the opportunities for heightened mutual attention and reciprocal exchange they provide (Bruner 1967, Jaffe, Stern and Parry 1973). But little systematic attention has been given to general changes in representative functioning underlying the infant's imitations and influencing the form of reciprocal exchange. These developing processes might be loosely described in terms of the child's ability to represent and direct the perspective of the other. Crucial changes occurring in this respect by the end of the sensori-motor period are possibly amongst the most significant for further developments in language use.

BIBLIOGRAPHY

ADELSON, E. & FRAIBERG, S., Self-representation in language and play: Observations of blind children, Psychoanalytic Quarterly, 1973, 42(4), pp. 539-562

BATES, E., CAMIONI, L. & VOLTERRA, V., The acquisition of performatives prior to speech, Merrill Palmer Quarterly, 1975, 1, p. 21

BLOUNT, B., Socialisation and prelinguistic development among the Luo of Kenya, Southwestern Journal of Anthropology, 1971, 27, pp. 41-50

BOWER, T.G.R., Development in infancy, San Francisco, Freeman, 1974

BRUNER, J. S., The Ontogenesis of speech acts, Journal of Child Language, 1975, 2, pp. 1-19

BURLINGHAM, D., Some notes on the development of the blind, Psychoanalytic study of the child, Vol. XVI, New York, International University Press, 1961, pp. 21-165

FRAIBERG, S., Parallel and divergent patterns in blind and sighted infants, Psychoanalytic study of the child, Vol. XXIII, New York, International University Press, 1968, pp. 266-300

FRAIBERG, S., Intervention in infancy: A program for blind infants, Journal of American Academy of Child Psychology, 1971, 3, p. 10

HABERMAS, J., Towards a theory of communicative competence, in DREITZEL, H. P. (Ed.) Recent Psychology, 2, MacMillan, 1970, pp. 115-148

JAFFE, J., STERN, D. N. & PARRY, J. C., Conversational coupling of gaze behavior in pre-linguistic human development, Journal of Psycholinguistic Research, 1973, p. 2

McTEAR, Repetition in child language: Imitation or creation? Paper presented at Nato Conference on the Psychology of Language, Stirling University, 1976

MELTZOFF, A., Unpublished doctoral dissertation, University of Oxford, 1976

NELSON, K., Structure and strategy in learning to talk, S.R.C.D. Monograph, 1973, 149, p. 38

REYNOLDS, P., Play, language and human evolution, in BRUNER, J. S., JOLLY, A. & SYLVA, K. (Eds.) Play: Its role in development and evolution, London, Penguin Books, 1976, pp. 621-637

SCAIFE, M. & BRUNER, J. S., The capacity for joint visual attention in the infant, Nature, 1975, 253, pp. 265-266

SCHAFFER, H. R., COLLIS, G. & PARSONS, G., Vocal interchange and visual regard in verbal and pre-verbal children, Paper presented at Loch Lomand Symposium, Strathclyde, Sept. 1975

SINCLAIR, H., Sensorimotor action patterns as a condition for the acquisition of syntax, in HUXLEY R. & INGRAM, E. (Eds.) Language acquisition: Models and methods, London and New York, Academic Press, 1971, pp. 121-130

SUGARMAN-BELL, Some organizational aspects of pre-verbal communication, in MARKOVA, I. (Ed.) The social context of language, London, Wiley, 1976

TREVARTHEN, C., HUBLEY, P. & SHEERAN, L., Psychological actions in early infancy, La Recherche, 1975

URWIN, C., Speech development in blind children: Some ways into language, Paper presented at Internationales Symposium des Blinden - Uno-Sehschwachen - Verbandes der D.D.R., 1976a

URWIN, C., The development of communication between blind infants and their parents, in LOCK, A. (Ed.) Action, gesture and symbol: The emergence of language, Academic Press (forthcoming)

WILLS, D., Vulnerable periods in the early development of blind children, Psychoanalytic study of the child, Vol. XXV, New York, International University Press, 1970, pp. 461-480

Part III

Personality and Representational Style

RATIONAL AND INTUITIVE FRAMES OF REFERENCE

Liam Hudson

I want to talk about evidence; especially about the kind of psychological evidence that relates the emotional organisation of the individual to those aspects of intellectual performance that we refer to by means of phrases like 'disposition', 'frame of mind' or 'frame of reference'.   And while I shall use two pieces of American evidence to stake out this territory in a general way, I shall then go on to concentrate on four pieces of work carried out in the Research Unit on Intellectual Development, and in which I have had a more direct hand.   In describing these, I will of course be trying to persuade you that 'frames of mind' or 'frames of reference' are aspects of intellectual functioning that can be explored in an orderly way.   But I also have a more surreptitious motive, because I want to say something, too, about the nature of psychological inquiry; about the kind of evidence that this throws up; and about the sorts of interpretative challenge that this evidence forces upon us.   At this surreptitious level, my thesis will be that the interpretative task of the psychologist has two facets, one of which we are alert to and the other of which we have neglected.   While we are quite good at wringing the interpretative significance from single, homogeneous bodies of evidence, we are less skilled, I think, at knitting together bodies of evidence that are totally dissimilar in character.   The contrast I have in mind, if you like, is that between 'parochial' and 'federal' interpretation. One tends to assume that the second of these is a more diffuse and messy version of the first.   But I want to demonstrate that in fact 'federal' argument offers us kinds of interpretative purchase that the more 'parochial' lacks; that it is in 'federal' argument that one of the special sources of vitality in psychological enquiry lies.

157

If psychology is to emerge from its present state of contention between mutually exclusive ideologies – the self-consciously hard-nosed versus the self-appointedly humane – I would argue that it is precisely towards such issues of interpretative competence that we must turn.   Towards the disciplines and rules of thumb often referred to as 'hermeneutic': a tradition that has its root, historically speaking, in Biblical scholarship; that is associated with men like Schleiermacher and Dilthey; and that consists in the search for the 'best reading' of the meaning that 'texts' convey.

This effort to grasp the intention of another intelligent being is one that can be viewed with more or less liberality.   In the strictest form of hermeneutic research, the 'text' must be a written document of some sort which the scholar does his best to make sense of, using only the concepts that its writer himself would recognise and accept.   The term 'hermeneutic' has been extended, though, to include other forms of interpretation.   The 'text' can be generalised to cover the record of any action that conveys meaning; tape recordings of conversation, for instance. And the interpretation that is reached can go beyond – well beyond – the categories that the actors would themselves accept.   Both historical and psychoanalytic interpretations are often of this sort.   I have even heard Darwin's work on the Beagle described as 'hermeneutic' in a somewhat extended sense.   In natural history, the patterns of meaning that form in the investigator's mind are not translations of patterns of meaning that have existed in other minds, but patterns perceived in aspects of the natural order that are not themselves sentient and may even be inanimate.   Whether or not one wishes to extend the concept of hermeneutics to this degree, or wishes to restrict it to the task of re-creating another's meaning, seems to me a matter of taste.   What matters is that it is the <u>interpretative</u> aspect of the investigator's activity that is seen as central: the feat of systematic intelligence whereby we use all sorts of evidence in making explicit the regularities that inform other creatures' actions.   And while the hermeneutic conception of psychology can be extended to overlap with traditional views of natural history, it is distinct from those models of psychology in which our work is seen as a branch of the technology of behavioural manipulation and control.

So, to begin at the beginning, let me declare an interpretative assumption: one about how worthwhile thinking occurs.   I would want to claim that all the more interesting exercises in the use of our wits arise from our attempts to resolve a tension: a generative tension between the dictates of intuition or impulse, and those of disciplinary constraint, of reasoned doubt.   Wherever you look, in art or science, you will find that the same state of generative tension occurs.   It follows, I think, that such creativeness as we possess flows not from the untrammelled expression of impulse, but

from an intimate negotiation, within the thinking of each
individual, between two frames of reference: between what seems
to us intuitively correct and what the constraining forces of
technique, material, tradition, or the marketplace require.

Stated in general terms, this idea of a generative tension
between frames of reference is a platitude; but at least it is a
platitude that one can set to work.   Let me begin with those two
pieces of American research, establishing the ground on which I
wish to argue.   Both are refreshingly bold in conception.   Both
grew from the fertile 'social relations' tradition at Harvard.
And together they make a strong prima facie case: a case for
looking at the personal life of the child as a determinant of the
attitude towards formal knowledge that the adult later displays.

The first of these is quite well known: Carlsmith's
ingenious study of the absent father.   Carlsmith realised that
during the Second World War, a large number of young men had left
home to fight, leaving infant sons behind them – and then, after a
few years' absence, had returned.   She thus had on her hands a
natural experiment.   For if the non-verbal bias of intelligence
that characterises young male students has its root in an identification with the father at an early age, such wartime sons should
grow up with this non-verbal bias of intelligence lacking.   By the
simple expedient of looking at the aptitude scores of Harvard
students whose fathers had been away at the War while they themselves were infants, she found just that: young men whose test
scores were what one might expect from a sample of highly intelligent young women.

Now this is not conclusive proof of a long-range effect of
early childhood experience on the intellectual disposition of the
young adult, but it is strongly suggestive.   So too is the second
Harvard Study – more recent, less well known, but in many ways more
remarkable and more sustained.   Frank Sulloway is a young Darwin
scholar who noticed that in the furore leading up to the publication
of the Origin of the Species in 1859, there was something odd about
the grouping of the antagonists: those for Darwin and those against.
This concerned their birth order.   There is, as we all know, a long-
standing accumulation of evidence to show that, in an academic context, first born and only sons do better than younger sons.   Also
that first born and only sons differ from the later born in
personality, tending in Alfred Adler's memorable phrase, to be
'power-hungry conservatives'.

On the basis of the accumulation, one would expect most of the
participants in the debate about evolution to be first born and only
sons; both those for, and those against.   But what Sulloway found
was that all those prominent Victorian intellectuals who were in

favour of Darwin's position were younger sons; and that all but
one of those who were opposed to him were first born or only sons.
In a sample of the twenty-three most eminent participants in this
debate, the discrimination between 'pros' and 'antis' is almost
perfect.   Using this finding as his corner stone, Sulloway has
gone on to collect further historical evidence to suggest that in
any scientific revolution in which there is a potent emotional
undertone - the Copernican revolution, the Darwinian revolution,
the Freudian revolution - those working for the new doctrine will
be younger sons, or sons whose position in the family was in some
sense conspicuously irregular.   He argues that this irregularity
will in its turn have disrupted the early identification with the
father that would otherwise have occurred, and will have fostered
a taste for a radical rather than a more conservative stance in the
face of new ideas; ones that threaten to overthrow traditional
assumptions about Man's special position - his position at the
centre of the universe, his Special Creation, or his power by acts
of will to govern the contents of his own head.

      Sulloway's study is of course far from conclusive.   But
together with Carlsmith's, it links together the emotional life of
the child with the intellectual disposition of the adult in a way
that intrigues me.   Using their work as a backdrop, let me now
deploy the four studies from the Unit.   The first is from the
field of mental measurement; another - miles away, academically
speaking - is from the sleep laboratory; another from the social
psychology of stereotyped beliefs; and the last from the demography
of marriage and divorce.   In each case, it is the resonances that
you should look for.   They are not four disparate pieces of
evidence, scattered across the academic landscape, each to be
accepted or rejected in its own terms.   Rather, they form a conglomerate of meaning; and, significantly, the kinds of interpretation they support, when taken together, are quite unlike those that
you would normally find in the separate literatures from which they
originally emerged.   To divide psychology into separate literatures,
in other words, is to foster interpretative patterns that are
continually at risk of becoming not merely parochial, but
misleadingly banal.

      As my first exhibit I want to take a distinction couched in
terms of mental tests that, in a sense, parodies the distinction
I have just drawn between discipline and impulse.   Discipline is
exemplified here by the I.Q. test; impulse by open-ended tests
that invite you, for example, to write down as many different uses
as you can for a brick or a paper clip.   Everybody possesses both
sorts of skill, but some show a marked preference for one rather
than the other.   Those who show a bias of ability towards the I.Q.
test are called 'convergers'; those whose bias is towards the open-
ended tests are called 'divergers'.   In the middle, there are the

'all-rounders'; those who possess a marked bias in neither direction.
Now it would be an unqualified conceptual disaster if this simple
distinction of types were treated as a system of pigeon-holes; the
basis for a parlour game of labelling. Rather, we use the distinction between convergers and divergers as a way of launching an
argument; a means of bringing the idea of generative tension
between discipline and impulse to bear on the kinds of thinking
people demonstrably display.

There exists a good deal of research to show that the people
we are here calling convergers and divergers differ in many ways.
Convergers, for example, are more conventional in their beliefs;
they show greater respect for authority. They also differ in the
kinds of academic work they find most congenial. In the English
educational system, convergers move naturally towards the physical
sciences, mathematics and classics; divergers towards history,
literature and modern languages. Biology seems to attract
convergers and divergers in roughly equal numbers. One of the
many personal differences that convergers and divergers display
concerns the uses they suggest for objects; convergers being less
likely than divergers to offer ideas that are violent. This is
not a particularly exciting result, though. It is what one would
expect; and in any case, the difference is not large. What is
more exciting is that when you look more closely you see that while
the convergers produce relatively few violent responses, a high
proportion of those they do produce are <u>very</u> violent; and from
time to time they are positively sickening. The three most
violent suggestions to come from a sample of convergers were:

   1) smash sister's head in (brick)
   2) wrap up dead wife so as blood does not stain
      car seats (blanket)
   3) to remove from baby sister's bed in mid-winter
      while asleep (blanket)

The most violent suggestions from the equivalent sample of divergers
were:

   1) suicide (paper clip)
   2) murder by smothering (blanket)
   3) nailing up one's study mate inside (barrel)

Convergers are more specific in what they suggest, and more concerned
with what one might call the intimate politics of the nuclear family.
So, if you plot the number of mildly violent responses from
convergers, all-rounders and divergers, you get a curve sloped in
one direction; if you plot extremely violent responses, you get a
curve - very prettily - sloped in the other. A result like this
is rather unusual in mental measurement; and the conventional
tactic of the psychometrician - to subject the result to factor
analysis, or to some other elaborate statistical procedure - in no
way helps to illuminate it.

Instead, we need to think.   If we do so, an interpretation beckons: one that is distantly dependent on Freud's notions of repression.   We already know that the converger is skilled in close analytical argument.   To achieve this, he seems to have learnt to control eruptions into his mind of content that is non-rational or 'strange'.   The diverger, by contrast, allows freer access to the non-rational; but the price he pays is an inability to concentrate on close, analytical argument.   In the language of ego defences, the converger is a 'repressor'; metaphorically, he is a mediaeval fortified town, with a massive perimeter wall.   In the same terms, the diverger is an 'intellectualisor', and his mental architecture is more open-plan.   The converger repulses the alien at the perimeter in forthright combat; the diverger has to rely more on the arts of collaboration with the aggressor and of guerilla war.   But in the converger, the very process of policing the boundary with the non-rational would seem to go with a heightening and focussing of the charge that the non-rational possesses.   Either the fierceness of the policing causes this heightening, or the policing is fierce in the first place because the tensions themselves are unusually potent.   We do not know. But something along these lines is clearly afoot.

Instead of elaborating a theory of defensive (and offensive) strategies in an ad hoc way, I would like to treat this first result as a bridge-head, and to conduct three forays from it. The first is to the frontier with physiology.   For the paradigmatic instance of the uncontrolled, non-rational, non-rule-bound thought is the dream.   And if the interpretation just put forward is heading in the right direction, you would certainly expect that convergers would repress not only their waking impulses but their dreams as well.

We know on excellent evidence that four or five times a night, we each enter a phase known as REM (or rapid eye movement) sleep. Our eyes flicker intermittently, as though we were watching some private film show.   If you wake people during this phase, they usually say that they were dreaming; and REM, as a consequence, has come to be accepted as the operational criterion that dreaming is taking place.

In two elegant studies conducted by graduate students of mine, Mark Austin and Michael Holmes, small groups of convergent and divergent students were put through the Edinburgh sleep laboratory. Divergers, they found, almost always recalled their dreams when woken in the midst of REM; convergers frequently did not - some-times claiming that they were not dreaming, but more usually acknowledging that they were dreaming yet being unable to remember what their dreams were about.   Precautions were taken to frustrate the various alternative explanations that can be put forward to

explain such a difference. I do not want to elaborate on these
refinements of design; rather to mention an even more intriguing
feature of the results they yielded.

Although the convergers recalled less than divergers, they
showed every physiological sign of dreaming more intensively.
They spent less time each night than the divergers in the REM
phase; but, within that phase, their eye movements were more
profuse. And the profusion of eye movement has itself been taken
in earlier research as an index of the vividness of the dream that
goes with it. So, interpretatively speaking, we have the same
pattern. Two sorts of study – one using mental tests, the other a
sleep laboratory – echo one another in a most satisfactory way: a
rigorous control of access to the non-rational is associated with a
greater head of steam.

Nor is this all. Holmes found that while convergers were
much less good at recalling their dreams while their eyes were
actually in movement, this weakness disappeared if awakenings were
timed so as to occur in the brief pauses between bursts of eye
movement. In fact, during these brief pauses, convergers' recall
was excellent – better if anything than the divergers'. Why should
they show such a remarkable improvement? The answer is conceptually
rather important. For it seems that while actual eye movements in
REM are associated with genuinely non-rational mental images, (with
'primary visual experience'), the brief quiescent pauses are
associated with the sleeper's more rational efforts to fit those
images into a sensible-seeming pattern ('secondary cognitive
elaboration'). If individuals are awakened during eye movement
and during quiescence, the dreams reported have a very different
character: Holmes found this, as had Molinaire and Foulkes in
earlier work. The convergers' weakness then is limited rather
strictly to mental events that accompany eye movement, and that are
patently non-rational. With the recall of more rational-seeming
thoughts they seem to experience no trouble at all.

The distinction between 'primary' and 'secondary', between the
arbitrarily impulsive and the more ordered and reflective, is of
real significance, then. But rather than venturing at this point
into Freudian theory, I would like to assay my next move from the
bridge-head, and look instead at the system of beliefs within which
self-consciously rational and more intuitive modes of thought are
embedded.* The measurement of such beliefs is in fact a relatively
well-rehearsed operation. You have available to you the semantic
differential, for instance, in which lists of nouns – Scientist,
Poet, Plumber – are associated with pairs of adjectives – hard/soft,

* For a detailed re-examination of this more neurological aspect of
Freudian theory, see Pribram & Gill (1976).

warm/cold, intelligent/stupid.   This technique gives rise to
regularities that are truly astounding.   Irrespective of their
knowledge of such people, citizens throughout the Western world
will agree that the Scientist, the embodiment of rationality, is
hard and cold, whereas the Poet, seen as a more intuitive creature,
is soft and warm.   I have found, in my own research, that they
will also elaborate on these woolly notions, rendering them quite
specific: the Science Graduate is seen as working long hours and
as being faithful to his wife; while the Arts Graduate is seen as
wearing fashionable clothes, flirting with his secretary, and
panicking in emergencies.

These systems of stereotypical beliefs have two remarkable
features.   The first of these is that they embody a sharp
discontinuity, in fact a positive semantic chasm, between ideas of
value and ideas of personal attractiveness.   In my own studies, I
have found that the virtues 'valuable', 'dependable' and
'intelligent' cluster so tightly together as almost to be serving
as synonyms.   Likewise with the virtues 'imaginative', 'exciting'
and 'warm'.   Yet the statistical connections between these two
clusters are virtually non-existent.

But there is an even odder aspect of this semantic chasm:
images built around each of the two clusters of meaning take shape
at different ages.   The image of the Scientist exists in its
fully-fledged form among intelligent English thirteen-year-olds;
and is readily detectable by the age of eleven - at which age many
of the children have had no formal science teaching at all.   All
agree that the Scientist is hard, cold, dull, intelligent, manly,
dependable, valuable.   The image of the Artist, in contrast, takes
shape later.   It is poorly etched in children's minds at thirteen;
but by seventeen is even sharper than that of the Scientist.   By
then, all are agreed that the Artist is soft, warm, exciting,
imaginative, feminine, undependable and lacking in value.

Nor is this all.   We know that the images of the Good Father
and Good Mother, overwhelmingly strong at thirteen, rapidly
fragment as adolescence progresses; but that meanwhile, the image
of the Good Teacher gets much more sharp.   Also, a more subtle
point, we know that we discriminate relatively poorly among those
adjectives that go to make up the image of the academic group to
which we ourselves belong.   Young scientists are more likely than
young specialists in the humanities to use 'valuable', 'dependable'
and 'intelligent' as though they were synonyms; whereas the young
humanists are more likely than young scientists to lump together
'imaginative', 'exciting' and 'warm'.   Looking for a generalisation,
we would want to say that our perception of images becomes more
stereotyped as the figures in real life that those images refer to
become of vital, personal concern.   Intense preoccupation is

associated with an indiscriminate use of language; mild preoccupation with discrimination that is greater.   And looking at the
results, we would also want to say that the stereotypes built
around the notion of impersonal authority and control are
established before adolescence sets in; while those to do with
artistic self-expression come into being only as adolescence
progresses.

Preadolescence, Piaget tells us, is the age at which children
are taken up with a stern authoritarianism of moral judgement, and
- as we can see for ourselves - with the acquisition of relatively
primitive, rule-bound intellectual skills.   Adolescence, in
contrast, is an age of emotional, personal discovery.   It seems
reasonable, then, to see the stereotypical scientist as the
personification of the preoccupying issues of the early school
years; and the stereotypical artist as the personification of the
preoccupations of adolescence.   There is a simple model of
intellectual development that now cries out to be released from
this argument: a model - obviously too simple, but too tempting to
resist - that sees the converger as someone whose characteristic
frame of mind fixates or gels before adolescence, during the
'latency period', when issues of control are paramount; and the
diverger as someone who fixates only later, in adolescence.

In terms of broad interpretative strategy, we have learnt something, I think, about why students of a convergent frame of mind
gravitate naturally towards science; while those whose disposition
is divergent move towards the humanities.   But more than that, we
have at least a toehold on the altogether more taxing issue of why
it is that convergent and divergent frames of mind take shape in
the first place.   We do not have answers, but we do have a new
notion of where to look, and of what questions to ask.   Why, for
instance, should some children's sense of themselves crystallize at
an earlier age than others?   What sort of pressure might it be that
leads a child to model himself on the ideal of impersonal authority
and control, while another bides his time, and waits?   And may it
be that cultures differ in this respect: the Russian, say,
encouraging an earlier fixation than the American?

However, despite factual studies like those of Carlsmith and
Sulloway, and despite cultural comparisons drawn so persuasively,
for instance by Bronfenbrenner, such questions are notoriously
difficult to handle.   This is partly because they are so easily
submerged in facile judgements of value: the assumption, in this
case, that it is worse to fixate early than late.   More immediately
accessible, I find, is another sort of question and another sort of
evidence.   Granted that the intellectual qualities of convergence
and divergence are linked to the personalities of the individuals
in question, what follows?   Will the lives that they lead be

different - not just as students, where we can get at them all too
easily with our tests and measurements, but as adults? If the
kind of story I have been telling is even approximately true, we
would expect specialists in different academic fields not only to
think differently, but to pursue different types of private life.
But before we look, we must draw breath - and be careful.

We know that the physical sciences have a convergent character,
in that they are perceived stereotypically as convergent, and that
they attract convergent students. But beware. The realities of,
say, physics, may be only tenuously related to the cultural stereotypes about physics. And although most of the students going into
physics are convergers or all-rounders, it is still true that a
minority are divergers - and that even among those who are
convergers or all-rounders, many have considerable abilities on the
divergent side. So, on a purely statistical basis, we must expect
those in a convergent discipline like physics to command a
considerable capacity for divergent thinking, should they feel
inclined to exploit it. And at the level of common sense as
opposed to statistics, we must also be wary, because the very act
of entering a profession that he sees as convergent - and therefore
'safe' - may set the convergent person free to exercise those
divergent aspects of his personality that he would otherwise hold
in reserve. Shifts of this sort are likely because we know, on
the basis of experiments, that the amount of divergent ability an
individual displays will depend to a considerable extent on his
reading of the setting in which he finds himself; on his sense of
what the occasion renders legitimate. Consequently, although we
may expect broad differences between disciplines, we would also
expect to find differences within a discipline between those whose
style of operation is predominantly convergent, and those whose
style is predominantly divergent.

With these provisos in mind, I would now like to turn to some
work of a purely demographic kind that I conducted together with my
wife. What we did, in practice, was to look through the 1969
edition of the British Who's Who, and pick out the academics. We
also had access to the results of the massive Carnegie Survey of
American Academic Life. And restricting ourselves to demographers'
evidence about births, marriages and social class, we found that
there were indeed huge differences to be found between the
disciplines. Those in the humanities, for example, proved
remarkably less likely than the scientists to marry, and to have
children. No less than 41% of eminent British classicists had no
children, either because they stayed single, or because they had
contracted childless marriages. The equivalent rates among
scientists were as low as 15% for physical scientists, and 8% for
biological scientists. So, between disciplines, we are forced to
consider differences not of a few per cent, but ones of three-,

four- or even five-fold.   Perhaps the most interesting group,
though, was the successful biologists.   They married more than
their colleagues in other disciplines, but they also divorced more.
Overall, they were between three and four times as likely as
colleagues in the humanities to divorce; and some six times as
likely to divorce as chemists or engineers.

The occupational hazard of the demographer is that of facts
floating free: of evidence that looks important, but that has no
anchorage in a body of understanding.   This danger became the more
acute when we discovered that, among the successful biologists, the
high rates of divorce were concentrated in a small group: those
who had been educated at private schools, and who had been born in
the first, rather than the second, decade of the century.   These
apparently arbitrary findings make good sense, however, when you
examine the names of the individuals in question.   For you see
that the group of biologists who were particularly divorce-prone
were also the ones who put experimental biology on its feet as a
discipline.   It may well be, in other words, that a field of
research makes particular use of those among its members who are
divorce-prone when it is itself in a formative phase.   And, of
course, vice versa: participating in a process of intellectual
upheaval may make domestic upheaval all the more likely.   The
evidence is perfectly congruent, then, with Thomas Kuhn's distinction between 'normal' and 'revolutionary' science, and the suggestion that convergers may rise to eminence through their contributions to 'normal' science, while divergers rise to eminence by
contributing to science that is 'revolutionary'.

There is a great deal more material that belongs in and around
the conglomerate that I have described so far.   There is clear
evidence, for example, that, for the eminent British doctor, his
social class of origin is closely related to the part of the body on
which he will eventually specialize.   Doctors from privileged homes
are more likely to achieve eminence through work on the head as
opposed to the lower trunk; the surface of the body as opposed to
its insides; the male body as opposed to the female body; and the
living body as opposed to the dead body.   And this effect would
seem to over-ride considerations of professional status: the
socially privileged, for instance, dominating dermatology, which is
a speciality enjoying relatively low esteem.   The explanation would
seem to be that doctors from privileged social backgrounds tend to
specialize in those parts of the body that - in our own culture, as
in the primitive societies studied by cultural anthropologists -
are considered as in some sense 'decent' or 'clean'.

But this is to launch another train of thought; another argument.   To pursue it systematically is to produce another conglomerate of evidence and interpretation adjacent to the first.   And it

seems to me that one of the profoundest difficulties of research
lies in judgements of precisely this kind: at what point to stop
trying to assimilate evidence to one body of ideas and understanding, and to allow another to form. The monomaniacs among us
assimilate every fact that moves to their own schemes and what they
cannot assimilate they ignore. The mindlessly promiscuous in
contrast, allow every conceivable permutation of variables, every
conceivable perspective, its own validity. Somewhere between
these two strategies there lies a more satisfactory balance; but
it is one that requires considerable tact to maintain.

At each step it is the 'best reading' we search for. At no
point can we sit back and allow our analytic, data-processing
procedures to tow us safely home. We judge, and judge again.
And we test the validity of our understanding not just by collecting
more evidence of the same kind, but by recasting our inquiries so
that our interpretations are challenged from quite a new point of
vantage.

Looking back over the evidence I have mentioned, some more
factual studies leap out at you: perfectly straight forward pieces
of work that we should have done, yet have not. We should have
looked closely, for example, at what happens to divergers who go
into science, and convergers who go into the humanities. But not
all pertinent questions about a body of understanding have that
comfortable, down-to-earth ring. I have made play, for instance,
with the notion of the discipline, but no one to my knowledge has
examined the contrasts and similarities of the disciplines that are
imposed on us by different intellectual pursuits: the discipline,
say, of the physiologist or surgeon faced with a human body, as
opposed to those that constrain a painter or photographer who are
similarly faced. And as each of our accomplishments - whether as
a surgeon, or psychologist, or painter - is embedded in a subtly
different set of relationships between intuition and disciplinary
constraint, it must follow that there is an ethnography of
intellectual activities to be performed. Both at the individual
and at the cultural level, we all negotiate some form of order, some
form of sense, that we can live with and find gratifying. It falls
to the psychologist to find where these different points of balance
and tension lie.

What the present evidence forces on our attention is a crucial
distinction: that between the rational and non-rational aspects of
our own thought. We differ among ourselves in the way we maintain
the boundary between the two, and in the traffic in ideas we permit
across it. And from this basic difference of strategy in the
management of impulse, a great deal else about us would seem to
flow: not just the way we respond to mental tests, and our ability
to recall our dreams; but the kind of marriage we have, the choices

we make about a field to work in, and the kind of contribution to that field we make once we are in it.   These widely diffused manifestations of our personal style look as though they are determined, at least in part, by our more general inclination either to admit to awareness, or to exclude from it, those emotionally charged ideas upon which we can place no rational construction.   And while the tendency of progressively-inclined psychologists has been to applaud openness, and to see restriction of access to the world of impulse as a form of stunting or immaturity, the evidence I have discussed suggests an altogether more complex picture, the strengths and weaknesses of the contrasting frames of mind counterbalancing one another in a most intricate way.

BIBLIOGRAPHY

AUSTIN, M.   Dream Recall and the Bias of Intellectual Ability, Nature, 1971, 231, p. 59

BRONFENBRENNER, U.   Two Worlds of Childhood, Russell Sage Foundation, 1970.

CARLSMITH, L.   Effect of Early Father-Absence on Scholastic Aptitude, Harvard Educational Review, 1964, 34, p. 3

HOLMES, M.A.M.   REM Sleep Patterning and Dream Recall in Convergers and Divergers, Occasional Paper 16, C.R.E.S., Edinburgh University, 1973.

HUDSON, L.   Contrary Imaginations, Methuen and Penguin, 1966.

HUDSON, L.   Frames of Mind, Methuen and Penguin, 1968.

HUDSON, L. and JACOT, B.   Marriage and Fertility in Academic Life, Nature, 1971, 229, p. 531

HUDSON, L. and JACOT, B.   Education and Eminence in British Medicine, British Medical Journal, 1971, 4, p. 162

HUDSON, L.   Human Beings, Cape and Doubleday, 1975.

MOLINARI, S. and FOULKES, D.   Tonic and Phasic Events during Sleep, Perceptual and Motor Skills, 1969, 29, p. 343

PRIBRAM, K. and GILL, M.   Freud's 'Project' Reassessed, Hutchinson, 1976.

SULLOWAY, F.   The Role of Cognitive Flexibility in Science, unpublished paper, Dept. of History of Science, Harvard, 1972.

Part IV

Philosophical and Cross-cultural Aspects

of Representation

REPRESENTATION :

THE PHILOSOPHICAL CONTRIBUTION TO PSYCHOLOGY

Richard Wollheim

1.   It is now, I hope, accepted as the outmoded view that it is that philosophy and psychology are totally independent disciplines. It seems to me that there are many philosophical questions that cannot be answered unless we know the relevant psychology, and there are many psychological questions answers to which await upon the relevant philosophy.   I think that one of the many reasons why the topic of representation is so interesting is that it illustrates extremely well the interdependence of the two subjects.   I shall be content if, in this paper which is necessarily schematic, I can make this view seem worth taking seriously.

2.   The first and most basic fact to be noted about representation is that every representation is a representation of something or other.   The Of-ness thesis - as I shall call the thesis that to be of something or other is an essential feature of representation - can also be expressed by saying that necessarily every representation has an object.

The Of-ness thesis lays itself open to three misinterpretations, all of which are serious.   The first and second misinterpretations are quite distinct, but the connection between the second and the third misinterpretations is at once intimate and problematic.   Each misinterpretation involves, initially, a distortion of the nature of the concept of representation and, derivatively, a contraction (so it turns out) in the extension of the concept of representation. However, it would be only pedantic if, in presenting these misinterpretations, I tried to segregate their consequences under these two separate headings.

The first misinterpretation, which I shall call, for a reason presently to emerge, the Figurative thesis*, insists that for every representation the something or other that it is of, or its object, can always be brought under some non-abstract concept. The Figurative thesis denies the possibility of there being representations whose objects cannot be brought under any concepts, and it also denies the possibility of there being representations whose objects can be brought only under abstract concepts. Whatever can be represented can also be described (according to this thesis) and, moreover, can be described in concrete terms.

The Figurative thesis puts as the central cases of representation cases where what is represented is e.g. a warrior, a bowl of apples, a garden, or some complex of such things. It displaces from the class of representations geometrical illustrations, such as the drawing of a cube, as well as the whole range of designs and 'abstractions' for which no verbal classification exists or is likely to exist. We might hope to capture the Figurative thesis if for a moment we narrow our attention upon the domain of art, for we might then say that the impact of the thesis is to exclude from representational art anything except figurative art - hence the name I have given it.

As a corrective to the Figurative thesis, and as a way of getting right both the nature and the extension of the concept of representation, I suggest the following rule of thumb**: that, confronted with a configuration on a two-dimensional surface, we should think of representation wherever we assign spatiality or a third dimension to what is in front of us - in so far, that is, as this assignment does not derive directly from the spatial properties of the stuffs of which the configuration is constituted.

The second misinterpretation to which the Of-ness thesis is exposed I shall call the Existential thesis, and it insists that for every representation there must exist an instance of the kind to which the something or other represented belongs. Probably for more reasons than one this formulation of the thesis is, even for the roughest purposes, too slack, and the thesis cannot be satis-factorily formulated without introducing the idea, which is not unobvious, that the something or other represented is always

---

* For the Figurative thesis, see e.g. Monroe Beardsley, Aesthetics (New York 1958). However, the thesis is also a commonplace in thinking about 20th century art and in 20th century art-educational theory.

** I have argued for this in my Art and its Objects (New York, 1968: London 1969) and in 'On Drawing an Object' reprinted in my On Art and the Mind (London 1973).

represented as something.   So what I have talked of so far loosely
as a representation of a warrior or a garden may now be thought of
as a representation of something or other as a warrior or as a
garden.   (Of course, there are or may be representations of a
warrior or a garden that do not represent them as warriors or
gardens – the warrior, say, is shown undressed and asleep, or still
in his cradle.   But these cases need not concern us.)   The
Existential thesis may now be reformulated thus: for every representation, there must exist an instance of the kind which the something or other represented is represented as belonging to.   So
there can be (according to this thesis) representations of
cardinals – that is, representations in which something or other
is represented as a cardinal – just because there are cardinals:
but there cannot be representations of unicorns – that is, representations in which something or other is represented as a unicorn –
since there are no unicorns.

The Existential thesis, unlike the Figurative thesis, has few
intrinsic attractions – though there may very well be philosophical
positions from which it appears difficult, if not impossible, to
resist.   However, the principal interest of the thesis lies in the
distinction that it embodies – that is to say, the distinction
between representation as indifferent to existence and representation as entailing existence – rather than in the stand that it
actually takes upon this distinction.   And much the same can be
said for the third misinterpretation of the Of-ness thesis*, of
which I have already said that it is very close indeed to, and some
would say that on any plausible interpretation of the two it is
identical with, the second misinterpretation.   The third misinterpretation, which I shall call the Portrayal thesis, holds that for
every representation, not only must there exist instances of the
something which the something or other represented is represented
as, but the question can always be legitimately raised, Which something is it that is represented?   Of course, the Portrayal thesis
allows that anyone of whom the question is asked in respect of a
given representation may in point of fact be unable to answer it:

---

* For the distinctions involved in the Existential thesis and the
Portrayal thesis, see e.g. Errol Bedford, 'Seeing Paintings',
Proceedings of the Aristotelian Society, Supplementary Vol. 40
(1966) pp. 47-62: Hidé Ishiguro, 'Imagination', Proceedings of
the Aristotelian Society, Supplementary Vol. 41 (1967) pp. 37-56:
Nelson Goodman, Languages of Art (Indianapolis and New York 1968):
David Kaplan, 'Quantifying In' in Words and Objections,
eds. D. Davidson and J. Hintikka (Dordrecht 1969):   Robert Howell,
'The Logical Structure of Pictorial Representation', Theoria,
Vol. XL (1974) pp. 76-109: Kendall L. Walton, 'Are Representations
Symbols?' The Monist, Vol. 58 (1974) pp. 236-54.

indeed the evidence required for answering it may, for contingent
reasons, no longer be available. But there is an answer to it, is
the point. For every representation there is a particular something or other that is represented: every representation is,
according to this thesis, a portrait.

If the Of-ness thesis is formulated as: if R is a representation, then there is some property f such that R is a representation
of an f - and it is important to see that by introducing properties
rather than concepts, the Figurative thesis is avoided - then the
Existential thesis may be formulated thus: if R is a representation
of an f, then there must exist fs, and the Portrayal thesis may be
formulated thus: if R is a representation of an f, then there must
be some particular f such that R represents it.

3.   Once the Of-ness thesis is granted, two questions immediately
suggest themselves as questions answers to which would go a very
long way towards providing a general theory of representation.
The questions are, what, in the case of any representation, is it
that is of the something or other that is represented? Or, what
(in the narrower sense of the term) is a representation? And,
what is the relation between the representation (in this narrower
sense of the term) and the something or other that it is of? Or,
what is it to represent?

If it is true that, in order to provide a general theory of
representation, it is necessary (if not sufficient) to answer these
two questions, a promising approach to existing theories would seem
to be to look at the answers that they actually give. However, we
find not only that some theories only laboriously divide themselves
up in this way, but some theories appear to concentrate exclusively
on one of these two questions.

But this last point is not necessarily the damaging point that
it might seem. For certain answers given to one or other of these
two questions virtually determine the answer that needs to be given
to the other, if anything like an overall theory is to emerge. So,
for instance, if we are told that to represent is to deliver to the
eye of an observer the same bundle of light-rays as would be
received from whatever is represented, the Arousal of Sensation
theory, we cannot be in much doubt what sort of thing a representation is. Or, if we are told that a representation is an illusion
(the Illusion theory) that pretty well provides an answer to the
question about the nature of the representational relation.

Of course, there will be theories of representation within
which the answers to the two questions are quite independent, one
of another. And there will be theories that constitute intervening
cases. And this in turn suggests a way - one way, that is - in

which theories of representation might be classified.   Theories of representation might be classified according to the degree of dependence or independence between the answers they provide to the two questions with which any such theory must concern itself.

However, I should like to draw your attention to another, though clearly related, way of classifying theories of representation.

Armed with a theory of representation, or with answers to the two questions.   What is a representation, and, what is it to represent?   We might imagine ourselves approaching a putative representation and asking of it, is it a representation?   And then, on the assumption that the answer is yes, going on to ask of it, what does it represent?   Now, the answers that such questions receive might be called the applied answers of the theory that we are armed with.   It is in terms of this notion - that of the applied answers of a theory - that we may introduce the second way of classifying theories of representation.   Theories of represen- tation might be classified according to the degree of dependence or independence between the applied answers they provide in the case of any given representation.

It should not be too hard to see that these two possible ways of classifying theories of representation, though related, are really not just different but very different.   For the first way of classifying these theories depends on considering the relations between two answers taken in themselves: whereas the second way depends on considering the relations between two answers in respect of the information that the theory says is at once necessary and sufficient for reaching them.   In the case of any given representa- tion, different theories of representation may very well deliver up precisely the same applied answers.   Indeed, if the theories attain to a minimal adequacy - what might be called material adequacy - they can be relied on to do just this.   But the theories will differ amongst themselves in respect of the information on which they prescribe that these answers are based.   With this firmly in mind we may say that the second way of classifying theories of representation amounts to this: that one should first consider the information that they stipulate as necessary and sufficient for determining, in the case of arbitrary R, that it is a representation, and then see how far this information goes - still, of course, on their reckoning - towards determining what the something or other is, that R is of.   The assumption to this way of classifying theories of representation is that there will be real differences in such reckonings: that with some theories there will be calculated to be a considerable overlap between the two pieces of information, and with other theories virtually none or none at all.

Examples of this second way of classifying theories of representation may now seem called for.   Let us consider the Illusion theory already referred to.   The information that the Illusion theory stipulates as necessary and sufficient for answering, in respect of given R, is R a representation? goes a long way, on this theory's account of the representational relation, towards answering, what is R of?   If, however, we turn to the Semiotic theory of representation, we get a very different result.   For the information that such a theory stipulates as necessary and sufficient for answering, is R a representation? gets us virtually nowhere at all towards answering, what is R of? - if, that is to say, we apply the Semiotic theory's account of the representational relation.   For, according to this theory, to know that R is a representation we have only to know that it is a character in <u>some</u> symbol system that satisfies certain formal requirements, whereas to know what R is of we need to know <u>what</u> actual symbol system R belongs to <u>and</u> we need to know its lexicon as well as its formal rules - and <u>that</u> is to know a great deal more.

(While on the subject of the Semiotic theory, it is worth pointing out that, though there is this very sizeable gap between the two applied answers that it delivers up in respect of any given representation, there is quite a narrow gap between the answers it gives to the two general questions, response to which constitutes the theory itself.   The answer that a representation is a character in a symbol system and the answer that to represent is to denote - to express the two answers in a way designed to be neutral between the varieties of the Semiotic theory - are clearly correlative. And this brings out a point I have made, that the two ways of classifying theories of representation, though related, are clearly very different.)

I shall now say of this second way of classifying theories of representation that it classifies them according to the <u>naturalness</u> that they assign to the representational relation.   The smaller the increment of information that a theory insists on if we are to be able (according to it) to determine what something already known to be a representation is a representation of, the more 'natural' account it gives of representation, whereas, the larger the increment of information that it specifies as requisite, the more conventionalist account the theory gives of representation.

My claim would only be that this captures a central part - it certainly would not be that it captures all - of our intuitive understanding of the dispute whether representation is grounded in

nature or rests on convention*.   It might, for instance, be said
that the dispute also concerns what counts as a representation, and
therefore concerns the information, absolutely reckoned, on which
we have to draw in order to determine whether something is a representation.

    If it were claimed, against me, that the notion of information,
as I have used it, is ultimately untenable, I would not be unduly
worried, for my suspicion is that, if this claim could be shown, it
could also be shown that the distinction between a natural and a
conventionalist account of representation is ultimately untenable.
And if it were claimed that the notion of information, as I have
used it, is tenable ultimately only inside some larger theory of
cognition, I should be positively delighted because I hold the
unsupported conviction that the same is true of the distinction
within accounts of representation.

4.   It should now be possible to assemble, out of the philosophical
ideas purveyed thus far, some requirements on any adequate theory of
representation.   I wish to propose two.

    The first requirement comes out of the immediately preceding
discussion.   It is that an adequate theory of representation should
assign to representation the degree of naturalness, conversely the
degree of conventionality, that it actually has.   In other words,
it should neither underestimate the difficulty nor fail to appreciate
the facility with which we can move from recognising that something
is a representation to identifying what it is a representation of.
(This, in effect, means that an adequate theory of representation
will not locate the phenomenon at, or perhaps even very close to,
either of the two ends of the natural-conventional spectrum.)

    The second requirement goes back to a point made somewhat
earlier.   Granted that it would be an error to think that all
representations are portraits, it is nevertheless true that some
are.   In other words, the concept of representation must allow
for the possibility of portraiture.   The requirement is, then,
that an adequate theory of representation must indicate how
portraiture is accommodated within representation.   It must
indicate the differential conditions of when we are, and when we

---

* For the discussion whether representation is natural or conventional, see e.g. Rudolf Arnheim, Art and Visual Perception (London
1956):   E. H. Gombrich, 'The Evidence of Images' in Interpretation:
theory and practice, ed. Charles S. Singleton (Baltimore 1969), and
'The What and the How: Perspectival Representation and the
Phenomenal World' in Logic and Art: Essays in Honour of Nelson
Goodman, ed. R. Rudner and I. Scheffler (Indianapolis and New York
1972).

are not, permitted to ask of R, which is a representation of an f, which f it represents, and it must indicate how this question is to be answered in a way that is consonant with the rest of what it says about representation*.

Choice of a theory of representation lies, as the current discussion stands, between about five or six alternative theories, depending on how precisely we individuate them.   I have mentioned already:

(a)   the Illusion theory**

(b)   the Arousal of Sensation theory+

(c)   the Semiotic theory++

---

* It is because of this requirement that I have not included in my list of theories of representation the causal theory, according to which a representation is of what has played an appropriate causal role in its production.   For it seems to me that, as things stand, this theory accounts exclusively for portraiture, and has to account for other forms of representation independently.   Some adherents of the theory (David Wiggins, private communication) hold to the belief that ultimately the causal theory can account for all kinds of representation, non-portraiture being exhibited as somehow derivative from portraiture.   For the theory, see e.g. Hidé Ishiguro, op. cit: David Kaplan, op. cit.

** For the Illusion theory, see e.g. S. K. Langer, Feeling and Form (London 1953):   E. H. Gombrich, Art and Illusion (London 1960). Art and Illusion, however, also contains other theories of representation.

+ For the Arousal of Sensation theory, see e.g. J. J. Gibson, 'A Theory of Pictorial Perception', Audio-Visual Communications Review, Vol. 1 (1954) pp. 3-23, and 'Pictures, Perspective and Perception', Daedalus, Vol. 89 (1960) pp. 216-27.

++ For the Semiotic theory, see e.g. G. Kepes, Language of Vision (Chicago 1944):   Richard Rudner, 'On Semiotic Aesthetics', Journal of Art and Art Criticism, Vol. X (1951) pp. 67-77:   Nelson Goodman, op. cit: John G. Bennett, 'Depiction and Convention', The Monist, Vol. 58 (1974), pp. 255-68.

To these we could add:

    (d) the <u>Resemblance theory</u>*, according to which a representa-
        tion is of what it resembles, or looks like. This theory
        is generally very unforthcoming, perhaps because it is al-
        together permissive, about what (in the narrow sense of the
        term) a representation actually is:

and

    (e) the <u>Information theory</u>**, according to which a representa-
        tion – which once again is generally left unspecified – is
        of something or other if and only if it delivers to the
        observer an optic array containing the same information as
        is found in the optic array of that something or other.

All these theories seem to me to be not implausible candidates, though I think that there are fatal objections to all, starting from the Resemblance theory, which certainly is the easiest to topple, and going right up to the Semiotic theory, for which I think there is most to be said and which certainly must, in part at least, find a place in the definitive statement of the true theory+.

---

* For the Resemblance theory, see e.g. Monroe Beardsley, <u>op. cit</u>:
Ruby Meager, 'Seeing Paintings', <u>Proceedings of the Aristotelian
Society</u>, Supplementary Vol. XL (1966) pp. 63–84.

** For the Information theory, see J. J. Gibson 'The Information
Available in Pictures', <u>Leonardo</u>, Vol. 4 (1971) pp. 27–35: John M.
Kennedy, <u>A Psychology of Picture Perception</u>, (San Francisco 1974).

+ The Illusion theory is criticised in Errol Bedford, <u>op. cit</u>:
Goran Hermeren, <u>Representation and Meaning in the Visual Arts</u>,
(Lund 1969): and in my 'Reflections on <u>Art and Illusion</u>'
reprinted in my <u>On Art and the Mind</u>. The Arousal of Sensation
theory is criticised in Nelson Goodman, <u>op. cit</u>: J. J. Gibson,
'The Information Available in Pictures': and John M. Kennedy, <u>op.
cit</u>. The Semiotic theory is criticised in my 'Nelson Goodman's
<u>Languages of Art</u>' reprinted in my <u>On Art and the Mind</u>. The point
that this theory must be incorporated in any sound theory is made
in that article very generally; some of the detail required for
working it out is provided in Kent Bach, 'Part of What a Picture
Is', <u>British Journal of Aesthetics</u>, Vol. 10 (1970) pp. 119–37, and
some in a forthcoming article by T. G. Roupas, 'Information and
Pictorial Representation', to appear in <u>The Arts and Cognition</u>,
eds. David Perkins and Barbara Leondar. The Resemblance theory is
criticised in Errol Bedford, <u>op. cit</u>: Nelson Goodman, <u>op. cit</u>:
my <u>Art and its Objects</u>: and Max Black, 'How do Pictures Represent?'
in E. H. Gombrich etc., <u>Art, Perception and Reality</u>, (Baltimore
1970). The Information theory is criticised in Nelson Goodman,
'Professor Goodman's New Perspective', <u>Leonardo</u>, Vol. 4 (1971)
pp. 359–60, and (more sympathetically) in T. G. Roupas, <u>op. cit</u>.

5.   I cannot hope within the confines of this paper to substantiate
these last remarks, which are therefore bound to seem dismissive,
and I shall have to rest my case on arguments that have been
produced elsewhere by myself and others.   I shall simply offer,
instead, in a necessarily crude version, what seems to me the best
available theory of representation.   It comes out well by the
criteria of adequacy that I have proposed, and it also seems to me
to have other things to recommend it.

     The theory is stated in terms of 'seeing in'.   For at least
central cases of representation, a necessary condition of R representing x is that R is a configuration in which something or other
can be seen and furthermore one in which x can be seen.   This gives
necessity not sufficiency for the simple reason that it covers such
cases as the cloud that is very like a whale or the photograph of
Charlie Chaplin that anyone might mistake for a photograph of Hitler.
Sufficiency (or something close enough to it for our purposes) is
reached only when we add the further condition that R was intended
by whoever made it to be a configuration in which something or
other could be seen and furthermore one in which x could be seen.
And this condition must be understood in such a way that whoever
made the representation was in a position or had the required competence, to form and act on this intention*.

6.   Perhaps the most natural way of demarcating philosophical and
psychological inquiry about representation is to think of
philosophy as characteristically interested in the nature of
representation and psychology as characteristically interested in
the various representational skills.

     What I have said so far, if accepted, should go some way
towards challenging the view that the two forms of inquiry, thus
demarcated, may be carried on with any real degree of autonomy.
If I am right about the nature of representation, if, that is, the
best available theory of the matter is in terms of 'seeing in', it
is at least an open question whether philosophical inquiry does not
run out into psychological inquiry.   For to see something or other
in a configuration is a representational skill - I shall call it
'representational seeing' - and the question is open in so far as
it remains uncertain how much of the substantive psychological
findings about representational seeing the philosophical analysis
of representation in its final state will need to incorporate.

---

* For this theory, see my Art and its Objects.   There, however,
the theory is stated in terms of the Wittgensteinian notion of
'seeing as' rather than in terms of 'seeing in', which I have now
come to see is more perspicuous.   I owe this insight largely to
Richard Damann.   The theory is restated in various essays in my
On Art and the Mind.

But however this turns out - and this is not an issue I shall or would be expected to pursue here - it should already be clear that even in its early state the philosophical analysis has constraints to lay down to which the relevant psychological findings must, on pain of insubstantiality, conform.

I shall specify some of these constraints, and in each case I shall, by referring you back to a point I made in discussing the nature of representation, locate the source of the constraint.

The first constraint is this: that the skill that psychology studies should have the appropriate scope - that is to say, it should be seen as in operation whenever anything three-dimensional is seen in a two-dimensional configuration.

This constraint derives, of course, from a consideration of the error involved in what I called the Figurative thesis. Since what is represented does not have to be brought under a concept, let alone under a non-abstract concept, the same must go for what is representationally seen.

It is the failure to respect this first constraint that vitiates, for instance, the well-known cross-cultural studies of W. Hudson and later workers on the perception of representations amongst various non-European populations*. For the kind of experimental situation in which a subject is shown a drawing of a huntsman, an antelope, and a mountain which is represented as being in the background but which configurationally lies between, and is then asked whether the huntsman can hit the stag, does not test by the answer given the subject's possession or otherwise of the skill of representational seeing. For in so far as the subject under-stands the question in relation to the drawing, he shows himself possessed of the requisite skill. In other words, to see the huntsman, to see the antelope, to see what does or does not lie between them, are all exercises of this skill**. (Of course, it is right to point out that it is no easy matter to determine whether

---

* E.g. W. Hudson, 'Pictorial depth perception in sub-cultural groups in Africa', Journal of Social Psychology, Vol. 52 (1960) pp. 183-208, and 'Pictorial perception and educational adaptation in Africa', Psychologia Africana, Vol. 9 (1962) pp. 226-39: A. C. Mundy-Castle, 'Pictorial depth perception in Ghanaian children', International Journal of Psychology, Vol. 1 (1966) pp. 290-300, which is (in part) reprinted in Cross-Cultural Studies, ed. D. R. Price-Williams, (London 1969).

** This point seems to have been appreciated in M. Wober, 'On cross-cultural psychology', Bulletin of the British Psychological Society, Vol. 25 (1972) pp. 203-5.

the subject does, as I have put it, understand the question in
relation to the drawing and whether he tries to answer it by
looking at the drawing and reporting on what he sees in it.   For
there could be certain cues from which the subject might infer
that a certain configuration must be a drawing of a huntsman or an
antelope – nevertheless he doesn't see the huntsman or the antelope
in it.   And then it would not be the case that he showed himself
capable of representational seeing.   He might be able to answer
the question in relation to the drawing, though not to understand
it in relation to the drawing.   The difference is, of course,
accessible to experiment.)*

The second constraint upon psychological findings about representational seeing is this: that the skill that psychology studies
should have the appropriate consequences – that is to say (and now
we have a weak and a strong version of these consequences, between
which I shall not adjudicate), weakly, that representational seeing
should be regarded as in operation only when the observer is not
necessarily led to believe that what he sees is actually there, and,
strongly, that representational seeing should be regarded as in
operation only when the observer is not led to believe that what he
sees is actually there.

The source of this constraint lies in something that has been
more implicit, I suppose, than explicit in what I said about the
nature of representation.   In enumerating the different available
theories of representation I distinguished between the theory that
I favour and what I called the Illusion theory.   Now the difference
(as I see it) that corresponds to this distinction is that, whereas
the Illusion theory defines, partially, a representation in terms of
the observer's being led to have an existential belief about what he
sees, a theory which defines, again partially, a representation in
terms of what the observer sees in it, does not additionally require
of the observer that he should have an existential belief about what
he sees.   My own view is that what representational seeing does
additionally require of the observer is that, as well as seeing
something or other in the configuration, he should be aware of the
configuration itself** – a possibility which, of course, an adherent
of the Illusion theory is intent to deny.   However, my view must
remain on the level of a suggestion, though, if the suggestion were

---

* E.g. Jan B. Deregowski, 'Illusion and Culture' in Illusion,
eds. R. L. Gregory and E. H. Gombrich (London 1973).

** I have argued for this in my 'Reflections on Art and Illusion'.
The point receives empirical support in M. H. Pirenne, Optics,
Painting and Photography (London 1970) and is used interestingly
in Michael Polanyi, 'What is a Painting?' British Journal of
Aesthetics, Vol. 10 (1970) pp. 225-36.

found acceptable, it would do something to fill out this **second** constraint upon the psychologist's inquiry into representational seeing.

I am not, of course, in a good position to say whether this second constraint is or is not likely to be respected by psychologists. Historically there is, I think, a disturbing omen. This omen is the tendency widespread in classical psychology and persisting well into our own day of employing experimental situations in which representational seeing is in point of fact in operation as though they were cases, indeed as though they were paradigms, of three-dimensional or non-representational seeing. Experiments in which our perception of solid objects is tested for its conditions on the basis of subjects being shown drawings of solid objects, or experiments in which the influence of shadow on perception of concave or convex surface is tested for its conditions on the basis of photographs of shadow - are cases in point. Such experiments seem to me misconceived in two related and important ways. In the first place, the phenomenon whose conditions they test is not what it is purported to be - that is, three-dimensional seeing - it is rather representational seeing. (Some-times, it is a different thing again: it is illusion - which must have its own distinct conditions.) And, secondly, the conditions that they purport to establish are not the conditions that they actually test: for the conditions they test are the representations of those conditions - indeed, in the nature of the experimental situation, this is all that they have available. (In the case of many conditions of perception, or perceptual cues, the distinction between conditions and represented conditions is an elusive one to make, but none the less vital. For instance, it is at first difficult to realise that in a drawing there is no such thing as overlap - there is only representation of overlap.)

Of course, the experiments that I have in mind do not actually violate the constraint under consideration. They do not assimilate representational seeing to three-dimensional seeing. They commit the converse error. They assimilate three-dimensional seeing to representational seeing. But what error and converse error have in common is a seeming indifference to whether what is tested is a form of perception that does, or a form of perception that does not, generate an existential belief: and either way round, the only thing that could justify the indifference is the theoretical conviction that from the point of view of psychology there is no difference between the two forms of perception. I doubt if this

conviction is ultimately true, and it certainly cannot be made an
assumption of the inquiry.*

The third constraint upon psychological findings about representational seeing is this: that the skill that psychology studies
should have the appropriate degree of flexibility - that is to say,
it must be capable of being controlled by different systems or rules
of representation. This, of course, derives from what I said about
whereabouts on the spectrum that runs from the natural to the conventional an adequate theory of representation should locate representation. My conclusion was, you will recall, that it should not
be located at, or, for that matter, too near, either of the two
ends of the spectrum: more relevantly, that it should not be
located at, or too near, the natural end. One thing that follows
from this conclusion is that any representation can correctly represent more than one three-dimensional thing and that any one three-
dimensional thing can be correctly represented by more than one
representation, and so an observer capable of representational
seeing must have assigned to him by psychology a skill that can
operate along these different pathways.

Of course any particular individual to whom such a skill is
assigned will not in point of fact be capable of seeing representationally along all these different pathways. Someone capable of
representational seeing is inevitably someone capable of one or
more modes of representational seeing.

The significance of this for psychology is, however, best
brought out in a somewhat broader context than that of mere representational seeing.

7.   I have suggested that the proper topic of psychological
inquiry concerning representation is the various representational
skills.   I have talked of representational seeing, and another
representational skill is the skill of producing representations,
or drawing skill as I shall call it.

Initially drawing skill and representational seeing might seem
to be linked rather like speaker's capacity and hearer's capacity
in the domain of language.   But a fatal objection to this analogy
is that someone (or so it seems) might have the capacity to see,
but no capacity to produce, representations: a possibility for

---

* The indifference shown by many perceptual psychologists between
real-scene perception and representational perception is inveighed
against in R. L. Gregory, The Intelligent Eye (London 1970).   The
point is taken account of in Julian Hochberg, 'The Representation
of Things and People', in E. H. Gombrich and others, Art,
Perception and Reality (Baltimore and London 1972) pp. 47-94.

which we do not wish to allow even theoretical room in the domain
of language - except in evidently degenerate cases.   Nevertheless,
even if the analogy is thus defective, it does not mean that it is
all bad.   Indeed it may very well have its value in pointing to a
dependence of drawing skill on representational seeing that is
closer than might otherwise be surmised.

     If the correct analysis of representation involves a reference
not only to what can be seen in a configuration but also to what is
intended to be seen in it, it is evident that the capacity to
produce representations presupposes in whoever has that capacity the
capacity to see things in them: for how else could he produce configurations intending this rather than that to be seen in them?   So
in a general way drawing skill requires representational seeing.

     However, the more interesting dependence of the productive
skill on the receptive skill occurs on a less general level.   It
follows from the fact that there are different systems or rules of
representation that not only are there different modes of representational seeing but there are different modes of drawing skill.
Now to claim that someone is capable of a certain mode of drawing
skill is also to make a claim about the mode of representational
seeing of which he is capable: it is to claim that the representational seeing of which he is capable is in a mode that integrates
with the kind of representation that he produces.   In so far as
this is not so, his capacity to produce representations that conform
to a certain system or fit certain rules is not a sufficient index
of his drawing skill and its mode.   This, of course, shows something
highly significant about the nature of the skill that drawing skill
is: it shows something (is how I would put it) about the kind of
internal mechanism that psychology needs to posit in order to
account for it.

     An example of this last point would not come amiss.   Someone,
say, draws representations in ordinary oblique projection.   If he
also in each instance sees that which the representation is of in
the configuration, and moreover does so with at least as great a
facility as he would with representations in some other projective
system, then there would be little doubt about the mode of drawing
skill that we should assign to him.   This is so because in this
case the mode of representational seeing integrates with the kind
of representation that he produces.   But imagine another case in
which someone produces similar representations but either he has in
each instance some difficulty in seeing that which the representation
is of in the configuration or (a more realistic alternative) he has
much greater facility in seeing things in representations made in
some other projective system, e.g. linear perspective.   In such a
case we surely would not think that the kind of representation that
he draws was a clear index of his drawing skill and its mode.   The

way he draws does not integrate with his mode of representational
seeing.   He recognizes not only that there are better, i.e.
representationally better, drawings than those which he does, he
thinks that there are better - once again, representationally
better - kinds of drawing than that which he does.

    Once it is recognized that an individual's drawing skill is
invariably within some mode, it is tempting to go on and try to
order the various modes in which drawing skill can be exemplified
into a hierarchy, so that some are more advanced than others.
This temptation is only strengthened when it is further recognized
that there is a standard temporal sequence in which the individual
passes through these various modes - a sequence which can be
correlated with cognitive progress.

    Nevertheless it might be misguided to give way too readily to
the temptation.

    For, even if the passage through the different modes of
drawing skill can be correlated with cognitive progress, it does
not follow that this passage is itself cognitive progress.   A
later mode of the drawing skill might serve cognitive interests
that are, on general grounds, held to be more advanced than those
served by an earlier mode.   But before we could conclude that the
transition from one mode to another was itself cognitive progress,
we would need to know the price paid for this transition.   We
should need to know, that is, to what extent the less advanced
cognitive interests which the earlier mode served well could still
continue to be served by the later mode.   It is only if the answer
is, to a considerable extent, that we should be clearly entitled to
think of the transition as itself cognitive progress, rather than a
concomitant of such progress.   And, notoriously, linear perspective,
though it may well correspond to advanced cognitive interests, must
fail to satisfy less advanced interests.   And the assumption, once
widespread, that only linear perspective can coherently or non-
inconsistently satisfy the different cognitive interests, since only
it provides a systematic way of representing space, cannot be introduced at this stage to justify the hierarchical conception of modes
of drawing skill.   For the assumption appears to be without
foundation.*

ACKNOWLEDGEMENTS

    In the writing of this paper I have benefitted greatly from
discussion with Patrick Maynard, Antonia Phillips, David Wiggins
and John Willats, to all of whom I have a debt of gratitude.

---

* Cf. Fred Dubery and John Willats, <u>Drawing Systems</u>, (London 1972)
The point is disputed in Jan B. Deregowski, <u>op. cit</u>.

HOW CHILDREN LEARN TO REPRESENT
THREE-DIMENSIONAL SPACE IN DRAWINGS

John Willats

ABSTRACT

In order to test the ability of children to represent three-dimensional space in a drawing, subjects of ages five to seventeen were given a real scene to draw from a fixed viewpoint.   Six classes of drawing system were identified in the drawings produced and it was found that with increasing age children were able to use an increasingly complex type of system.   These drawings were discussed in relation to two theories of representation: that drawing depends on the ability to imitate the appearance of the scene, and that drawing depends on the ability to imitate culturally determined stereotypes.   It is argued that both these theories are inadequate to explain the drawings produced, and that drawing depends less on imitation than the ability to invent abstract rule-governed systems. In this respect the acquisition of drawing ability seems to resemble the acquisition of verbal language.

Although children nearly always draw pictures purporting to represent three-dimensional objects, this does not necessarily mean that they are able to represent the third dimension in their pictures.   For example, although nearly all children draw pictures of people, they can do this by manipulating picture elements which are largely symbolic and in which there are no references to the third dimension;   so that not only are all the relationships on the paper surface two-dimensional, but all these relationships refer to two-dimensional relationships in the scene.   The ability to draw the human figure in such a way that there is a genuine representation of its extension in three dimensions in space is as a rule an ability which has to be slowly and painfully acquired in the life

class at an art school – the case described by Selfe (Chapter 2)
forming a remarkable exception to this general rule.   In more
formal terms the ability to draw the human figure in this way
depends on the ability to handle a complex 'language' in which
features of the scene – contours of continuous smooth forms,
discontinuities, wrinkles, puckers, changes of colour, hairs, etc.
– all have to be represented by more or less abstract pictorial
elements (Huffman, 1970).   Mature artists have to be able to
handle a variety of similar pictorial devices such as the various
drawing systems, the use of overlap and the use of the various
types of atmospheric perspective;   and the pictures of any particular individual or culture may, in theory at any rate, be for-
mally described by an account of the pictorial devices which go to
make up the pictorial structures characteristic of these individuals
or cultures.   Children do not normally have these pictorial devices
available to them, either because from a performance point of view
they lack the skill to handle the media, or because the devices for
representation are too complex to be available at the level of
competence.

    Perhaps the simplest of all pictorial devices is the represen-
tation of three-dimensional objects with plane facets by the use of
line.   It is significant that in the development of the automatic
representation of three-dimensional objects by machine this was the
first problem to be tackled.   The problem in drawings of this kind
is to so dispose the lines on the picture surface that the relationships between the positions of the lines on the paper map the
relationships between edges of the objects in the scene in a
meaningful and coherent way.   The system of mapping used in any
particular picture may be described as the 'drawing system' upon
which the structure of that picture is based.   There are a number
of drawing systems in common use;   for many people in the West the
most familiar of these systems is likely to be what is loosely
known as 'perspective' but practitioners in specialist fields such
as painting, engineering or architecture may be equally at home with
other systems (Dubery and Willats, 1972).   A picture may also be
recognised as being in one system or another by reference to
relationships between lines representing edges on the picture
surface, and a knowledge of the object being represented.   Drawings
of objects in perspective for example may be recognised by the fact
that lines in the pictures which represent edges in the scene normal
to the picture surface (the 'orthogonals') appear to converge to a
point.   Two other drawing systems which turned out to be particularly important in this study were orthographic projection and
oblique projection.   In oblique projection the orthogonals,
instead of converging as they do in perspective, remain parallel.
Normally these lines lie at an oblique angle to the horizontal, but
in the special case known as vertical oblique they appear vertical.
In orthographic projection orthogonals cannot be depicted, because
the projection of edges normal to the picture plane appear as points.

In order to test the child's ability to handle these devices
we need to provide him with a scene consisting of an arrangement of
objects made up of plane facets, and a particular viewpoint from
which to draw.   In this study the task was made as easy as possible
by providing the children with familiar objects in which all the
facets were made up of edges at right angles.   The question also
arises of a possible conflict between the child's own frame of
reference and the frame of reference provided by local 'landmark'
features in the scene (Harris Chapter 6).   This problem was sim-
plified by arranging the scene so that the child's own frame of
reference related as simply as possible to the obvious frames of
reference in the scene.

Subjects in the experiment were one-hundred-and-eight children
aged five to seventeen taken from State schools in East London.
Most of these subjects were taken at random from mixed ability
classes;   the remaining fifteen children, all girls, were balanced
within their age groups for academic ability on the basis of their
teachers' reports.   There were equal numbers of boys and girls in
each age group.

The scene they were asked to draw consisted of a radio, a box
and a saucepan standing on a table, and subjects were seated so
that they faced one of the long sides of the table.   The view they
had of the scene from this position corresponded to that shown in
Figure 1.   This drawing, which is referred to as the 'canonical
drawing', was obtained by placing a vertical sheet of clear plastic
between the subjects' viewpoint and the table, and tracing round
the outlines of the scene as perceived through the plastic, keeping
the eye fixed at the viewpoint by a small ring sight.   Subjects
were tested individually, and, as far as possible, all subjects had
the same view of the scene.   Each subject was given a ballpoint
pen, a sheet of A4 paper, and the instruction: "Please do me a
drawing of that table and the things on it".

The drawings produced were divided into six classes according
to the type of drawing system used.   These classes corresponded to
drawing systems already identified in various cultures and disciplines throughout the world;   but in addition each succeeding class
of system was more complex than the preceding one in the way in
which spatial relationships were represented.   The results showed
that this sequence of systems in terms of logical complexity corresponded to a developmental sequence related to the chronological age
of subjects tested.

In the first class were a relatively small number of drawings
in which the children had been unable to bring the depictions of the
individual objects represented into any coherent relationship on the
picture surface;   although in a number of drawings the individual
objects in isolation were drawn in quite a complex way.   An example
of a drawing in this class is shown in Figure 2.

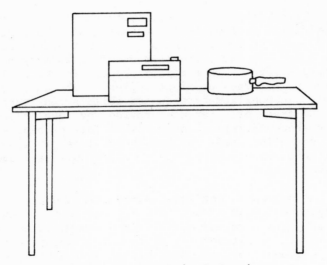

Figure 1. Canonical drawing

Figure 2. Typical drawing class 1: no projection system

In the second class were drawings in orthographic projection. In these drawings spatial relations in an 'up and down' direction in the scene are represented by 'top to bottom' relationships on the picture surface, and 'side to side' relationships in the scene are represented by 'side to side' relationships on the picture surface.   'Front to back' relationships in the scene are simply ignored.   Thus, since all points on the table top in the scene are equidistant from the floor, all points on the table top are represented as equidistant from the bottom of the paper.   This results in the table top being represented by a single straight line (Figure 3).

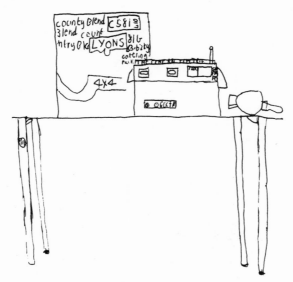

Figure 3.   Typical drawing class 2:   orthographic projection

In the third class were drawings in vertical oblique projection.   In this system the table top is represented by a rectangle, and we can think of this as the result of either of two possible approaches to the problem of representation of the third dimension. According to the first approach the child knows that the table top is a rectangle in a literal sense and, wanting to include this important feature of the scene, simply tacks it on to the front view of the table in orthographic projection.   According to the second approach 'front to back' relationships in the scene can be represented in a symbolic way by 'top to bottom' relationships in the picture.   The application of either of these 'rules' results in the table top being drawn as a rectangle, so that the lines representing the side edges of the table top (the orthogonals) are not only parallel, but run from top to bottom across the picture surface (Figure 4).

Figure 4.   Typical drawing class 3:   vertical oblique projection

Figure 5.   Typical drawing class 4:   oblique projection

Figure 6. Typical drawing class 5: naive perspective

Figure 7. Typical drawing class 6: perspective

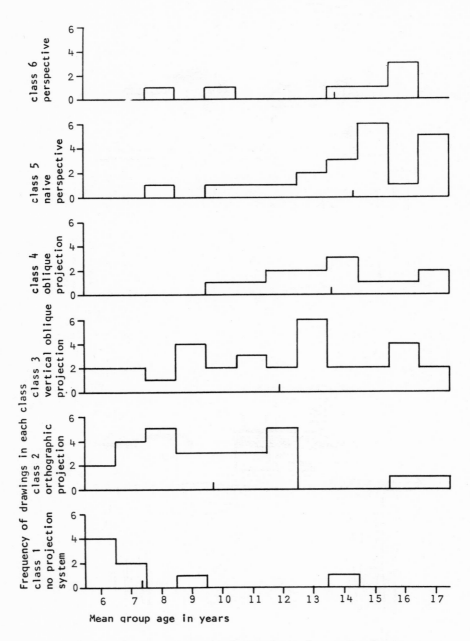

Figure 8. Frequency of drawings in each class

In the fourth class were drawings in oblique projection, and in these drawings the lines representing the side edges of the table top were also parallel; but instead of running from top to bottom they ran obliquely across the picture surface.   The simplest way of describing these drawings is to say that whereas top to bottom relationships in the scene are represented by top to bottom relationships on the picture surface and side to side relationships in the scene are similarly represented by side to side relationships in the picture (as in the two preceding systems) front to back relationships are represented by oblique relationships on the pic- ture surface.   The result of applying this rule is that the table top is represented by a parallelogram (Figure 5).

In the two final classes the orthogonals converged, and the 'sense' of their inclination on the picture surface was the same as that shown in the canonical drawing, i.e. they converged towards a point more or less vertically above the table top; but whereas in class five (naive perspective, Figure 6) this convergence was only just sufficient to distinguish the drawings from those in class three (vertical oblique projection), in class six (perspective, Figure 7) the convergence was much more apparent.

Figure 8 shows the frequency of drawings in each class for each age group, and the mean age for each class.   (A more detailed account of the task and results appears in Willats, 1977.)

A number of theories concerning the nature of representation have been proposed (Wollheim, Chapter 12).   For the most part these theories lay more emphasis on the perception of pictures than on their production.   While it seems plausible to assume that the underlying competence required for production is related to that required for perception we cannot necessarily assume that these processes are the same; so that theories about perception cannot automatically be transformed into theories about production.   With this proviso, it seems that the theories so far proposed seem to fall into two broad types: those in which the underlying assumption is that drawing arises as the result of imitating the appearance of the scene; and those in which the assumption is that drawing depends on learning how to recognise and imitate a fixed set of stereotypes. Theories of the first type can be illustrated by reference to J. J. Gibson's point projection theory (Gibson, 1971).   According to this theory the way to make a faithful picture is to so organise the picture surface that the optic array it presents to the eye of a spectator perfectly matches the optic array from the real scene. Of course, this theory can really only apply to paintings rather than line drawings, as Gibson acknowledges, but we might perhaps modify the theory by saying that in a faithful line drawing the angular displacements of the rays from points on edges of objects in the scene, measured relative to the observer's frame of reference, match the angular displacements of rays from corresponding

points on lines in the picture.   Line drawings of this kind can be
obtained easily enough by tracing over a photograph of the scene, or
using a drawing machine similar to the one used to produce the
canonical drawing shown in Figure 1.   Artists sometimes do this in
a rough and ready way by holding up a pencil at arms length and
adjusting the distance between points on the drawing so as to match
apparent distances between corresponding points in the scene as
measured along the pencil.   Drawings of this kind are, or can be,
produced by a mechanical process.   The variety of drawings which
can be produced by this means is not the result of any generative,
productive process in the Chomskian sense, but is a result of the
infinite variety of available scenes to copy.   Many teachers
actively discourage children from drawing 'from life' (i.e. from
real scenes) on the assumption that copying is bad for them.

An alternative and entirely different theory is that drawing
realistic pictures depends on being able to imitate stereotypes
learnt, not from nature, but from the prolonged experience of pictures.   According to this theory, since conventional stereotypes
vary from one culture to another, as do words in verbal language,
these stereotypes are culturally determined and have to be learnt.
This theory, or something like it, is usually ascribed to Nelson
Goodman, but it is difficult to decide (Goodman, 1968) whether
Goodman believes that it is isolated pictorial elements, images
('the way a table is drawn' for example), or the mapping rules from
scene to picture which are culturally determined.   However, since
Goodman states that 'realism is a matter of habit', it seems that
he believes that some process of conditioning is central to the
perception of pictures if not their production.   There is no doubt
that children do learn to draw stereotypes (how to draw Donald Duck,
for example).

The results of this experiment seem difficult to reconcile with
either of these two types of theory.   The first theory seems to
ascribe the inadequacy of children's drawings to their lack of
ability to copy from nature.   However, from the point of view of
'resemblance' many drawings in class 1 (orthographic projection)
seem to resemble the canonical drawing more closely than any other
drawings except those few in class 6.   It could be argued that
drawings in class 3 result from the attempt to imitate the appearance
of the scene but that this appearance is so modified by the constancy
mechanisms that the table top appears to the child as a rectangle and
so is drawn as such; but it seems that if anything young children
are actually better at estimating 'apparent' (i.e. projective) size
(such as the apparent size of the far edge of the table compared with
the apparent size of the front edge) than older children (Piaget, 1969,
p. 220).   In any case, it is difficult to see how any constancy mechanism could operate so that at the point of view from which the children drew their pictures both edges of the table appeared to lie at an
oblique angle to the horizontal in the same direction, so this argument cannot account for pictures in oblique projection.

Alternatively, it could be argued that the children had learnt stereotyped ways of drawing tables, and, when confronted with a real table produced these drawings as a response.   In that case it is difficult to see where children learnt these stereotypes.   Drawings in vertical oblique projection are almost unknown in our culture and drawings in oblique projection are quite rare.   Drawings in ortho- graphic projection are common enough in engineering and architectural drawing offices, but children would normally have less access to these than adults.   In any case there seems to be no reason why children should adopt different stereotypes at different ages.

Both these theories seem to suffer from an undue concentration on perception, while the process of production is regarded as a rather mechanical skill;   whereas any painter knows that the problem in drawing is not so much perception as finding a way in which three dimensions can be represented on a two-dimensional flat surface.

The classes of drawings produced in this experiment can be seen as stages in the child's attempt to solve this problem, each stage being more complex than the previous one, and requiring greater powers of abstract thought.

In the first stage the child is unable to form any coherent relationships on the picture surface, either literal or symbolic, which represent relationships in the scene.

In the second stage the problem of representing top to bottom and side to side relationships in the scene is solved by representing these relationships in a literal way by top to bottom and side to side relationships on the picture surface, and in our study this persisted through all the succeeding stages.   In the second stage the problem of representing front to back relationships in the scene is left unresolved and in the drawings in this class these relation- ships are not represented.

Stage three is an intermediate stage between literal and sym- bolic representation: the rectangular table top can result either from a literal representation of the table top as a rectangle or as the result of representing front to back relationships in the scene in a symbolic way by top to bottom relationships in the picture.

In the fourth stage, in which the third dimension is represen- ted by a direction diagonally across the surface, the representation is clearly symbolic;   it accords neither with what the child knows of the table top (that it is rectangular) nor with what he sees of it (that the side edges appear to converge).

Stages five and six are less easy to account for especially since they seem to be alternative rather than succeeding stages of development.   In all the previous stages the problem has apparently

been to find a way to represent the three dimensions inherent in
the scene; what Harris (Chapter 6) calls adjacent landmark or
framework features.   The question of reconciling this with the
child's self-related frame of reference has been ignored.   We can
probably account for stage 5 (naive perspective) by saying that the
child has learnt the rule that in adult pictures the orthogonals
converge but has not learnt to connect this rule with the appearance
of the scene.   Possibly we can say that in stage six the child has
learnt to connect this rule with the appearance of the scene;   that
is, in Harris's terms, the child has learnt in perspective drawing
to co-ordinate his own framework of reference with the local frame
of reference of the scene;   as he earlier had to learn to do in the
development of perception.

A rectangular or 'carpentered' set of objects in the scene
naturally suggests a local or landmark reference system similar to
Cartesian co-ordinates, whereas if we think of the child's self-
centred frame of reference in terms of direction of gaze as Harris
implies this naturally suggests a system of polar co-ordinates.
Further, the third dimension in a system of Cartesian co-ordinates
easily and naturally maps onto a set of parallel directions on a
flat surface.   Not so a set of polar co-ordinates, which suggests
the interpenetration of a plane by a ray at a target point.   Perhaps it is the difficulty of reconciling two fundamentally different
co-ordinate systems which seems to make perspective such a difficult
task;   out of twenty subjects in the last two age groups only nine
used some form of perspective, and of these only three were in true
perspective.   The difference between the mean angle of convergence
of drawings in this class (about $80°$) and that of the canonical
drawing in strict or 'scientific' perspective (about $115°$) can
probably, on this account, be explained by the operation of the
constancy mechanisms (Vernon, 1971, p. 63).

To what extent is this process of development influenced by
teaching in schools?   The answer as regards the first four stages
is probably 'very little'.   Vertical oblique projection is never
taught in schools, and orthographic and oblique projections are
taught only to boys in mechanical drawing classes, which usually
begin at about the age of twelve.   Most of the drawings in orthographic projection appeared well before this age (see Figure 8),
and of thirteen drawings in oblique projection six were produced by
girls.

If this account of the developmental sequence of stages is
correct, then drawing, far from being a mechanical process is, particularly for younger children, an active, creative, problem solving
activity in which the child invents successively more complex and
abstract rule-systems for the concepts which he wishes to communicate.
In this respect the acquisition of drawing ability seems remarkably

similar in its developmental pattern to the acquisition of verbal
language.   We might illustrate this by a quotation from Cromer
(1974) which is taken from a study of language but, it seems could
equally well apply to drawing:

> "It would appear, then, that the child does not learn words,
> but that he invents them for the things he wants to communi-
> cate.   Furthermore, imitation does not appear to be a
> mechanism of acquisition.   This does not mean that these
> inventions are totally independent of the language he hears
> about him;   they are closely related to it, but are neverthe-
> less independent of it in important respects, the most impor-
> tant appearing to be the creativity which he brings to bear
> on the acquisition process, and this creativity has to do
> with the communication of concepts which he is cognitively
> able to handle." (p. 206)

ACKNOWLEDGEMENTS

    I am most grateful to Professor N. S. Sutherland of Sussex
University for his help and criticism in the preparation of
Willats, 1977 on which this paper is based.   I would also like
to thank Sarah Hurn, Harry Fisher and Allan Hooker of North East
London Polytechnic, the head teachers and staff of the schools in
which this experiment was carried out, and the Quarterly Journal
of Experimental Psychology for permission to reproduce Figures 1
and 8.

BIBLIOGRAPHY

CROMER, R. F.,   The development of language and cognition: The
    cognition hypothesis, in FOSS, B. (Ed.) New Perspectives in
    Child Development, Penguin, 1974

DUBERY, F. & WILLATS, J.,   Drawing systems, London and New York,
    Studio Vista, 1972

GIBSON, J. J.,   The information available in pictures, Leonardo,
    1971, 4, pp. 27-35

GOODMAN, N.,   Languages of art, Indianapolis, Bobbs Merrill Co Inc,
    1968

HARRIS, P. L.,   The child's representation of space, Chapter 6
    in this volume

HUFFMAN, D. A.,   Impossible objects as nonsense sentences, in
    MELTZER, B. & MICHIE, D. (eds.) Machine Intelligence, 1970,
    6, Edinburgh University Press

PIAGET, J.,   The mechanisms of perception, Routledge & Kegan Paul,
     1969

SELFE, L.,   A single case study of an autistic child with
     exceptional drawing ability, Chapter 2 in this volume

VERNON, M. D.,   Experiments in visual perception, second edition,
     Harmondsworth, Penguin Books Ltd, 1966

WILLATS, J.,   How children learn to draw realistic pictures,
     Quarterly Journal of Experimental Psychology, 1977, (in press)

WOLLHEIM, R.,   Representation: the philosophical contribution to
     psychology, Chapter 12 in this volume

PICTORIAL   RECOGNITION   AS   AN   UNLEARNED   ABILITY:

A   REPLICATION   WITH   CHILDREN   FROM

PICTORIALLY   DEPRIVED   ENVIRONMENTS

G. Jahoda, J. B. Deręgowski, E. Ampene and N. Williams

ABSTRACT

In Experiment 1 children aged about three years were studied
in rural areas of Ghana (N=34) and Rhodesia (N=12), where pictorial
material is rare.   Subjects were trained to identify a set of
common objects; on subsequent testing with coloured photographs
the overall correct recognition rate was 86%.   Experiment 2 was
carried out in a small urban area in Ghana with thirty-nine children,
of whom twenty-five attended a pictorially rich model nursery school.
Photographs only were presented, and the rates of correct identification were almost exactly the same for attenders and non-attenders.
These results confirm the conclusions of Hochberg and Brooks (1962),
lending no support for the view that differential experience with
pictures influences pictorial object recognition.

The literature on cross-cultural aspects of pictorial perception contains an apparent, and as yet unresolved, contradiction.
On the one hand there is ample evidence, ranging from anecdotal to
experimental, indicating that many pre-literate people experience
difficulties in interpreting pictures as two-dimensional representations of three-dimensional objects.   This evidence, which has
been summarized by Miller (1973), led him to suggest "that the
ability to perceive anything in a pictorial representation requires
some experience with pictures in order to acquire the set that
pictures can represent more than a flat surface" (p. 148).   A
similar view was taken by Goodman (1968), and it has even been said
by Segall, Campbell and Herskovits (1966, p. 33) that a photograph
can be regarded as an arbitrary convention, that has to be learnt.

On the other hand the recent study of subjects with minimal exposure to pictures by Deręgowski et al. (1972) obtained results which could be regarded as demonstrating that even such people can, albeit with considerable effort, make sense of pictures.   There is, of course, also the famous study by Hochberg and Brooks (1962) which maintains that there is a native ability for pictorial recognition, so that it is the deficiencies reported from some cultures which require special explanation.   The major weakness of this heroic study is its N of one.   The aim of the present study was to take advantage of natural settings in which there is very little pictorial material for replication with a larger sample.

EXPERIMENT   1

Methods

Samples.   The main study was undertaken in four remote rural Ghanaian villages in the Accra plain, bordering the Akwapim region. For the purpose of comparison an additional sample was tested in a rural area in Rhodesia, some twenty-five miles from Salisbury.   In these settings exposure to Western-type pictorial material is minimal.   The traditional dwellings are devoid of pictures, with the occasional exception of photographs of persons, though even these are rare.   However, both in Ghana and Rhodesia copies of newspapers find their way into the villages; but these seldom contain pictures of objects.   Moreover, no small child was ever observed to be in possession of a newspaper.   Apart from this a few posters were seen, usually without any pictures or featuring only people.   The only source of pictures of objects that was found were labels on tins, but since these are not widely used by subsistence farmers children are unlikely to see them regularly.   It should be mentioned that one of the Ghanaian villages had a school, so that children might have had access to some books from their older siblings, and the results for this location were therefore separately analysed. While it cannot be claimed that the subjects' environment was totally devoid of pictorial material, the amount that could be observed was negligible by Euramerican standards.

As regards subjects, initial attempts were made to test children aged around two years (eight in Ghana and five in Rhodesia).   This proved unsuccessful: the children were terrified by the situation and either tried to escape or remained sitting petrified, unable to pay any attention to the stimulus materials.   It was therefore decided to test children aged about three who mostly proved able to cope quite well, though some remained rather shy and inhibited.   A total of five children had to be eliminated (only in Ghana) because they 'dried up' in the course of the first stimulus series and could not be persuaded to continue.   This is unlikely to have produced

any bias, since some of these children made correct responses while
they were still functioning. Altogether thirty-four children completed the test in Ghana (twenty boys and fourteen girls) and twelve
in Rhodesia (four boys and eight girls).

Materials. These consisted first of sets of small common
objects familiar to the children, and accordingly differing somewhat
in Ghana and Rhodesia. The objects were photographed against a
neutral background with a Polaroid camera to produce 8 X 8 cm colour
prints. Objects used in Ghana were as follows: BANANA*, basket*,
BOTTLE*, calabash, coin, EGG*, *ladle*, LEAF, ORANGE*, pants*, *sandal*,
stone, *tin*, twig. Those capitalized were identical in Rhodesia,
whilst for those italicized a local form was substituted (the
asterisk will be referred to later); additional items in Rhodesia
were: enamel bowl, cup and spoon.

In Ghana only a further set of colour pictures was prepared,
which showed a large object in a natural setting: bicycle*, hoe*,
house*, lorry*, man, stool*, tree*, woman. In all these cases the
object occupied most of the picture space. In addition there were
two pictures featuring animals (chicken*, goat*) which were quite
small in the centre of the picture. Examples of the stimulus
pictures are shown in Figures 1a and 1b*. In Ghana the pictures
were first presented in five sets. These consisted of 3,4,3,4
items for which objects were initially shown; the remaining set of
4 was confined to large objects in natural settings. This was the
'long'version, subsequently modified to the 'short' one where two
of the sets involving prior object presentation were eliminated,
and one additional set of photographs of large objects in natural
settings included; the sequence thus became 3,4,4,4. In both
versions the presentation followed four systematically varied
orders. In Rhodesia there were always three sets consisting of
4,4,3 stimuli, preceded by the actual objects.

In the case of the sets consisting of photographs only in
Ghana it is not possible to arrive at a chance model. For sets
linked with the presentation of objects one can assume that subjects
randomly named the objects previously shown. On this basis the
chance expectation of rate of success would be 29% in Ghana and
27% in Rhodesia. Since the actual success rate obtained and
reported below ranged from two to three times the chance expectation,
significance testing was superfluous.

Procedures. In Ghana the child sat at a specially constructed
low table opposite the African experimenter, with the European

---

* For technical reasons it was not possible to reproduce the
pictures in colour in this volume.

Figure 1a.   Example of small common object: sandal

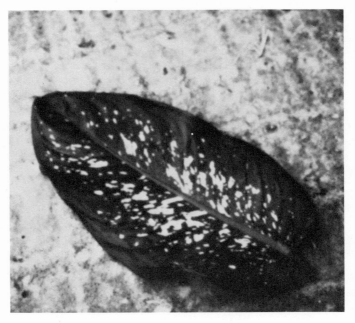

Figure 1b.   Example of small common object: leaf

Figure 2.   Example of large object in natural setting: lorry

Figure 3.   Testing situation, Experiment One

experimenter located diagonally behind the child's seat so as to be able to record the responses and communicate by signs with the other experimenter without himself being seen.   The mother or another member of the child's family was usually in the vicinity to provide reassurance, but at some distance.   In Rhodesia the child sat on a blanket on the ground, between his mother and the African assistant. The observer (J.B.D.) occupied a chair some two paces from the blanket.   Otherwise the basic procedure was the same.

After putting the child at ease, the experimenter placed a set of three or four objects in front of him.   It was explained that the 'game' consisted of handing to the experimenter any object she names.   This was an initial control device to ensure that the child was acquainted with the name of the object;   if not (which was very rare) the name was given.   The child then handed the objects over as instructed;   when only a single object remained, the child was told to name it.

Next, the corresponding set of colour photographs was laid out in a different random order in front of the child.   An object shown in one of the pictures was named, and the child had to pick out the appropriate photograph and hand it to the experimenter as before. The photograph was then returned to its position whether or not the response had been correct and another object was named, until the whole set had been completed.

In Ghana there was a further stage where children were merely given sets of photographs without prior presentation of objects, the task being otherwise identical.   Since errors could have been the result of lack of attention or confusion rather than of incorrect perception, a check procedure was adopted with pictures wrongly selected: at the end of each set such pictures were shown to the child with a request to name the object.   If this was correctly done, the subject was credited with it in spite of previous failure.

Children were rewarded with a small packet of biscuits at the end of their testing.

RESULTS

In Ghana the procedure varied slightly in different locations Thus it was found that the number of stimuli in the first two villages seemed too large, with children showing signs of becoming restive;   in the other two villages a shorter presentation was there- fore used.   Hence the results for these will be presented separately, and given in terms of rounded mean percentage scores;   these were arrived at by expressing the number of correct responses as a pro- portion of the total possible ones.   The findings are presented in Table 1.

Table 1. Mean percentage of correct picture responses

Sample	Procedure	School in Village	N	Mean per cent correct
GHANA:				
Villages A and B	long	no	10	83
Village C	short	no	12	89
Village D	short	yes	12	79
RHODESIA:	short	yes	12	94
Overall			46	86

For the Ghana data a further analysis was carried out in order to answer the question whether pictures of objects handled by the children were easier to recognise than the others. For this purpose the mean number of errors per picture was calculated; the initially surprising result was a mean of 3.9 errors for objects handled, as compared with 2.7 for larger objects seen only in pictures. On scanning the data it became evident that the main factor responsible was the extremely high error rate for the picture of a stone, which seems to have been highly ambiguous for the children. When the error rate is recomputed omitting this one picture, the respective rates are 2.8 versus 2.7; there is thus no indication that the handling of objects was necessary to help the children in recognizing pictures.

EXPERIMENT   2

In the course of conducting the final experiment in Ghana it became obvious that the children experienced no serious difficulty in recognizing pictures, even in the absence of the corresponding objects. It was therefore decided to run another experiment whose primary purpose was to throw further light on the possible effects of education. Being a very simple exercise, it will only be briefly described.

The location of this second study was a small urban area some eight miles from Accra which has a model nursery school and, unlike most schools and nursery schools in Ghana, is lavishly equipped with pictures and picture books. A sample of twenty-five children attending this nursery school (mostly for a minimum of about six months) was selected, as well as fourteen children who had never attended. Moreover, parents of the nursery school children mostly came from a higher socio-economic background; twenty-one of the nursery school children came from homes where both parents had an education, whilst only two of the others had such a background.

Thus the nursery school children were almost certainly exposed to a much richer pictorial environment. Most of the children were somewhat younger than those in the first experiment, ranging from two-and-a-half to three.

The children were tested individually by an African experimenter (E.A.), no white stranger being present. They were given a set of sixteen pictures, consisting of those in the lists given above which are marked with an asterisk. It will be noted that half of these were of common objects, though on this occasion no actual objects were presented, merely the pictures; the other half consisted of the larger objects shown in their natural setting.

In order to facilitate comparison, scores will again be given as percentages correct. For the nursery school children the mean score was 73%, and for those not attending nursery school 71%. This is of course not a significant difference, so that there is no indication that a substantial contrast in richness of pictorial environment has any discernible effect.

The difference in the proportion of correct responses between Experiments 1 and 2 approaches significance, so that it is perhaps appropriate to consider possible reasons. One may be that the initial experience with objects may provide some slight training, or at any rate help to familiarize children with the nature of the task; another reason is probably that the children taking part in Experiment 2 included more younger ones aged about two-and-a-half.

                              DISCUSSION

It should be pointed out that the original Hochberg & Brooks (1962) study dealt with line drawings and black-and-white photographs, whilst the present one employed only colour photographs. There is little doubt that colour provides an important additional cue for recognition, and to that extent it may be considered that the task was somewhat easier. However, Forge (1970) reports of the Abelam of New Guinea that they were unable to recognise even coloured pictures.

It cannot be maintained that all the children in Experiment 1 have been totally devoid of any contact with pictures. It would therefore still be possible to argue that there could exist a very low threshold of pictorial experience, in the nature of one-trial learning, which is sufficient to trigger off the ability to recognize pictures. Whilst possible in principle, this seems rather unlikely because it is difficult to envisage any mechanism whereby it could come about. On the other hand the study offers clear evidence that the amount of exposure to pictorial material bears no observable relationship to the ability to recognize pictures of objects;   and this fact contradicts Miller's (1973) emphasis on the importance of experience with pictures.

Apart from the limitations mentioned, the outcome of the present study is entirely consistent with the view arrived at by Hochberg & Brooks (1962) that visual experience of objects in the real world is sufficient to lay the foundation of an ability for picture recognition.   The results also fit in with those of Kennedy & Ross (1975) who studied the Songe of Papua, using outline drawings;   their sample consisted partly of school children, but even the older subjects with little or no education had a high rate of success with recognition of the drawings.   All this supports the view put forward by Hochberg & Brooks (1962) that it is not the understanding of pictures, but the difficulties encountered with such understanding which require to be examined further.   Although a detailed discussion of this problem would be beyond the scope of the present report, some possible factors that might be considered in this connection will be briefly reviewed.

Such difficulties as arise in comprehension of pictures can be divided into two categories: the difficulties encountered when a picture is used as a substitute for a depicted object and difficulties which arise when a subject is required to interpret relationships between various parts of the same picture.

The first type of difficulty has been found in a variety of cultures, including those in which pictures are readily labelled, and even relatively sophisticated subjects are not entirely free of it.   Thus, Deręgowski and Jahoda (1975) have shown that Scottish women find it easier to learn location of objects than to learn location of pictures depicting them;   Ekman and Junge (1961) observed that Swedish students were not capable of judging relative volumes of depicted cubes as well as those of solid cubes, and Klapper and Birch (1969) found that children responded more vehemently to tools than to their portrayals when requested to mime the manner in which the tools were used.   In a cross-cultural comparison Deręgowski and Serpell (1971) noted that Scottish subjects were superior to Zambian subjects on sorting of pictures but equal to them on sorting of objects.   It seems therefore that on a variety of tasks pictures are not equivalent to objects.

Difficulties with relationships within a picture are shown by Hudson's studies (1967), wherein subjects are reported to have labelled various elements of a picture correctly, yet failed to grasp adequately the relationship between them.   Sometimes they misinterpreted the implicit spatial relationships and, occasionally, the depicted activities.   Similarly Doob (1961) found that his African subjects had no difficulty in recognizing and even categorizing human figures in pictures and drawings, but they seemed unaware of what these people were doing.   Defective grasp of a complex picture showing a Bantu family scene was also demonstrated by Duncan et al. (1973).

Both these sets of studies suggest that simple recognition of pictorial elements, though a necessary step towards full pictorial perception, is not sufficient to ensure that pictures as wholes are fully understood.   Such a process calls for more complex skills, which so far have been insufficiently analyzed.

ACKNOWLEDGEMENT

This study forms part of a larger project supported by the U.K. Social Science Research Council, whose assistance is gratefully acknowledged.

BIBLIOGRAPHY

DEREGOWSKI, J. B. & SERPELL, R.,   Performance on a sorting task: a cross-cultural experiment, International Journal of Psychology, 1971, 4, pp. 273-281

DEREGOWSKI, J. B., MULDROW, E. S. & MULDROW, W. F.,   Pictorial recognition in a remote Ethiopian population, Perception, 1972, 1, pp. 417-425

DEREGOWSKI, J. B. & JAHODA, G.,   Efficiency of objects, pictures and words in a simple learning task, International Journal of Psychology, 1975, 10, pp. 19-25

DOOB, L. W.,   Communication in Africa, New Haven, Yale University Press, 1961

DUNCAN, H. F., GOURLAY, N. & HUDSON, W.,   A study of pictorial perception among Bantu and White primary school children in South Africa, Johannesburg, Witwatersrand University Press, 1973

EKMAN, G. & JUNGE, K.,   Psychophysical relations in visual perception of length, area and volume, Scandinavian Journal of Psychology, 1961, 2, pp. 1-10

FORGE, A.,   Learning to see in New Guinea, in MAYER, P. (ed.) Socialization, London, Tavistock, 1970

GOODMAN, N.,   Language of art: an approach to a theory of symbols, Indianapolis, Bobbs-Merrill, 1968

HOCHBERG, J. & BROOKS, V., Pictorial recognition as an unlearned
    ability: a study of one child's performance, American Journal
    of Psychology, 1962, 75, pp. 624-628

HUDSON, W., Study of the problem of pictorial depth perception,
    International Journal of Psychology, 1967, 2, pp. 89-107

KENNEDY, J. M. & ROSS, A. S., Outline picture perception by the
    Songe of Papua, Perception, 1975, 4, pp. 391-406

KLAPPER, Z. S. & BIRCH, H. G., Perceptual and action equivalence
    of photographs in children, Perceptual & Motor Skills, 1969,
    29, pp. 763-771

MILLER, R. J., Cross-cultural research in the perception of
    pictorial materials, Psychological Bulletin, 1973, 80,
    pp. 135-150

SEGALL, M. H., CAMPBELL, D. T. & HERSKOVITS, M. J., The influence
    of culture on visual perception, Indianapolis, Bobbs-Merrill,
    1966

DISCUSSION OF THE PAPERS BY

WOLLHEIM AND JAHODA

Professor Jahoda was unable to attend the conference. His paper was read by Dr Deręgowski who answered questions.

Wollheim. It wouldn't be easy to say from Jahoda's results whether the children exercised representational seeing or whether they used various other cues to arrive at a solution. I wonder whether you have considered this distinction.

Deręgowski. I am not sure that I have grasped your notion of "seeing in". It seems to me that if a person recognises something and consistently calls it by a name, he is "seeing in" even though he may not be "seeing in depth". For example, you could look at a Victorian silhouette and say: "This is Disraeli". He would be recognised as a specific person but I don't think we would be able to say anything from the silhouette about the width of Disraeli's cheekbones. The perception of depth in that sense isn't there.

I would distinguish between two aspects of pictorial representation. The first is representation of pictorial depth without any meaning being evoked. In these cases it would be easier if the person were to forget that a three-dimensional interpretation is possible. If you take the two-pronged trident illusion (Figure 3, Chapter 15) subjects from Western culture have difficulty because they see it in depth. If they saw it merely as a pattern of lines it would be as good as any other pattern. If one takes subjects from a non-pictorial culture, where one knows there are consistent differences in perspective interpretation, they find it easier to draw the three-pronged figure than Western subjects. The depth is there although it hasn't any meaning.

The second aspect is recognition of something.   If one were
to draw a schematic outline of a boot, the majority of people would
say it was a boot but is it a number 7 fitting?   The depth cues
aren't there.

Wollheim.   Well it would give us rather sparse information
but of course there would be many representations which would not
give us much more.   There could be representations which give us
three-dimensional information without giving us information about
size.   There could be other cases, e.g. cross-cultural ones, where
someone does indeed recognise that this is a huntsman (referring to
Hudson's (1960) ambiguous figure of a hunter).   He recognises that
but he doesn't recognise it at all in the sense that he sees it in
the representation.   He might recognise it because he knows beforehand for example, that the experimenter is only going to show him a
limited number of alternatives.   He can eliminate various possi-
bilities straight off.   There may be certain cues that tell him it
is a huntsman but that needn't be a case of representational seeing.

Deregowski.   If the cues arise from outside the picture then
perhaps it wouldn't.   But, as Elizabeth Newson pointed out earlier,
a tick is regarded by children as a very good representation of a
bird.   It is one of those things which children cotton onto once
they have seen it.

Gopnik (Oxford).   I would like to make a point which relates
both to Professor Wollheim's original question and to Professor
Jahoda's paper.   One of the things Dr Deregowski mentioned was
that colour was quite relevant in children's picture recognition.
If the experimenter says: "Give me a picture of a banana", even
if the child had only a red square, a green square and a yellow
square to choose from, the child might be clever enough to work
out: "Someone says give me a picture of a banana and they want
me to do something with these coloured pictures in front of me".
Well probably the child would give you a yellow square for the
banana or a green square for a leaf.   That would be a case where
it wouldn't be an arbitrary response but it would be difficult to
say whether they were "seeing in".

Wollheim.   Yes.

Deregowski.   As far as Jahoda's data is concerned I think he
controls for it because he has various possible items of the same
colour.   I agree that it is possible that subjects cotton on to
one cue only.   One could check for it experimentally.

McGurk (Surrey).   Jahoda and I did a study (Jahoda and McGurk,
1974) in which the recognition of objects in pictures depended on
the response to depth cues in the picture.   Under these conditions

young Ghanaian, Zambian, Rhodesian and English children all recognised identical objects at different depths as different things,
depending on the depth cues.   The children were responding to
intra-picture spatial information, I think that may answer the
earlier criticism of Gopnik.

    Greene (Open University).   I think one issue being raised is
how far to take the concept of representation.   Is it a resemblance?
Are you establishing whether children think that a picture resembles
an object?   How far are you taking the concept toward conventional
signs?   Does one count a tick as a representation of a bird or
stick men as representations of men?   If you go in that direction
you end up by saying that language is a form of representation.

    Wollheim.   Well obviously one has to draw the line somewhere
but we don't want to do so in any kind of arbitrary way.   There
are different kinds of theoretical considerations to be met, both
philosophic and also to do with what we would recognise as the
unity of a perceptual skill.

    Freeman.   Isn't it up to psychologists to ask what represen-
tational criteria may be used in any given task and not to generalise
across task demands?   Otherwise you end up in the position Judith
Greene pointed out, where you have to say that all language is
representational because you think there are sufficiently good
criteria for representation within the language to meet the other
criteria as well.

    Wollheim.   I totally sympathise with that.   I think that the
philosophers' definition of representation is going to be influenced
by psychological findings.   There must be commerce in both directions.

BIBLIOGRAPHY

HUDSON, W., Pictorial depth perception in sub-cultural groups in
    Africa, Journal of Social Psychology, 1960, 52, pp. 183-208

JAHODA, G. & MCGURK, H., Development of pictorial depth perception:
    cross-cultural replications, Child Development, 1974, 45,
    pp. 1042-1047

See also Deręgowski's paper (Chapter 15).

CLOSING ADDRESS

PICTURES, SYMBOLS AND FRAMES OF REFERENCE

J. B. Deręgowski

It would be impossible for me, even if I had the capacity to
do so, to comment cogently upon all the issues which we have heard
discussed and to touch upon all the papers which were presented.
Such an attempt would at best lead to a cumbersome catalogue of
proceedings. I shall therefore confine my remarks to a small
number of papers.

The theme of the conference was: "The child's representation
of his world". The key term in this title, representation, has
to an empirical psychologist, I think, at least two distinctive
meanings. One of these refers to the artifacts created by the
child which are intended to represent the external world, the other
to the internal schema or frames of reference which the child uses
in his interaction with the external world. Unlike the former,
the latter are not directly accessible, and have to be elicited by
a variety of techniques, including analysis of children's artifacts.

Drawings are a case, par excellence, of representations (artifacts) serving as a key to internal representation, because they
convey very clearly the essential difficulty with which a psychologist has to deal, namely that there are likely to be two sets of
schemata which he may have to disentangle from each other. One of
these sets governs the way in which a subject perceives and the other
the way in which the subject expresses himself.

Let us consider Dr Freeman's study (Chapter 1). This is
concerned with the rules which govern the act of drawing, but not
of drawing in general, but drawing of a man. The indefiniteness
of the article must be stressed, for there is an essential

difference between the implications of the request to draw the cup,
as in Freeman and Janikoun's (1972) study, and a request to draw a
cup or a man.   This distinction, which has been pointed out in a
paper by Vurpillot and Brault (1959), arises from the fact that,
whilst in the former case a child has to reproduce a real object,
in the latter he is merely asked to reproduce a pictorial sign for
an object which he might have acquired without ever attempting to
draw from a model.   This could have happened in several ways.
For example, his attention might have been drawn to the fact that
a tick is a passable representation of a bird in flight or that two
circles embellished with a few short lines make an equally acceptable
representation of a cat.   Indeed it could also happen that a child
without any instruction encountered such simple devices, found them
to be apposite and adopted them.

In other words, he might have learned to produce a clearly
recognisable pictorial sign standing for a three-dimensional object
without attempting to draw a model and hence without translating
from three to two dimensions.   Now, whenever he is asked to draw
a man or a cup he reproduces an appropriate sign.   Such a sign may,
of course, change with the passage of time owing to maturation and
in the large majority of cases owing to socialization.   These
changes, however, need not affect its essential nature, which is
that of a symbol perceptually intimately connected with a category
of three-dimensional objects in the outer world (such as cups or
men), but not derived from them by the draughtsman.

The resultant symbolist style of representation is, of course,
common in children, and its nature is well described in a very
recent paper by Barrett and Light (1976), which ingeniously disen-
tangles the differences between three styles recognized in
children's drawings:

1) Symbolism,
2) Intellectual Realism, and
3) Visual Realism.

These can best be described by adducing an example.   Let us assume
that a child is presented with two cups: a cup without a handle and
another cup so placed that the handle is invisible to the draughtsman, although he has been shown that this cup has a handle.   The
drawings obtained in response to these stimuli define the three
types of response as follows:

Assuming that the 'symbolist' identifies both objects as cups
and that his symbol for a cup incorporates a handle;   both his
drawings will then show a handle.

An 'intellectual realist', on the other hand, who draws what
he knows to be there, will under these circumstances draw a handleless cup in response to the first stimulus and a 'proper' cup in
response to the second.

Not so the 'visual realist', who draws what he sees and would therefore make two 'handleless'drawings.

In the main, in terms of this terminology, the drawings presented by Dr Freeman seem to me to fall into the symbolic category.   Further, one could argue that, although such symbols are not immutable (and, indeed, this is clearly demonstrated in Mr Willsdon's paper on drawings (Chapter 4), they do not change greatly, as shown by the evidence of Cameron (1938) that even sophisticated adults do not necessarily show great advance in these matters.   Indeed, the difficulty which adults encounter when learning to draw seem often to be that of abandoning the well habituated symbolic styles.

We must now ask the inevitable question in psychology, if it is to be regarded as a science of human behaviour in general: is there any evidence to show that Dr Freeman's findings may not have universal applicability?   There are suggestions in the literature (Kellogg, 1959, Baker and Kellogg, 1967) which purport that such drawings are the result of slow evolution from meaningless scribbles which are used to build increasingly more meaningful units. According to these speculations, the drawings of Dr Freeman's subjects represent one of the higher levels of this evolutionary process.   According to these suggestions, too, one would not expect such drawings to occur in those cultures where drawings are unknown.   The data relevant to the issue are very scarce.   This is so because cultures which would satisfy the above requirement are rare and because, regrettably, little work has been done in such cultures.   There is, however, one very relevant study.

Fortes (1940) collected drawings from a number of Tallensi subjects, who, as far as one could ascertain, had never drawn before.   These subjects when first presented with a pencil, scribbled profusely, but they also drew from imagination a variety of figures.   Their drawings (Figure 1) do not possess the features commonly associated with first drawings of our children.   They leave one in no doubt, however, as to their symbolic nature.   Since these subjects had never received any instruction in drawing, such symbolism as their efforts contained must have been spontaneous. Drawings obtained by Fortes from schoolchildren of the same genetic stock (Figure 2) are, on the other hand, similar to drawings made by Western schoolchildren.   It seems that even little schooling causes abandonment of symbolism in its purest form, or at least causes it to be modified.

Two points need to be made about Fortes' data: 1) the age range of his unschooled subjects extended well into adulthood, hence the mode of representation observed cannot be said to be characteristic of childhood;   and 2) the drawings of the unschooled

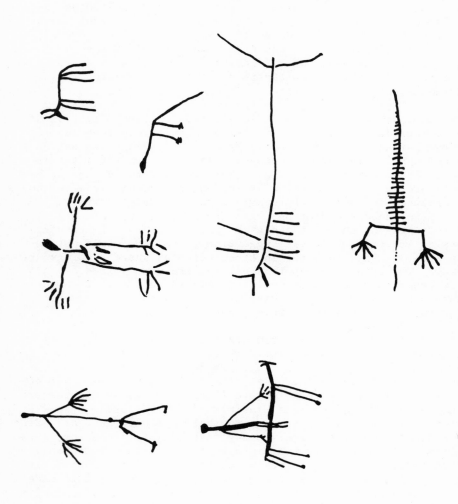

Figure 1. Drawing of men and animals obtained by Fortes (1940) from Tallensi who have never drawn before and whose culture is pictureless

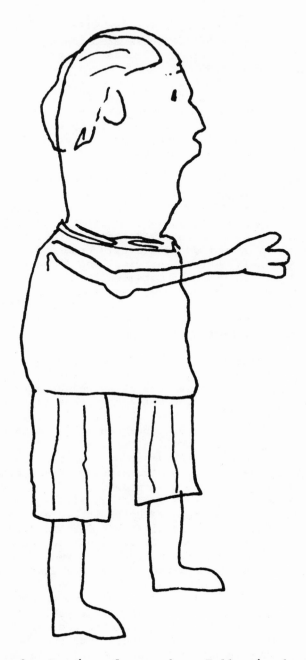

Figure 2.   Drawing of a man by a Tallensi schoolboy

Tallensi differ markedly from those of English and Welsh children.
The Tallensi human figures are microcephalic and have long stick-
like bodies. Their facial features are missing. (On the other
hand, certain other features are exceedingly prominent!) None of
them has arms growing from his head.

These observations limit the range of applicability of
Dr Freeman's conclusions. They do not diminish their value. On
the contrary, they enhance them for it is by observing such contrasting results that we can chart our progress. We would be utterly
lost on a boundless plane of agreement.

It has been mentioned before that symbolic drawings may be
arrived at by a different process than drawing from a model and
may therefore not be regarded as evidence that a draughtsman is
capable of translating from three dimensions into two. This
argument obviously does not apply to the Tallensi drawings.
Admittedly these were not drawn directly from models but from
recall of such models, but the original models were real three-
dimensional objects. (One can dismiss as unlikely, I feel, the
hypothesis that when drawing, say, men, the Tallensi recalled what
shadows of men looked like and drew these, thus letting the Good
Sun make 3D-2D translations for them.) It follows therefore that
such translation has been achieved.

This was a specific type of translation which can perhaps
tentatively be called 'epitomist'. In this type of translation
the picture conveys the appearance of an object without using
pictorial depth cues. A silhouette of a head is recognised as a
silhouette of a three-dimensional object, not because the perceptual
cues involved in the figure make one see it as three-dimensional,
but because it is reminiscent of a head, and heads are three-
dimensional. In contrast with this an eidolic translation occurs
independently of the meaning of the picture, sometimes even in spite
of the absence of any conceivable meaning, as in the case of the
two-pronged trident (Figure 3). In this figure, the persistent
attempts of the perceptual apparatus to interpret the configuration
as a meaningful three-dimensional figure lead to puzzlement. If
the perceptual mechanism were able to accept such a stimulus as a
meaningless, flat, pattern its difficulties would probably disappear
(Deregowski, 1969). The distinction between these two translations
becomes apparent in Hudson's (1960, 1967) studies to which
Professor Wollheim referred (Chapter 12) (and to which I shall
return). Some of Hudson's subjects were capable of an 'epitomist'
translation (that is, they could recognize the depicted figures: the
hunter, the elephant, the duiker, etc.), but they were incapable of
the 'eidolic' translation: i.e. they could not see depth in the
picture which was implied by the various depth cues. (Support for
this interpretation will be found in Deręgowski and Byth, 1970, and
Deręgowski, 1973.)

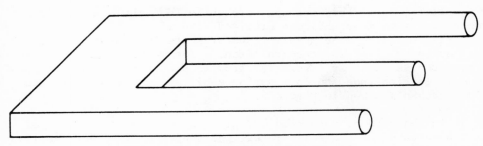

Figure 3.   'Two-pronged trident'

The instances described deal, however, with the drawing-to-object translations.   Let us now consider what happens, or is likely to happen, when a translation in the opposite sense is involved, that is the same sense as that used by the Tallensi and by Dr Freeman's subjects.

Let us imagine that a subject is required to draw three cubes resting upon a table.   Such information as can be derived from the surface of the table (from its density gradient, for example) and from other sources conveys to the subject the truths that the cubes are not equidistant from him, and that all the faces of the cube are square.   Now, to arrive at a picture which approximates to his retinal projection, that is, a picture conventionally (but not, in my view, arbitrarily) accepted as correct, the draughtsman has to space the cubes on his drawing in accordance with the cues of distance provided, but also to draw their faces not as squares, but as rhombi.   He has to do so in spite of the fact that those very cues which convey to him the distance between the cubes also convey to him the fact that the faces are square.   There is something irrational, even perhaps magical, about this process to untutored minds.   How otherwise can a collage of 'incorrectly' drawn elements lead to a drawing which (even to such untutored minds) is patently superior to a drawing which consists of 'correctly' drawn faces?   Why are such 'incorrectly' drawn elements perceived as correct representations once the drawing is completed?

These questions are especially vexing if the Piagetian obser-vation that children find it difficult to adopt other perspectives than their own is considered, since drawing a cube as an array of squares may be taken to suggest exactly the opposite, i.e. that a child is capable of assuming a multiplicity of perspectives.

It is, therefore, perhaps worthwhile to dwell a moment longer on drawings made by children provided with either cubical or 'para-cubical' models. The observations presented here are derived from responses by Scottish schoolchildren. The models used ranged in completeness of their 'cubicity' from a 'plasticine' cube, through a wire lattice cube, to four variants of vestiges of a cube (the 'para-cubes') shown in Figure 4.

In the case of both cube stimuli, as well as in the case of the para-cubes having solid faces, the subjects (aged between five-and-a-half and six-and-a-half) reproduced the models by drawing simple quadrilaterals, which were in all probability approximations to squares, the dominant geometric shapes of the models. Older subjects (aged between eight-and-a-half and eleven-and-a-half) tended to abandon these simple outlines in favour of more complex figures approximating more closely to the retinal projection of the models.

A similar difference was observed between the responses of the younger and the older groups in the case of the wire para-cubes. There, however, the subjects did not use a square of its approxima-tion to depict the model nearly as often as they did in the case of the stimuli described above, but tended to accentuate the fact that the squares constituting the figure were, objectively, readily apparent. They did so by either drawing these figures as connected quadrilaterals or by representing them in a side view, using a single line, as U-shaped arrangements. It thus appears that the representation of a cube (or near-cube) by a square is not derived by a choice of one of its square faces and a decision that it should be taken pars pro toto to represent the cube, but rather that such a drawing conveys the gist of the model as seen by the subjects, showing subjects' ability to abstract this gist. This ability is essentially similar in essence to that which enabled both Bristol and Tallensi subjects to abstract the important characteristics of a human figure.

Furthermore, the quadrilateral outline drawn in response to the cubes was, in the case of the younger group, generally left empty. In the older group a variety of sub-divisions of this out-line occurred. Although the present data do not allow one to examine these statistically it is probably worthwhile to arrange the observed data in a possible taxonomic table. This is done in Figure 5.

The initial and simplest division of a square is that achieved by drawing a line parallel to two of its sides (Figures 5b and 5c). Division is further elaborated by drawing two such lines at right angles to each other (Figure 5d) and finally by drawing two such

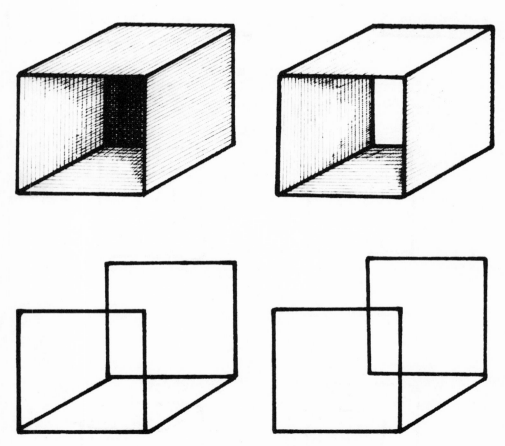

Figure 4. A set of 'para-cubes' used as models
with Scottish schoolchildren

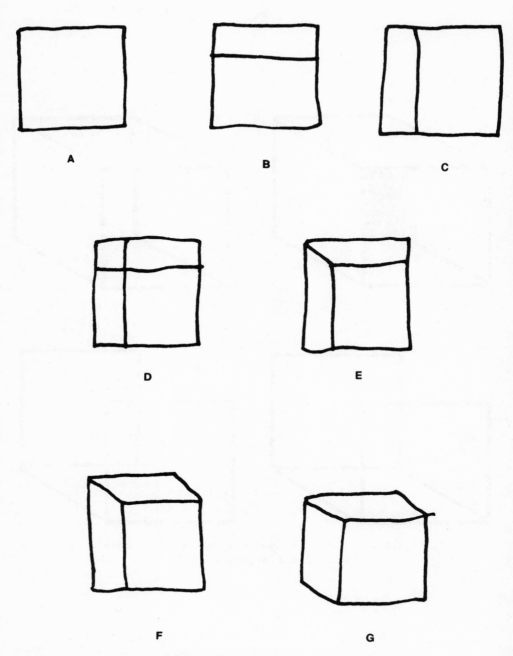

Figure 5.   Putative taxonomy of children's drawings of a cube

lines so that they meet within the square and by connecting their
junction to the nearest corner (Figure 5e).   All these developments
do not affect the shape of the outlines, the conceptual dominance of
which forms a major obstacle to the achievement of what is generally
taken to be the correct representation of the model.   Such representation can only be achieved by abandoning the square outline.
This process, the data suggest, is not immediate but is mediated by
the pentagonal outline.   Whenever this occurred it was the result
of chamfering of the upper corner of the square with the line parallel
to the sloping line drawn in Figure 5e.   The resulting drawing
is shown in Figure 5f.   The chamfering of the appropriate bottom
corner and hence the arrival at correct representation appears to
take place last, perhaps because it involves alteration to the
drawing of the base of the figure, and the base rests palpably on a
horizontal table top, with all the bottom members in the same plane.

If this is a correct interpretation of the difficulty, then
this brings us back to the problem of frames of reference, for it
shows a degree of conflict between the cube in isolation and the
cube perceived on the background of a table, reminiscent of the
conflict described in the paper on children's coding of stimulus-
to-background ratios presented to this Conference.*

Thus one cannot escape the possibility that the frame of
reference used by a draughtsman undergoes gradual changes which
eventually lead to such skilful use of background cues that it
enables him to adopt a unique spatial position and construction
of his drawing from that point of view only.

This element of space travel is, of course, central to
Dr Harris' thesis (Chapter 6).   Before I discuss it, however, let
me present to you a model of extreme simplicity.   In this model I
have reduced to one dimension the notions which are used to describe
our three-dimensional space.   Let S denote the subject, and therefore a point relative to which all egocentric references are made;
let X denote the allocentre; and let A and B denote two objects.
Furthermore, let all these be co-linear and let the only admissible
measurement be in the direction away from the appropriate reference
point.   Therefore, for a configuration:

$$S - X - A - B - (S^1)$$

the subject's responses are:

     egocentric: B is further than A.
     allocentric: B is further than A.

---

* See LAWRENSON, W., Children's coding of stimulus to background
ratios, <u>British Journal of Psychology</u>, 1977 (in press)

Consider now what happens when a subject is required to imagine that he occupies position S^1 and to make appropriate responses.   Such a request may lead to one of the following consequences:

1) Failure to imagine such a shift and hence no change in responses.

2) Imaginary movement of the egocentre only and hence the following responses:

> egocentric: A is further than B.
> allocentric: B is further than A.

3) Movement of the allocentre only and hence the following arrangement:

$$S - A - B - (X^1)$$

which leads to the following responses:

> egocentric: B is further than A.
> allocentric: A is further than B.

4) Imaginary movement of the egocentres and movement of the allocentre:

$$A - B - X^1 - S^1$$

and again consistency of the two types of response, both yielding that A is further than B.

In the usual experimental setting we are facing the task of determining the frame of reference which the subject uses from his responses and our knowledge of the position of the egocentre.   We do not know where the allocentre is.   The above simplistic schematisation suggests that under such circumstances we cannot be sure of a subject's point of reference, for whatever response we obtain it is compatible with either of the two descriptions. Experimental procedures do not, however, impose upon the subject as severe constraints as those prevailing in the above model.   A subject can make a response which is clearly neither egocentric nor allocentric and which, therefore, if one accepts that these are the only influences which can prevail, shows a compounding of these effects.

Such is, of course, the line of argument adopted by Dr Harris in interpreting the data obtained jointly with Basset in a noteworthy extension of the paper by Huttenlocher and Presson (1973). There is a feature of the latter paper which was not discussed during the Conference and which is relevant in the present context. In the second of the two experiments reported by Huttenlocher and Presson subjects responded under all possible combinations of two variables.   One of these was the presence (H+) or absence (H-) of

an external marker (a toy horse) in the position from which the
subjects had to imagine that they were seeing the display, and the
second was the subject's own position.   In half of the cases the
judgements were made with the subject actually moving to the position from which the judgement had to be made (M+) and in the other
half he remained stationary (M-).   In half of the cases the
marker was used, and in the other half it was absent.

Now, the conditions of the experiment were such that it seems
very likely (but of course not certain) that if an allocentric
reference point had been used it was provided by the position of
the toy horse.

The results reported show the following percentages of erroneous
responses under each experimental condition:

1) H+; M+: 9.9 (1.6)
2) H+; M-: 31.4 (3.9)
3) H-; M+: 14.1 (0.8)
4) H-; M-: 40.2 (2.5)

The figures in brackets give the ratios of egocentric errors
to other errors, the egocentric errors being those responses which
would have been correct, had they been made from the subject's
original position.

Huttenlocher and Presson concentrate their analysis on the
ratios obtained and admit puzzlement by the evidence that in the
H+ condition the ratios were higher, and that the horse significantly affected the difficulty of the task.   It seems to me that
this result cannot be taken as yielding unequivocal support for the
theory that a child's difficulties arise solely out of its egocentricity.   In this negative sense it does offer, however, a modicum
of support for the hypothesis that the difficulty is one of co-
ordination of the two possible perspectives (if there are only two
possible perspectives).

Dr Cox's (Chapter 7) results can also be seen as in agreement
with such an interpretation, for they can be said to show that it
is easier to teach a subject to visualise a view from a different
stance than that occupied by him by allowing him to remain at his
original position and providing either visual or verbal feedback
than by allowing him to move to the position which he was to occupy
in his imagination and derive the feedback himself.   In the former
case both the subject's ego- and allocentres remain, presumably,
unaltered throughout the experiment.   In the latter case, the egocentre moves and such a stable relationship no longer holds.

Accordingly, if I were to question the theory of spatial
development so ably advanced by Dr Harris, I should do so, not by

querying the general nature of the contestants for the dominance of
a child's frame of reference, but by wondering about their exact
nature and their relative strength at various ages of the child.
It is this aspect which calls for further attention.*

    My remarks about the manner in which Hudson's results illustrate
the distinction between the two ways of translating from picture to
reality may have left you with the impression that the translation
which I called 'eidolic' is of necessity the more difficult.   I
hasten to dispel such an impression.   Both types of cues, the
epitomist and the eidolic, can vary in intensity and it just so
happens that in the picture in question the latter appear to be
weaker.   In other circumstances they exercise considerable
influence.   Thus, if I were to ask you to choose one of the shapes
shown in Figure 6 to match the shape shown in Figure 7, and the
shape shown in Figure 8, your responses would show a predictable
influence, the chosen shape being more squarish when matching
Figure 7 (Deręgowski, 1976).

Figure 6.   A selection of rhombi from which one is to be chosen
            to match Figure 7 and one to match Figure 8

* As implied by the simple linear model an empirical determination
of the frame (s) of reference is likely to prove difficult.   Does
a child use the same frame for all the objects within a sitting
room?   Or does he code his grandmother in relation to a fireside
chair and his grandfather in relation to a bottle of port?   If
several distinct frames are used how are they chosen?   How are they
related, and how are they remembered?

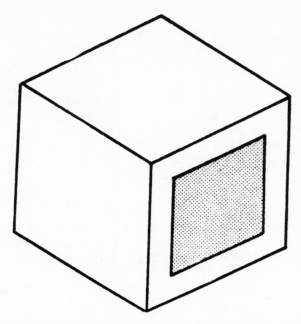

Figure 7.   Stimulus rhombus to be matched with one of rhombi
            shown in Figure 6

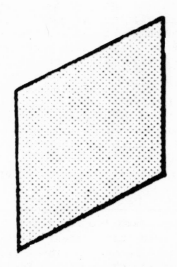

Figure 8.   Stimulus rhombus to be matched with one of the rhombi
            shown in Figure 6

Both types of stimuli, the epitomist and the eidolic, cause, I think, specific difficulties at times measured against Professor Wollheim's criteria (Chapter 12).   The 'perceptual', or eidolic, type, does so.   It could be argued that it is closely related to visual illusions and whilst one can say with a considerable degree of plausibility that in 'seeing-in' into Figure 7 the observer sees something like a box and that the draughtsman who constructed the stimulus did so in response to instructions to draw a cube, one cannot say such things about the Müller-Lyer illusion.   Neither an intention nor 'seeing-in' is present in the latter instance.   Yet the underlying psychological process is probably the same in both instances and psychological processes are of great interest to psychologists.

Some of them would therefore be inclined to argue that this shows the distinction between representational and non-representational designs to be more blurred than at first appears, and that essentially the same figures in statu nascendi should not be classified as radically different from their fully developed counterparts.

The difficulties with epitomic elements are of a similar marginal nature.   They result, from a philosophical point of view, from the problem of 'intent' in representation and perception, and arise in the specific cases when the creator of an image has the general intention to create something which has the potential of evoking 'seeing-in', but which does not define in any appreciable manner the nature of such seeing.   I refer, of course, to Rorschach's blots.*   Here, some psychologists would say, a search for meaning is essentially the same as a search for meaning in a silhouette, and would ask: Can we confine to strictly differentiated categories stimuli which evoke the same perceptual processes? Such questions, stimulated by a discipline sometimes unfortunately regarded by psychologists as alien, are, I think, of fundamental importance.

The failure to note this psychologically important distinction between the epitomist and eidolic representations is responsible, I suspect, for Professor Wollheim's overhasty condemnation of Hudson's work.   Hudson would freely admit that all his subjects were to some degree capable of epitomist 'seeing-in';   indeed, this type of 'seeing-in' was an essential prerequisite for effective assessment

---

* In case this example seems too far fetched, let me mention here that Shaw (1969) observed that a clear picture of a tortoise was sometimes called a snake because of the shape of its head, sometimes an elephant because of the shape of its feet, and occasionally a crocodile because of the pattern of its shell.

of their eidolic 'seeing-in', and it is in the 'eidolic' mode that
the cultural differences were observed.*

It may well be that this distinction between the two modes
just stressed sends the ball back into the philosopher's side of
the court.   If it does, it is, I hope, to the benefit of both
disciplines.

---

* For examples of epitomist difficulties in a cross-cultural
setting, see Doob (1961), Forge (1970), Deręgowski, Muldrow and
Muldrow (1972).   The last of these studies describes the responses
of subjects drawn from an entirely pictureless culture to pictures,
and reports some noteworthy failures as well as some surprising
successes.   Professor Jahoda's paper (Chapter 14) is also of
importance in the present context.   Comprehensive reviews of
cross-cultural studies in pictorial perception will be found in
Miller (1973) and Deręgowski (1977).

ACKNOWLEDGEMENTS

    I am indebted to my colleagues Mr J W Shepherd and Dr N E
Wetherick for the comments on a draft of this paper.

BIBLIOGRAPHY

BAKER, H. & KELLOGG, R.,   A developmental study of children's
    scribblings, Pediatrics, 1967, 40, pp. 382-389

BARRETT, M. D. & LIGHT, P. H.,   Symbolism and intellectual realism
    in children's drawings, British Journal of Educational
    Psychology, 1976, 46, pp. 198-202

CAMERON, N.,   Functional immaturity in the symbolizations of
    scientifically trained adults, Journal of Psychology, 1938,
    6, pp. 161-175

DERĘGOWSKI, J. B.,   Perception of two-pronged trident by two and
    three dimensional perceivers, Journal of Experimental
    Psychology, 1969, 82, pp. 9-13

DERĘGOWSKI, J. B. & BYTH, W.,   Hudson's pictures in Pandora's box,
    Journal of Cross-Cultural Psychology, 1970, 1, pp. 315-323

DERĘGOWSKI, J. B.,   Illusions and culture, in GREGORY, R. L. &
    GOMBRICH, E. H. (Eds.) Illusion in nature and art, London,
    Duckworth, 1973

DEREGOWSKI, J. B., Implicit shape constancy as a factor in pictorial perception, British Journal of Psychology, 1976, 67, pp. 23-29

DEREGOWSKI, J. B., Perception, in TRIANDIS, H. et al. (Eds.) Handbook of Cross-Cultural Psychology, Vol. 2, Boston, Allyn and Bacon, 1977

DEREGOWSKI, J. B., MULDROW, E. S. & MULDROW, W. F., Pictorial recognition in a remote Ethiopian population, Perception, 1972, 1, pp. 417-425

DOOB, L. W., Communication in Africa: a search for boundaries, New Haven, York University Press, 1961

FORGE, A., Learning to see in New Guinea, in MEYER, P. (Ed.) Socialization, London, Tavistock, 1970

FORTES, M., Children's drawings among the Tallensi, Africa, 1940, 13, pp. 239-295

FREEMAN, N. H. & JANIKOUN, R., Intellectual realism in children's drawings of a familiar object with distinctive features, Child Development, 1972, 43, pp. 1116-1121

HUDSON, W., Pictorial depth perception in sub-cultural groups in Africa, Journal of Social Psychology, 1960, 52, pp. 183-208

HUDSON, W., The study of the problem of pictorial perception among unacculturated groups, International Journal of Psychology, 1967, 2, pp. 89-107

HUTTENLOCHER, J. & PRESSON, C., Mental rotation and the perspective problem, Cognitive Psychology, 1973, 4, pp. 277-299

KELLOGG, R., What children scribble and why, Palo Alto, 1959

MILLER, R. J., Cross-cultural research in perception of pictorial materials, Psychological Bulletin, 1973, 80, pp. 135-150

VURPILLOT, E. & BRAULT, H., Étude expérimentelle sur la formation des schemes empiriques, L'Année Psychologique, 1959, 59, pp. 381-394

INDEX

237